Henry Leon
Tom Inskip

2004 Jack Austin

# ACTIVE MATHEMATICS 3

| TOW HOUSE OL | |
|---|---|
| T. Inskip | A |
| T. Russell | B |
| Philip Lis | C |
| Peter Davies | |
| Andrew Walichnowski | D |
| Hashem G. | D |

Ben Parker

**ACTIVE MATHEMATICS**

Pupils' book 1      0 582 08439 3
Teacher's guide 1    0 582 08444 X

*B. V. Hony*


Pupils' book 2      0 582 08440 7
Teacher's guide 2    0 582 08445 8

*B. V. Hony*


Pupils' book 3      0 582 08441 5
Teacher's guide 3    0 582 08446 6

*B. V. Hony and D. A. Turner*


Pupils' book 4      0 582 08442 3
Teacher's guide 4    0 582 08447 4

*D. A. Turner, B. V. Hony, I. A. Potts, K. D. Oakley and P. S. Lane*


Pupils' book 5      0 582 08443 1
Teacher's guide 5    0 582 08448 2

*D. A. Turner, B. V. Hony, I. A. Potts and K. D. Oakley*

# ACTIVE MATHEMATICS 3

**B. V. Hony and D. A. Turner**

*Oundle School*

LONGMAN

Longman Group UK Limited
*Longman House, Burnt Mill, Harlow, Essex CM20 2JE, England*
*and Associated Companies throughout the world.*

First published by Active Publications 1988
© Active Publications

Second edition first published by Longman Group UK Limited 1992
© Longman Group UK Limited

First published 1992
ISBN 0 582 08441 5


Set in Times by Ellis Associates
Printed and bound in Great Britain by
Butler & Tanner Ltd, Frome and London

# CONTENTS

**To the user of this book**
**Acknowledgements**

## —— Chapter 1 ARITHMETIC I

**1.1**  Basic principles  *1*
**1.2**  More calculator buttons  *8*
**1.3**  Percentage profit and loss  *10*
**1.4**  Problem solving  *15*

Revision Exercise 1  *18*
Basics Test 1, Puzzlers  *20*
Coursework: Kit Kat bars  *21*

## —— Chapter 2 GRAPHS I

**2.1**  Basic principles  *22*
**2.2**  Graph relationships  *23*
**2.3**  Understanding graphs  *26*
**2.4**  Investigating graphs  *29*
**2.5**  Travel graphs  *32*

Revision Exercise 2  *37*
Basic Algebra Test 1, Puzzlers  *39*
Coursework: World sprint record  *40*

## —— Chapter 3 ALGEBRA I

**3.1**  Basic principles  *41*
**3.2**  Brackets  *46*
**3.3**  Symbolic expression  *47*
**3.4**  Problem solving  *50*
**3.5**  Simplifying algebraic fractions  *52*
**3.6**  Solving algebraic fractions  *53*
**3.7**  Simultaneous equations  *54*
**3.8**  Inequalities  *56*

Revision Exercise 3  *58*
Aural Test 1, Puzzlers  *60*
Coursework: Motoring costs  *61*

**FACT FINDERS**: The UK hurricane  *62*

## —— Chapter 4 GEOMETRY I

**4.1**  Basic principles  *64*
**4.2**  Angles of a circle  *67*
**4.3**  Similar triangles  *70*
**4.4**  Gradients  *76*

Revision Exercise 4  *79*
Basics Test 2, Puzzlers  *81*
Coursework: The Cross-staff  *82*

## —— Chapter 5 TRIGONOMETRY

**5.1**  Basic principles  *84*
**5.2**  Tangent ratio  *85*
**5.3**  Sine and cosine ratios  *90*
**5.4**  Miscellaneous problems  *96*

Revision Exercise 5  *98*
Basics Test 3, Puzzlers  *100*
Coursework: Aviation flight paths  *101*

## Chapter 6 PROPORTION

**6.1** Basic principles *102*

**6.2** Change of units *105*

**6.3** Exchange rates (mental) *107*

**6.4** Comparative costs *108*

**6.5** Problem solving *110*

**6.6** Inverse proportion *113*

**6.7** Science problems *115*

Revision Exercise 6 *118*

Basic Algebra Test 2, Puzzlers *120*

Coursework: The solar system *121*

## Chapter 7 ALGEBRA II

**7.1** Equations *122*

**7.2** 'Trial and improvement' solution *125*

**7.3** Inequalities *127*

**7.4** Circumference of a circle *129*

**7.5** Area of a circle *133*

**7.6** Pythagoras' theorem *137*

**7.7** The cylinder *141*

**7.8** Formulae *143*

**7.9** Rearranging formulae *144*

Revision Exercise 7 *146*

Aural Test 2, Puzzlers *148*

Coursework: The Active Maths puzzle *149*

**FACT FINDERS**: The Channel Tunnel *150*

## Chapter 8 GRAPHS II

**8.1** Basic principles *152*

**8.2** Graphs of $y = ax$ *153*

**8.3** Graphs of $y = ax + b$ *155*

**8.4** Graphs of $y = ax^2$ *157*

**8.5** Graphs of $y = \frac{a}{x}$ *160*

Revision Exercise 8 *162*

Basics Test 4, Puzzlers *164*

Coursework: Bicycle gears *165*

## Chapter 9 ARITHMETIC II

**9.1** Tolerance *166*

**9.2** Percentages *167*

**9.3** Wages and salaries *170*

**9.4** Taxation *171*

**9.5** Interest and loans *173*

**9.6** Discount and hire purchase (HP) *174*

Revision Exercise 9 *176*

Basics Test 5, Puzzlers *178*

Coursework: World population *179*

# CONTENTS

## ▬ Chapter 10 STATISTICS AND PROBABILITY

**10.1** Basic principles  *180*
**10.2** Misuse of statistics  *183*
**10.3** Scatter graphs  *184*
**10.4** Calculating averages  *185*
**10.5** Frequency distributions  *188*
**10.6** Probability: single events  *193*
**10.7** Probability: combined events  *198*

Revision Exercise 10  *205*
Aural Test 3, Puzzlers  *207*
Coursework: Traffic flow problem  *208*

## ▬ Chapter 11 GEOMETRY II

**11.1** Basic principles  *209*
**11.2** Enlargements  *215*
**11.3** Loci  *219*
**11.4** Maps and bearings  *222*
**11.5** Scale drawing  *225*
**11.6** Drawing three-dimensional figures  *227*
**11.7** Networks  *229*
**11.8** LOGO  *232*

Revision Exercise 11  *236*
Basic Algebra Test 3, Puzzlers  *238*
Coursework: Surveying with a Silva compass *239*

**FACT FINDERS**: Wimbledon  *240*

## ▬ Multiple Choice Tests  *242*

## ▬ Active Mathematics and the National Curriculum

| Level | 4 | 5 | 6 | 7 | 8 | 9 | 10 |
|---|---|---|---|---|---|---|---|
| Book 1 | ■ | ■ | ■ | | | | |
| Book 2 | | ■ | ■ | ■ | ■ | | |
| Book 3 | | | ■ | ■ | ■ | ■ | |
| Book 4 | | | | ■ | ■ | ■ | ■ |
| Book 5 | | | | | | | ■ |

# TO THE USER OF THIS BOOK

If you have understood the basic work of the previous two books in this series, you should enjoy developing the skills in this book.

## About this book

Most chapters begin with a comprehensive BASIC PRINCIPLES section which revises previous work which is used in the chapter, followed by worked EXAMPLES of every type of problem. The REMEMBER boxes give useful hints. ACTIVITIES help to apply the principles.

The questions in each EXERCISE are carefully graded and include many real challenges in the MASTERMNDER sections.

At the end of each chapter, there are TESTS of many types, a comprehensive REVISION EXERCISE, and finally, some PUZZLERS to have some fun with.

## Coursework

The Coursework in this book is of the standard required for the GCSE exam. Each Coursework is about one topic and you should find it interesting as well as challenging. The maths skills required are based on those covered in previous chapters. Coursework can and should be done as part of the course, in order to:
- **apply** the skills learned in the text
- **consolidate** the skills of the text
- **discover** things for yourself.

Each Coursework should be written up as you would write up the results of an experiment in science. The finished product should therefore be self-explanatory. Remember, you must **communicate** your ideas on paper so that someone else can follow your method, your explanations, your calculations and your argument.

Marks will be given for method, accuracy, explanation, neatness and, if the Extension is done (Higher level only) initiative and content. These categories are explained more fully below.

| CALCULATION | Method | (M) | You must show **how** you arrived at your answer. |
| | Accuracy | (A) | The **correct** answer, units and degree of accuracy. |
| COMMUNICATION | Explanation | (E) | Include a title, introduction and a brief but relevant concluding paragraph. Remember you must **communicate** your ideas on paper. Words of explanation must precede all workings, tables, diagrams and graphs. All practical work should be explained. |
| | Neatness | (N) | **Spread out** your work. Write on one side of the paper only. Use a sharp pencil and box up tables of information. |
| EXTENSION | Initiative | (I) | This is for your original ideas. Explore any aspect of the problem, quoting relevant facts and figures. |
| | Content | (C) | Use mathematics to illustrate your ideas. |

For the Higher Level examination, each piece of Coursework is marked out of 20, but for the Standard Level the 'Extension' work is omitted and it is marked out of 15. The following table shows the allocation of marks for each piece of Coursework.

| Page | Coursework | Maximum marks per category | | | | | |
|------|------------|---|---|---|---|---|---|
| | | M | A | E | N | I | C |
| 21 | Kit Kat bars | 4 | 5 | 4 | 2 | 2 | 3 |
| 40 | World sprint record | 3 | 5 | 4 | 3 | 2 | 3 |
| 61 | Motoring costs | 3 | 5 | 4 | 3 | 2 | 3 |
| 82 | The cross-staff | 2 | 4 | 5 | 4 | 2 | 3 |
| 101 | Aviation flight paths | 4 | 6 | 3 | 2 | 1 | 4 |
| 121 | The solar system | 4 | 6 | 3 | 2 | 1 | 4 |
| 149 | The Active Maths puzzle | 3 | 6 | 3 | 3 | 1 | 4 |
| 165 | Bicycle gears | 3 | 5 | 4 | 3 | 2 | 3 |
| 179 | World population | 5 | 5 | 3 | 2 | 3 | 2 |
| 208 | Traffic flow problem | 4 | 5 | 4 | 2 | 2 | 3 |
| 239 | Surveying with a Silva compass | 1 | 8 | 3 | 3 | 3 | 2 |

## ACKNOWLEDGEMENTS

The authors would like to thank their respective wives Marion and Melissa for tolerating the many long hours of commitment which have been necessary in writing this book. They are also extremely grateful to the large number of teachers who have used the material prior to publication and who have made so many helpful comments about it, especially Ian Potts, Keith Oakley, Nick Owens and Richard McKim, to mention but a few. They would also like to pay tribute to the critical questioning and inspiration they have received from the pupils they have taught while developing ideas and concepts. And last, but by no means least, to the team from Longman, Nina Konrad, Sophie Clark and Hendrina Ellis, who launched this edition.

## Photographs

Barnaby's Picture Library 95; Boeing 49, 103; Bruce Coleman 117; The Duke of Edinburgh's Award photo: Alan Russell 224; Dunlop 6; Frank Lane Picture Agency 115, 159; Michael Holford 169 top, 169 bottom, 228; B. V. Hony 60; Birmingham Evening Mail 15; Kutztown Bologna Comnpany 142; QA Photos 150, 151; Rex Features 36, 218, 241; Science Photo Library 121; Topham Picture Source 78, 113, 240; D. A. Turner 13; The Independent 62.

# 1 ARITHMETIC I

## 1.1 Basic principles

### The calculator

A calculator possesses many different buttons. You will probably have used the following:

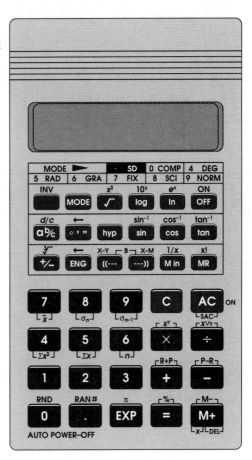

| + | add | | − | subtract |
| ÷ | divide | | = | equals |
| $x^2$ | square | | $1/x$ | reciprocal |
| √ | square root | | ∛ | cube root |
| $x^y$ | $x$ to power $y$ | | +/− | changes sign |
| [( | open bracket | | )] | close bracket |

The order in which you carry out a calculation is important.

REMEMBER

| | |
|---|---|
| Brackets | B |
| Indices | I |
| Division | D |
| Multiplication | M |
| Addition | A |
| Subtraction | S |

Answers can be written to the nearest 100, nearest 10, nearest whole number, etc. Or, a more convenient way of indicating the amount of accuracy is to use either decimal places (DP) or significant figures (SF). Look carefully through the tables below to remind yourself of these methods.

**Decimal places DP**

| Number | Number written to | | |
|---|---|---|---|
| | 1 DP | 2 DP | 3 DP |
| 30.586 | 30.6 | 30.59 | 30.586 |
| 0.04907 | 0.0 | 0.05 | 0.049 |

**Significant figures SF**

| Number | Number written to | | |
|---|---|---|---|
| | 1 SF | 2 SF | 3 SF |
| 30.586 | 30 | 31 | 30.6 |
| 0.04907 | 0.05 | 0.049 | 0.0491 |

**■ EXAMPLE 1**

Give your answers to 3 SF: **a** $\frac{4.38 - 2.97}{9.873}$ **b** $\frac{28.43}{9.04 + 11.875}$ **c** $\left(\frac{1}{0.035}\right)^3$ **d** $\sqrt{4.7^3 - 0.6^2}$

**a** $\boxed{[(}$ 4.38 $\boxed{-}$ 2.97 $\boxed{)]}$ $\boxed{\div}$ 9.873 $\boxed{=}$ 0.143 (3 SF)

**b** 28.43 $\boxed{\div}$ $\boxed{[(}$ 9.04 $\boxed{+}$ 11.875 $\boxed{)]}$ $\boxed{=}$ 1.36 (3 SF)

**c** 0.035 $\boxed{1/x}$ $\boxed{x^y}$ 3 $\boxed{=}$ 23 300 (3 SF)

**d** $\boxed{[(}$ 4.7 $\boxed{x^y}$ 3 $\boxed{-}$ 0.6 $\boxed{x^2}$ $\boxed{)]}$ $\boxed{\sqrt{\phantom{x}}}$ 10.2 (3 SF)

## — Approximations

> **REMEMBER**
>
> When making an approximation: first change all numbers to 1 SF.

**■ EXAMPLE 2**

Find the approximate answer to: **a** $0.087^2 + \frac{4.83}{8.7}$ **b** $\frac{6.87}{7.83 \times 0.478}$

**a** $0.09^2 + \frac{5}{9} \approx 0.1^2 + 0.5 \approx 0.5$

**b** $7 \div (8 \times 0.5) \approx 7 \div 4 \approx 2$

## — Directed numbers

Your teacher says 'I'm not, not giving you a test today.' Are you pleased, or not?

> **REMEMBER**
>
> When subtracting with directed numbers, two negatives become a positive.
> ('Subtract $-3$' means '$-(-3) = +3$'.)

**■ EXAMPLE 3**

**a** Subtract $-4$ from 6. **b** Add $-6$ to $-3$. **c** Subtract $-5$ from $-8$. **d** Evaluate $5 - (-7)$.
**e** Evaluate $-8 + (-10)$.

**a** $6 - (-4) = 6 + 4 = 10$

**b** $(-3) + (-6) = -3 - 6 = -9$

**c** $(-8) - (-5) = -8 + 5 = -3$

**d** $5 - (-7) = 5 + 7 = 12$

**e** $(-8) + (-10) = -8 - 10 = -18$

---

*REMEMBER*

When multiplying or dividing with directed numbers:
- **Like** signs give a **positive** result: $(-3) \times (-2) = +6$
- **Unlike** signs give a **negative** result: $(-3) \times (+2) = -6$

■ *EXAMPLE 4*

**a** Multiply $-5$ by $-7$.    **b** Divide 12 by $-4$.    **c** Divide $-15$ by $-3$.    **d** Divide $-21$ by 7.

**a**  $(-5) \times (-7) = 35$

**b**  $12 \div (-4) = \frac{12}{-4} = -3$

**c**  $(-15) \div (-3) = \frac{-15}{-3} = 5$

**d**  $(-21) \div 7 = \frac{-21}{7} = -3$

## Index form

We use index form for writing very large and very small numbers.

*REMEMBER*

$10\,000 = 10 \times 10 \times 10 \times 10 = 10^4$     *Index form*: $10^4$

$0.01 = \frac{1}{100} = \frac{1}{10^2} = 10^{-2}$     *Index form*: $10^{-2}$

## Standard form

*REMEMBER*

In standard form a number is written in the form
$$a \times 10^b$$
where $a$ is 1 or greater than 1 but less than 10, and $b$ is an integer.
(An 'integer' is a whole number (including zero), and can be positive or negative.)

■ *EXAMPLE 5*

Write the following in standard form and correct to 2 SF: **a** 68 970    **b** 0.0506

**a**  $68\,970 = 6.9 \times 10^4$ (2 SF)     **b**  $0.0506 = 5.1 \times 10^{-2}$ (2 SF)

## ___ Exercise 1

**1** Correct each of the following to 1 DP:
    **a** 4.26      **b** 6.718      **c** 8.572      **d** 0.163      **e** 0.856
    **f** 0.987      **g** 0.049      **h** 0.051      **i** 0.009

**2** Correct each of the following to 2 SF:
    **a** 4.729      **b** 6.29      **c** 7.009      **d** 480.7      **e** 309
    **f** 45 678      **g** 0.249      **h** 0.0842      **i** 0.0846

**3** Correct each of the following to 3 SF:

    **a** 3.617      **b** 6.076      **c** 7.696      **d** 456.9      **e** 456.4
    **f** 45 678      **g** 0.1234      **h** 0.1357      **i** 0.02 468

**4** Without using your calculator, work out:

    **a** $\frac{8 \times 9}{10}$      **b** $\frac{5 \times 10}{0.1}$      **c** $\frac{0.3}{6} \times 3$      **d** $15 \times \frac{0.6}{5}$      **e** $\frac{4 \times 0.2}{10}$

    **f** $\frac{0.3 \times 6}{0.2}$      **g** $\frac{0.8}{2} \div 4$      **h** $\frac{5}{0.5} \div 10$      **i** $6 \times 0.1 \div 0.01$   **j** $20^2 \div (0.5 \times 4)$

    **k** $30^2 \div (0.3 \times 0.5)$          **l** $(0.1^2 - 0.01^2) \div 0.001^2$

**5** Work out an approximate answer to:

    **a** $\frac{172 \times 49.3}{8.5}$      **b** $\frac{4.97 + 92.4}{24.9}$      **c** $\frac{0.08 \times 74}{3.09}$      **d** $746 \div \frac{8.7}{48.9}$

    **e** $\frac{38.7}{7.68} \div 53.8$      **f** $9.02^2 \div 7.85$      **g** $\frac{0.4891^2}{3.82 + 1.89}$      **h** $\frac{0.9}{(0.9^2 + 0.9)^2}$

**6** Use your calculator to work out each of the calculations in Question 5. Give each answer correct to (i) 2 SF (ii) 3 SF.

**7** Write the following numbers in standard form and correct to 2 SF:
    **a** 235      **b** 1260      **c** 5460      **d** 845 000
    **e** 0.025      **f** 0.106      **g** 0.000 36      **h** 0.000 056 5

**8** Use your calculator to work out the following correct to 4 SF:

    **a** $\frac{24.71 \times 0.153}{0.94}$      **b** $\frac{105.6}{2.75 \times 3.51}$      **c** $\frac{11.5 - 3.14}{21.3 + 1.74}$      **d** $(1.08)^5$

    **e** $\sqrt{11.4 + 0.375}$   **f** $(12 \div 11)^7$      **g** $3.7^2 - 2.8^2$      **h** $(0.8)^6 - 1$

**9** Use your calculator to work out the following. Give your answers in standard form to 3 SF.

    **a** $\sqrt{8^2 + 5.6^2}$      **b** $45 - \sqrt{4.5}$      **c** $\sqrt{4.5} - 45$      **d** $(23.456)^2$

    **e** $\left(\frac{4.7}{0.75}\right)^5$      **f** $\frac{(1.09 - 0.85)^5}{0.000\,987}$      **g** $\left(\frac{1}{4.3^3} + \frac{1}{2.3^4}\right)^2$      **h** $\frac{(3.5 + 1.7 \times 2.3)^3}{3.5 \times 1.7 - 2.3}$

**10** Without using your calculator, work out:
    **a** $36 + (-14)$      **b** $(-36) - (+14)$   **c** $36 - (-14)$      **d** $(-36) \div 9$
    **e** $108 \times (-2)$      **f** $(-5.6) \div (-7)$   **g** $10^2 \times 10$      **h** $10^4 \div 10^2$
    **i** $10^2 \div 10^4$      **j** $10^{-2} \times 10^2$      **k** $10^3 \div 10^{-1}$      **l** $10^{-1} \div 10^{-2}$

MASTERMINDERS

**11** Use your calculator to work out, to 3 SF:

   **a** $\sqrt{\dfrac{1}{7.2^2} + \dfrac{1}{3.9^3}}$    **b** $\sqrt{(\tfrac{5}{7})^3 - (\tfrac{4}{7})^3}$

**12** In the sixteenth century, Italian mathematician and gambler Girolamo Cardano devised the formula below for a solution to a cubic equation of the form $x^3 + ax = b$.

$$x = \sqrt[3]{\sqrt{(\tfrac{a}{3})^3 + (\tfrac{b}{2})^2} + \tfrac{b}{2}} - \sqrt[3]{\sqrt{(\tfrac{a}{3})^3 + (\tfrac{b}{2})^2} - \tfrac{b}{2}}$$

Use this formula to find a solution to the equations below (give your answers to 4 SF and check your solutions).

   **a** $x^3 + 4x = 2$
   **b** $x^3 + 5x = 3$

## ▃ Problem solving

> **REMEMBER**
>
> You should solve problems in three stages:
> 1 Write down in **words** what you are trying to find.          [W]
> 2 Show all your **working**.          [W]
> 3 Write your **answer** with the correct units and to the correct degree of accuracy.   [A]

### ■ EXAMPLE 6

In 1989, 6 million people formed a human chain across America. The chain was 6300 km long. Find the mean 'link' length per person.

   [W]     Mean link length per person

   [W]     $= \dfrac{6300 \times 1000}{6\,000\,000}$ m

   [A]     $= 1.05$ m

### ■ EXAMPLE 7

During the first months of its release in America in 1975, the film *Jaws* made about 5 million pounds per week. How much did the film make per second during this period, to the nearest pound?

   [W]     Pounds made per second

   [W]     $= £\dfrac{5\,000\,000}{7 \times 24 \times 60 \times 60}$   (Change 1 week into seconds)

   [A]     $= £8$ to the nearest pound

## — Exercise 2

1  1 million cans of baked beans are sold every day in the UK. Find the mean number sold per second to 2 SF.

2  Concorde uses 360 litres of fuel every 45 seconds. How many litres would you expect it to use each second?

3  A gold bar has a mass of 11.4 kg. If gold is valued at £25 per gram, find the value of the bar.

4  A 450 g tin of tomatoes costs 81p. Find **a** the cost per gram  **b** the mass per penny correct to 1 SF.

5  Each year an average of 250 thousand people are injured on the UK roads. If these people were placed end to end in a straight line, estimate the length of the line.

6  A room measures 6 m by 7 m by 4 m. 1 m$^3$ of air has a mass of 1.2 kg; find the mass of air in the room.

7  When travelling at full speed the QE2 uses 864 m$^3$ of fuel per day. Approximately, how many litres per second are used? (1 m$^3$ = 1000 litres.)

8  Human hair grows at a rate of about 0.43 mm per day. How long would it take, to the nearest year, for a man to grow a 10 m beard? (The photograph shows J. B. Dunlop, Scottish vet and inventor, who originated the pneumatic rubber tyre.)

9  An electron microscope magnifies the length of an object 4000 times. If the image is 80 mm long, calculate the actual length of the object in metres.

## — Percentages

'Per cent' means per hundred: so 1% means $\frac{1}{100}$ and 10% means $\frac{10}{100}$.

> ### REMEMBER
>
> When finding a percentage of a quantity:
> - A percentage less than 100% decreases a quantity.
> - A percentage greater than 100% increases a quantity.

■*EXAMPLE 8*

A standard bottle of shampoo contains 200 ml. The small bottle contains 50 ml less and the large bottle contains 70 ml more. Find, as a percentage, **a** how much less there is in the small bottle **b** how much more there is in the large bottle.

**a**  (We are comparing the capacity of the small bottle with the standard bottle. Therefore we say the standard size is 100%.)
The capacity of the small bottle is $(200 - 50)$ ml = 150 ml. Let $x$ = 150 ml as a percentage.

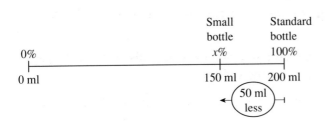

From this ratio line we can write:
$$\frac{x}{150} = \frac{100}{200}$$
$$200x = 100 \times 150$$
$$x = \frac{100 \times 150}{200}$$
$$x = 75\%$$

Therefore the small bottle contains 25% less than the standard bottle.

**b**  (We are comparing the capacity of the large bottle with the standard bottle. Therefore we say the standard bottle is 100%.)
The capacity of the large bottle is $(200 + 70)$ ml = 270 ml. Let $y$ = 270 ml as a percentage.

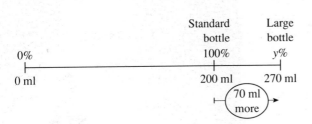

From this ratio line we can write:
$$\frac{100}{200} = \frac{y}{270}$$
$$270 \times 100 = 200y$$
$$\frac{270 \times 100}{200} = y$$
$$y = 135\%$$

Therefore the large bottle contains 35% more than the standard bottle.

---

*REMEMBER*

1  Represent the facts on a ratio line.
2  Relate the **original** quantity to 100%.
3  If you are finding a percentage, put the percentage on the top line.
4  Ask yourself if your answer is sensible.

---

## ▬ Exercise 3

1  What is 12.5% of 30?

2  Increase 54 by 15%.

3  Decrease 87 by 20%.

**4** What percentage of 80 is 54?

**5** Find as a percentage how much smaller £12 is than £15.

**6** Find as a percentage how much larger £15 is than £12.

**7** Find the length which is 15% less than 45 cm.

**8** Find the mass which is 15% more than 45 kg.

**9** At the beginning of a term Maggie put the shot 13.50 m. At the end of the term she put it 14.58 m. What was her percentage improvement?

**10** Tom runs the 100 m in 14.5 s. After training he shows an 8% improvement. What is his improved time?

**11** **Investigate** these facts. A 522 g jar of Marmite is sold as a special offer. On the label is written '15% free'.

# __ 1.2 More calculator buttons

## __ Standard form

Your calculator has a special way of dealing with very large or very small numbers. Such numbers can be entered in standard form.

For example, on your calculator the display `1.2345   09` means $1.2345 \times 10^9$, or $1\,234\,500\,000$.

The display `1.2345   −04` means $1.2345 \times 10^{-4}$, or $0.000\,123\,45$.

Most calculators have a button which produces numbers in standard form. This is the 'exponent' button, shown as `EXP` or `EE`.

■*EXAMPLE 1*

Calculate $(4.1 \times 10^7) \div (2.3 \times 10^{-4})$ in standard form correct to 2 SF.

4.1 `EXP` 7 `÷` 2.3 `EXP` 4 `+/−` `=` `1.7826   11` $= 1.8 \times 10^{11}$ (2 SF)

## __ Exercise 4

**1** Write as ordinary numbers:
   a `6.789   05`   b `2.34   −02`

**2** How would your calculator display the following numbers in standard form?
   **a** 523 000   **b** 7 030 100 000   **c** 0.003 15   **d** 0.000 002 15

**3** Copy and complete the following:

| | Question | Calculator instructions | Answer to 3 SF |
|---|---|---|---|
| **a** | $\sqrt{19} + 89$ | 19 ☑ ➕ 89 🟰 | |
| **b** | $\sqrt{19 + 89}$ | ▐ ( 19 ➕ 89 ) ▌ ☑ | |
| **c** | | 19 ☑ ✖ 89 🟰 | 388 |
| **d** | $(1.989 \times 10^5)^5$ | | $3.11 \times 10^{26}$ |
| **e** | $19^2 - 89$ | | 272 |
| **f** | $\sqrt{198 - 9^2}$ | | 10.8 |
| **g** | $(1.9 \times 10^3) \times (8.9 \times 10^2)$ | | 1 690 000 |
| **h** | | 19 EXP 8 $x^y$ 9 🟰 | $3.23 \times 10^{83}$ |
| **i** | | 19 EXP 8 +/− $x^y$ 9 🟰 | $3.23 \times 10^{-61}$ |
| **j** | $\sqrt{19^4 - 89^2}$ | | 350 |

For Questions 4 to 20, give your answers in standard form to 2 SF.

**4** $(3.1 \times 10^5) \times (2.1 \times 10^3)$      **5** $(1.4 \times 10^{-1}) \times (3.2 \times 10^4)$

**6** $(7.51 \times 10^6) \times (2.5 \times 10^{-2})$      **7** $(5.03 \times 10^{-7} \times (3.25 \times 10^{-3})$

**8** $(4.2 \times 10^3) \div (3.8 \times 10^2)$      **9** $(3.7 \times 10^{-4}) \div (5.6 \times 10^5)$

**10** $\dfrac{1.03 \times 10^3}{6.1 \times 10^{-1}}$      **11** $\dfrac{2.1 \times 10^{-2}}{5.3 \times 10^{-8}}$

**12** $\dfrac{(4.1 \times 10^3) \times (6.21 \times 10^4)}{2.1 \times 10^5}$      **13** $(7.3 \times 10^8) + 10^9$

**14** $(6.2 \times 10^{-5}) - (2.4 \times 10^{-7})$      **15** $(2.5 \times 10^4)^4$

**16** $(5.9 \times 10^{-3})^3$      **17** $(5.8 \times 10^5)^{-3}$

**18** $(3.6 \times 10^6)^4 \times (6.3 \times 10^{-4})^6$

## MASTERMINDERS

**19** $\dfrac{(4.1 \times 10^{-1}) \times (8.9 \times 10^{-3})}{(2.1 \times 10^{-2}) \times (6.1 \times 10^{-4})}$

**20** $\sqrt{\dfrac{(3.2 \times 10^{-2}) \times (9.7 \times 10^2)}{5.6 \times 10^{-3}}}$

## ___ The memory buttons

### ___ *Activity 1*

When you want to carry out a number of similar calculations, you can use the memory buttons on your calculator. This flow diagram shows you how.

To put a number into the memory, you enter the number and then press the 'enter memory' button, `Min`.

`MR` is the 'memory recall' button.

`M+` is the 'add to memory' button.

To clear the memory, you enter 0 into the memory.

Use the flow diagram to multiply each of the following numbers by 1.456 (give your answers to 2 SF):

34, 35, 37.4, 35.9.

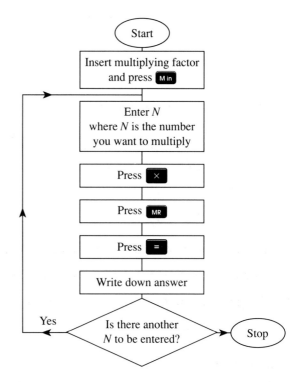

## ___ **1.3** Percentage profit and loss

We can use percentages to work out the profit or loss when something is sold. We are comparing the selling price with the cost price (the original price). Therefore we say the cost price is 100%.

### ___ *Activity 2*

We want to compare the profitability of two young entrepreneurs, Nina and Matthew, who have both made a profit of £4.80.

Nina makes a skirt from materials which cost £6, and she sells it for £10.80.

Matthew makes a go-cart from materials which cost £60, and he sells it for £64.80.

We can use percentages to investigate **comparative** profits.

**1** The cost price (original price) of Nina's skirt was £6. We are comparing the selling price of the skirt with the cost price, therefore we say that the cost price is 100%.

The selling price is £10.80. Let $x$ = £10.80 as a percentage.

First we draw a ratio line like this:

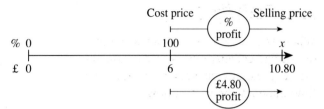

From this ratio line we can write:

$$\frac{100}{6} = \frac{x}{10.80} \quad \text{(Multiply by 10.80 and 6)}$$

$$10.80 \times 100 = 6x \quad \text{(Divide by 6)}$$

$$\frac{10.80 \times 100}{6} = x$$

$$x = 180\%$$

The profit is the difference between the selling price and the cost price, that is:

Percentage profit = 180% − 100% = 80%

**2** Use this method to work out the percentage profit which Matthew made on selling his go-cart.

**3** Who was more successful?

## ■ EXAMPLE 1

A tennis racket is bought for £37.50. It is sold for £30. Find the percentage loss.

We are comparing the selling price with the cost price. The cost price is £37.50 which we call 100%. Let $x$ = £30 as a percentage.

First we draw a ratio line:

From the ratio line we can write:

$$\frac{x}{30} = \frac{100}{37.50}$$

$$x = \frac{100}{37.50} \times 30$$

$$x = 80\%$$

Therefore the percentage loss = 100% − 80% = 20%.

■*EXAMPLE 2*

A woman advertises her food processor in the local newspaper for £45. If she sells it at this price, she makes a 32% loss. Find the price she paid for the food processor to the nearest penny.

We are comparing the selling price with the cost price. Let the cost price = £$x$, which we call 100%.

First we draw the ratio line:

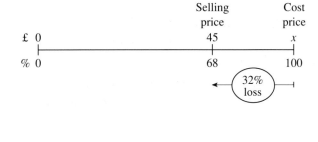

From the ratio line we can write:

$$\frac{45}{68} = \frac{x}{100}$$

$$\frac{45 \times 100}{68} = x$$

$$x = £66.176$$

Therefore the cost price to the nearest penny is £66.18.

---

*REMEMBER*

1 Represent the facts on a ratio line.

2 Relate the **cost price** to 100%.

3 If you are finding a percentage, put the percentage on the top line.

4 Ask yourself if your answer is sensible.

---

## Exercise 5

1  Copy and complete the table. Remember to show all your working.

|   | Cost price | Selling price | % loss or profit |
|---|---|---|---|
| **a** | £38 | £43.70 | |
| **b** | $25 | $29.50 | |
| **c** | £30 | | 12% loss |
| **d** | $45 | $31.50 | |
| **e** | $62 | | 35% profit |
| **f** | £43 | | 90% profit |
| **g** | $67.50 | | 80% loss |
| **h** | | £0.42 | 98.5% loss |
| **i** | £8.10 | £4.05 | |
| **j** | | $69 | 250% profit |
| **k** | £324 | | 140% profit |
| **l** | £3.20 | £12.40 | |

**2** A house is bought for £185 000 and sold for a 32% profit. What is the selling price?

**3** A house is sold for £166 056. If the owner makes a 32% loss, find the original price he paid for the house, to 4 SF.

**4** Lucy makes a 35% loss when she sells her hatchback for £7800. What price did she buy the car for?

**5** A car is bought for £7654. Calculate (to 2 SF) the percentage loss if it is sold for:
**a** £7000  **b** £6500  **c** £6000  **d** £4000. (Remember to use the memory buttons on your calculator.)

**6** A rare stamp increases in value by 35%. What was its value before the increase, if it is now valued at £81?

**7** A CD player decreases in value by 45%. What was its value before the decrease, if it is now valued at £220?

**8**

## Who gets what from the price of a book?

Details from the article were as follows:

| | |
|---|---|
| Retailer | £5.83 |
| Author | £1.29 |
| Distributor | 65p |
| Publisher | £3.24 |
| Printer/Binder | £1.94 |

Use percentages to compare these figures. Comment.

**9** The population of a rabbit warren increases by 20%, and then increases by a further 20%. If there were originally 150 rabbits in the warren, calculate the new population.

**10** A shopkeeper sells a bicycle for £145, making a profit of 16% of his cost price. What price should he sell it at to make a profit of 20%?

**11** A shopkeeper has articles for sale at the following prices:
£3.40, £4.60, £5.98, £6.07, £7.89
Calculate (to 2 DP) what she paid for each of the articles if she makes 14% profit on each article.

**12** A pair of shoes is sold for £46.23. If this price includes VAT at $17\frac{1}{2}\%$, which the shopkeeper adds to the price he paid for the shoes, find the amount of VAT paid.

MASTERMINDERS

13 The table shows, for France and the UK, the relative price of alcohol (relative to take-home pay), the consumption (litres of pure alcohol per year) and the death rate from cirrhosis of the liver per 100 000 of the population.

|  | France | UK |
|---|---|---|
| Consumption | 24.66 | 7.66 |
| Death rate | 51.7 | 4.1 |
| Relative price | 0.016 | 0.057 |

a Work out as a percentage:
  (i) How much less alcohol is consumed in the UK.
  (ii) How many fewer deaths there are from cirrhosis in the UK.
  (iii) How much cheaper alcohol is in France.
b How much more expensive is alcohol in the UK compared with alcohol in France? Give your answer to 2 SF.
c Comment on your answers.

14 In the January sales, a video recorder is reduced by 20% and then by a further 10% of the original price. What was the original price of the video recorder if it was sold for £324 after the second reduction?

15 The usual profit made by a shop on an article is 35%. During a sale 20% is taken off the marked price (this is called a '20% discount'). What is the cost price to the shop of an article which sells for £2.70 during the sale?

16 A shopkeeper sells a pen for 99p and makes a 10% profit. He sells another pen for 99p and makes a loss of 10%. On the two sales together, did the shopkeeper gain, lose or break even?

17 Curry powder is sold at one store for 36 pence per gram and at another for 45 pence per gram. Find the percentage saving of the better buy.

18 The rate of inflation in Eculand fell from 15% to 5%. What effect does this have on shop prices?

## ___ *Activity 3*

Collect examples of percentages that you come across from newspapers and magazines. **Investigate**.

# 1.4 Problem solving

■ *EXAMPLE 1*

An electronic printer can print 12 000 words a second. Approximately, how long would the printer take to print the Bible which contains about $7\frac{1}{2}$ million words?

[W]    Time to print $7\frac{1}{2}$ million words

[W]    $= \dfrac{7.5 \times 10^6}{1.2 \times 10^4 \times 60}$    (Convert to minutes)

[A]    $\approx 10.42$ minutes
(10 minutes 25 seconds)

> *REMEMBER*
>
> [W]   Words
> [W]   Working
> [A]   Answer

■ *EXAMPLE 2*

A common cough virus is $9.144 \times 10^{-6}$ mm long. How many can be placed in a straight line across a pin which has a diameter of $6 \times 10^{-4}$ m?

[W]    Number in a line across a pin

[W]    $= \dfrac{6 \times 10^{-4} \times 10^3}{9.144 \times 10^{-6}}$    (Change to millimetres)

[A]    $= 65\,617$ to the nearest whole number

# Exercise 6

1   Austrian Johann Hurlinger walked from Vienna to Paris on his hands in 55 days. What was his mean speed in mph, to 2 SF, for the 871 mile journey?

2   The world record for the most press-ups in 24 hours is held by Paddy Doyle (UK) who managed 37 350. How many did he do per minute, to 2 SF?

**3** Paul McCartney, songwriter and ex-Beatle, earns an estimated £25 million a year from his compositions. How much does he earn a minute, to 3 SF?

**4** The average British television viewer watches 25 hours 21 minutes of television per week. How many days of viewing, to 3 SF, will a person have watched in a lifetime of 75 years?

**5** The United States Library of Congress houses 63 million books on 860 km of shelving. What is the mean thickness in centimetres, to 3 SF, of a book in the library?

**6** Gold is a very soft metal and can be hammered into sheets $1 \times 10^{-4}$ mm thick. How many sheets are needed to make a pile 25 cm high?

**7** The average mass of a grain of sand is $1 \times 10^{-7}$ kg. How many grains of sand are there in 2 kg? (2 kg is the standard mass of a bag of sugar.) Give your answer to 1 SF.

**8** The radius of the nucleus of the hydrogen atom is $1 \times 10^{-12}$ mm. How many would fit in a straight line across a human hair of diameter 0.06 mm?

**9** The population of the world is $4.5 \times 10^9$. The Isle of Man has an area of 540 km$^2$.
**a** How many cm$^2$ are there in 1 km$^2$?
**b** If every person in the world moved to the Isle of Man, how much space would each person have to stand on? (Give your answer in cm$^2$.)

**10** A woman breathes a mean of 22 times each minute. If she inhales a mean of 650 cm$^3$ of air at each breath, calculate the total volume of air she inhales in a lifetime of 70 years. Give your answer in m$^3$ in standard form to 2 SF. Compare your answer to the volume of your classroom.

**11** The remotest heavenly body visible with the naked eye is the 'Great Galaxy of Andromeda'. It is about 2 150 000 light years away from Earth.
Given that a 'light year' is the distance light can travel in a year, calculate the distance of Earth from Andromeda in km, to 2 SF.
(Speed of light: $3 \times 10^5$ km/s.)

**12** There are on average 90 blades of grass per cm$^2$ on a lawn. Twickenham rugby ground measures 144 m by 69 m. Estimate the number of blades of grass at Twickenham. Give your answer in standard form to 2 SF.

**13** A professional golfer plays 40 tournaments a year, each averaging three rounds.
If the courses are about 5500 m long, how many miles would he hit a golf ball in competition in a year? (Take 1 mile $\approx$ 1600 m.)

**14**

## PROFITS PLUNGE BY $200m

In the article it was revealed that this year's profits were $3.5 billion and the total sales were up by $2.8 billion to $28 billion.

**a** What was last year's profit?
**b** What were last year's total sales?
**c** What was this year's profit expressed as a percentage of this year's total sales?

## MASTERMINDERS

**15** When we stare up at the sky at night we see the stars as they were in the past. This is because they are so far away it takes a long time for the light to travel to Earth.
Through her telescope, Sara looks at Pluto as it was how many hours ago?
(Distance to Pluto $\approx 6.12 \times 10^9$ km; speed of light $\approx 3 \times 10^5$ km/s.)

**16** The Amazon Basin covers an area of 5 million km$^2$ and receives an average of $12 \times 10^{15}$ kg of rain per year. (1 m$^3$ of water has a mass of 1000 kg.)
**a** How many kilograms of rain does 1 m$^2$ of the Amazon Basin receive per day?
**b** How many centimetres of rain fall per day?

**17** A large sheet of paper is 0.1 mm thick. It is cut in half and one piece placed on top of the other. These two pieces are then cut in half again and placed on top of each other. How high is the resulting pile of paper if this is done in total:
**a** (i) 2 times   (ii) 3 times   (iii) 5 times   (iv) 50 times?
**b** The distance from the Earth to the Moon is $3.84 \times 10^5$ km. Compare your answer to part (iv) to this distance.

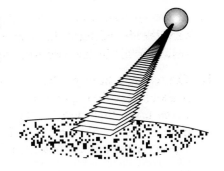

**18 Investigate** the 1988 Olympic medals table shown below. Should the UK be placed last and the USSR first?

| Country | Gold | Silver | Bronze | Population millions |
|---|---|---|---|---|
| USSR | 55 | 31 | 46 | 262 |
| E. Germany | 37 | 35 | 30 | 17.1 |
| USA | 36 | 31 | 27 | 227 |
| S. Korea | 12 | 10 | 11 | 34.7 |
| W. Germany | 11 | 14 | 15 | 60.7 |
| Hungary | 11 | 6 | 6 | 10.3 |
| Bulgaria | 10 | 12 | 13 | 8.73 |
| Romania | 7 | 11 | 6 | 21.6 |
| France | 6 | 4 | 6 | 52.7 |
| Italy | 6 | 4 | 4 | 53.7 |
| China | 5 | 11 | 12 | 983 |
| UK | 5 | 10 | 9 | 59.5 |

## ━━ Revision Exercise 1

**1** **a** Give your answers to 4 SF:

    (i) $\sqrt{2.3^2 + 3.5^2}$                       (ii) $1.89^5$

    (iii) $\dfrac{3.7 \times 10^9}{7.3 \times 10^{11}}$             (iv) $\sqrt{\dfrac{3.51 + 1.72}{3.51 - 1.72}}$

  **b** Give your answers to 3 SF:

    (i) $\sqrt[3]{\dfrac{2.512}{1.253}}$                  (ii) $\dfrac{5.5 \times 10^{-4}}{2.5 \times 10^{-2}}$

    (iii) $\dfrac{10^6}{1.5 \times 10^3}$              (iv) $\dfrac{2.5 + 3.1 \times 2.7}{2.5 \times 3.1 - 2.7}$

**2**

           Sun      Earth    Saturn

The Earth is approximately 150 million km from the Sun, and Saturn is approximately 1430 million km from the Sun.

  **a** When the three planets lie in a straight line, as shown above, how far is Saturn from Earth? (Give your answer in kilometres and in standard form.)

  **b** The spacecraft Voyager 1 sent signals back to Earth from near Saturn enabling us to see new and clearer pictures. Radio waves travel at about 300 million m/s.
    Approximately, how long did it take the signals from Voyager 1 to reach Earth? (Give your answer in minutes.)

**3** Five pupils' examination scores were as follows:

    Steven:  96 out of 120     Anne:    84 out of 112     Mark:  12 out of 16
    Pat:       34 out of 40      Melissa:  96 out of 160

  **a** Convert these scores to percentages.
  **b** Rearrange the pupils in order of attainment from first to fifth.
  **c** A mistake has been made in marking. Melissa's score should have been 10% higher. What is her corrected score out of 160, and her new position?

**4** **a** A chair is bought at an auction for £56.50, and a week later is sold for £71.19. Find the percentage profit.
  **b** A table is bought at the auction for £275. What must the selling price be to make a profit of 16%?
  **c** A dealer bids for a picture at the auction. She thinks that she will be able to sell it later for £350. If she needs to make a profit of 28% when she sells it, what is the maximum price that she should bid for it at the auction?

**5** Jamal places £1200 in a Building Society savings account which pays 12% p.a. (per annum, or per year) on the money in the account.
  Assuming that all interest is left in the account at the end of each year, calculate how much Jamal will have in his account after: **a** 1 year   **b** 2 years   **c** 3 years.

**6** For a school production of 'Hamlet' the costs were:

Script hire:   30 scripts at £1.75 each
Set design:    £325
Costumes:      £160
Programmes:    £94

Tickets for the play cost £1.50 each and programmes were 50p each.
The numbers of tickets sold for the three performances were:

|          | Tickets | Programmes |
|----------|---------|------------|
| Thursday | 112     | 73         |
| Friday   | 153     | 97         |
| Saturday | 180     | 110        |

**a** Calculate the total gain or loss made by the production.
**b** Express this figure as a percentage of the production cost.

**7** A survey was carried out in a school to find out how many pupils regularly watched the Six O'Clock News on BBC1. The results were:

|                  | Boys | Girls | Total |
|------------------|------|-------|-------|
| Do watch News    | 223  | 252   | 475   |
| Don't watch News | 110  | 95    | 205   |
| Total            | 333  | 347   | 680   |

**a** What percentage of boys watch the News?
**b** What percentage of girls watch the News?
**c** What percentage of all the pupils don't watch the News?
**d** What percentage of pupils watching the News are girls?
**e** What percentage of pupils not watching the News are boys?

**8** The distance to the Sun from the Earth is about 150 million km. This distance is called an 'astronomical unit'. If a car could travel to the Sun at 70 mph (miles per hour), how long would it take to cover one astronomical unit? (Take 1600 m ≈ 1 mile.)

**9** The mechanical clock in Salisbury Cathedral dates back to 1386. After repairs in 1956, it is still working. The end of the minute hand describes 630 cm per revolution. Assuming that the clock has never stopped, how far will the end of this hand have travelled by the year 2000? (Give your answer in kilometres in standard form to 3 SF.)

**10** The Seiken railway tunnel links the two main northern islands of Japan. It replaced the dangerous ferry crossing which took about four and a half hours to cover a 112 km sea journey. The tunnel is 37 km long and the train takes 10 minutes to pass through it. Calculate:
**a** The mean ferry speed in km/h.
**b** The mean train speed in km/h.
**c** How much faster the train is than the ferry, in mph. (Take 1600 m ≈ 1 mile.)

## Basics Test 1

**A** Calculator
Give all your answers to 3 SF.

**1** $\frac{6.9}{36.1-21.9}$        **2** $\left(\frac{2.09}{2.19}\right)^5$

**3** $\sqrt{14.9} + 1.49 \times 10^2$        **4** $(3.4 \times 10^{-4}) - (4.3 \times 10^{-3})$

**5** $28.6^3 + 10^4$        **6** $\frac{5.8 \times 10^6}{3.9 \times 10^3}$

**B** Paper and pencil

**7** $\frac{5}{100} + 0.08$        **8** $\frac{5}{6} - \frac{1}{5}$

**9** Find the area of a rectangle whose sides are 19 cm and 23 cm.

**10** A book was bought for £15 and sold for a profit of 12%. What was the selling price?

**11** How many minutes are there in 1740 hours?

**12** How long does it take to travel 198 km at 44 km/h?

**13** Seventeen CDs cost £161.50. What is the mean cost of a CD?

**14** A grain of sand has a mass of $1 \times 10^{-4}$ g. How many are there in 1 kg?

**15** Increase 15 cm by 12%.

**C** Mental
Ten questions will be read out to you.
You need the following information for Questions 16 to 20:

Half a pint of lemonade costs 45p. One packet of biscuits cost 55p.

## Puzzlers

**1** **Practical** Devise a suitable method, and use it, to measure the thickness of a page in your dictionary.

**2** Chris has four different types of coin in her savings, and exactly the same number of each type. If the coins are in general use in the UK and total £18.81, how many of each type does she have?

**3** If the rope attached to the pedal is pulled in the direction shown, in which direction would the bicycle move?

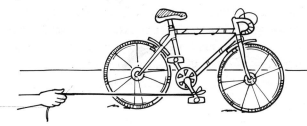

# Coursework: Kit Kat bars

This Coursework is about Kit Kat bars. Each bar costs 25p and has a mass of 47.2 g. 1277 million bars are sold every year.

(For all calculations you should assume that each bar has the shape of a cuboid.)

1 A special promotional packet contains four Kit Kat bars.

   **a** The diagram above shows one way in which these bars can be packed. Draw separate three-dimensional diagrams to show the six different practical ways they can be packed. Which way would you choose for the promotional packet? Briefly explain your reasons.

   **b** Printed on the packet is '4 for the price of 3'. Use percentages to comment on this statement.

2 Forty eight bars are tightly packed into a box whose internal dimensions are 12.6 cm by 24.8 cm by 10.3 cm. If the thickness is 1.05 cm and the width is 6.2 cm, find the length of a bar.

3 Devise a method to measure the dimensions of your classroom, using only a 30 cm ruler. Use it to **estimate** the maximum number of Kit Kat bars which could be stored in the room. Compare your answer to the number of bars sold each day.

4 Compare the total mass of Kit Kat bars sold each year with the mass of a Jumbo jet (approximately 375 tonnes).

5 Copy and complete the following table and give your answers to 2 SF. Assume that Kit Kat bars are sold only during an 8-hour period each day.

|  | Day | Hour | Minute | Second |
|---|---|---|---|---|
| Mean number sold per Mean cost sold per Mean mass sold per |  |  |  |  |

6 Each bar is wrapped lengthwise by a strip of paper. Compare the total length of paper used in a year's production with the circumference of the Earth (approximately 40 000 km).

7 Each bar is wrapped in a sheet of thin foil. If the area of foil used is 10% more than the surface area, work out the total area of foil used in a year's production. Compare your answer to another area of your choice.

## EXTENSION

8 **Investigate** whether a Kit Kat bar is good value for money.

# 2 GRAPHS I

## ___ 2.1 Basic principles

Graphs can be drawn to illustrate the relationship between two quantities. You have probably used conversion graphs (for changing litres into pints, for example) and travel graphs.

### ___ Plotting a graph

In this book a graph of 'distance against time' means distance plotted on the vertical axis, and time plotted on the horizontal axis. Similarly, a graph of 'mass against height' means mass plotted on the vertical axis and height on the horizontal axis.

> ___ *REMEMBER*
>
> When drawing a graph:
> 1 If necessary, work out a table of data from the information given.
> 2 Draw the axes, divide each into equal parts and label each axis clearly. If you are not given the scale, choose a suitable one.
> 3 Plot the points with a neat cross and join them up using a sharp pencil.
> 4 Give the graph a title.

■ *EXAMPLE 1*

This travel graph of distance against time shows part of a race between two cyclists A and B.

**a** Which cyclist is faster?
**b** How far did A travel in 1 second?
**c** What are the speeds of A and B?

**a** Cyclist A is faster because the line A has the steeper slope.

**b** A travels 15 m in 1 second.

**c** [W]    Speed of cyclist A
     [W]    $= \frac{60}{4}$
     [A]    $= 15 \, \text{m/s}$

     [W]    Speed of cyclist B
     [W]    $= \frac{20}{8}$
     [A]    $= 2.5 \, \text{m/s}$

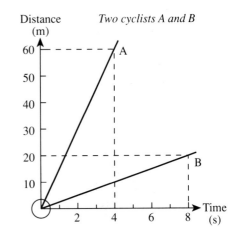

Distance (m) — *Two cyclists A and B* — Time (s)

# — 2.2 Graph relationships

In this section we shall see how the relationship between two quantities can be shown on a graph. We will be looking at both straight-line graphs (such as conversion graphs) and other shapes of graph.

Quantities that can change are called 'variables' (because they can vary!) and we use letters to represent them. For example, we use '$d$' for distance and '$t$' for time. You will come across many other variables in this chapter.

## ■ EXAMPLE 1

$x$ and $y$ are two variables. The graphs of $y$ against $x$ below show different sorts of relationship between $y$ and $x$. Describe these relationships in words.

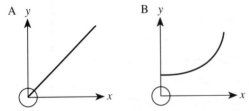

Graph A shows that as $x$ increases, $y$ **constantly** increases.
Graph B shows that as $x$ increases, $y$ **gradually** increases more rapidly.

Can you think of everyday examples which could be represented by each of these graphs?

## ■ EXAMPLE 2

The graph shows how the depth of a sea-wave, at a stationary buoy, is related to time.
Describe this relationship in words.

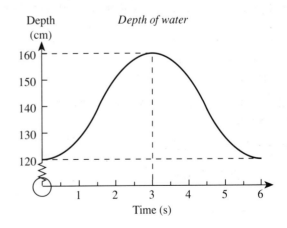

We could say that, 'In the six seconds, the depth of water increases from 120 cm to 160 cm and then decreases to 120 cm'.

23

## ___ Exercise 7

1   Describe an everyday situation to match each of these graphs.

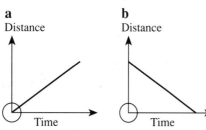 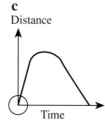 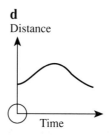

**a**
Distance

**b**
Distance

**c**
Distance

**d**
Distance

2   Which of the graphs (i) to (iii) best fits each situation?

**a** Andrew throws a ball to Ben.

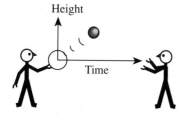

Height

Time

**(i)**
Height

**(ii)**
Height

**(iii)**
Height

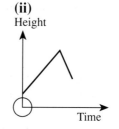 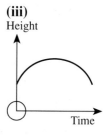

**b** A young tree is planted and grows successfully. Its height is measured each week.

**(i)**
Height

**(ii)**
Height

**(iii)**
Height

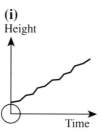 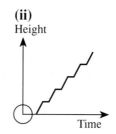 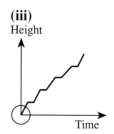

**c** A car accelerates away from rest and then makes an emergency stop.

**(i)**
Speed

**(ii)**
Speed

**(iii)**
Speed

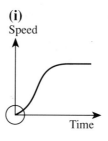 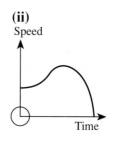 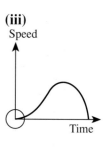

**d** An air-bed is inflated by a hand-pump.

**(i)**
Volume

**(ii)**
Volume

**(iii)**
Volume

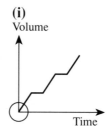 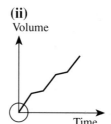 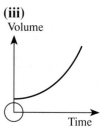

**3** A stone is thrown nearly vertically upwards from a cliff so that it eventually falls to the beach below. Sketch a graph showing how the height of the stone above the beach is related to time.

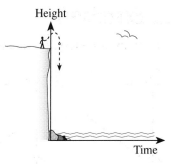

**4** Here is a plan of a Grand Prix motor-car racing circuit. Sketch the speed against time graph that a racing car would produce over one lap of the circuit.

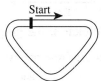

**5** Sketch separate graphs of $y$ against $x$ showing how each of the following are related.
**a** $y$ decreases constantly as $x$ increases.
**b** $y$ increases constantly, then gradually decreases more rapidly as $x$ increases.
**c** $y$ decreases constantly, then gradually increases more rapidly as $x$ increases.
**d** $y$ increases constantly, then remains constant, then increases constantly again as $x$ increases.

## MASTERMINDER

**6** The diagrams show vertical cross-sections through two cylindrical containers A and B, and two containers, C and D, each of which is part of a cone.

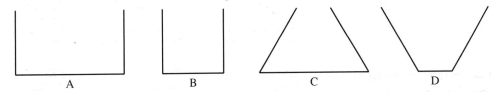

Each container is filled from a tap from which water is flowing at a constant rate. The graphs below show the depth of water measured against time in each of three containers.

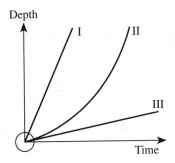

Which container is represented by **a** Graph I   **b** Graph II   **c** Graph III?

## __ 2.3 **Understanding graphs**

In this section you will be given various graphs, each telling a different story. Make sure you understand the graph **before** attempting the question.

---
*REMEMBER*

- Look at the title of the graph.
- Look at the labels on the axes, and the units used.
- Look at the line of the graph

---

■*EXAMPLE 1*

The two lines on the graph below show the **total** lengths of two springs when different weights are hung from them.

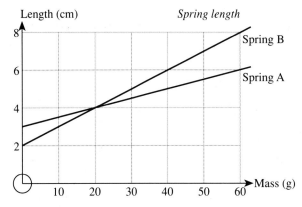

**a** What is the unstretched length of spring B?
**b** What is the extension of spring A when a mass of 60 g is hung from it?
**c** What mass produces the same length in both springs?
**d** What mass, when hung from spring B, increases its length by 1 cm?
**e** When a mass of 40 g is hung from each spring, what is the difference in their lengths?

**a** Unstretched length of spring B = 2 cm.
**b** Extension of spring A with mass of 60 g = 6 − 3 = 3 cm.
**c** Mass producing same length on both springs = 20 g.
**d** Mass which increases length of spring B by 1 cm = 10 g.
**e** Difference in length for mass of 40 g = 6 − 5 = 1 cm.

(Always remember to use **words** to explain each of your answers.)

26

## Exercise 8

1 Sam and Penny monitored their changes in mass over eleven months. Their results are shown on this graph.
   **a** Who was the heavier in June?
   **b** When were Sam's and Penny's masses equal?
   **c** What was Penny's mean monthly increase in mass between 1st January and 1st September?
   **d** Between which months do you think Sam might have been on a diet?
   **e** When was the greatest difference between their masses?
   **f** In which month did Penny's mass remain unchanged?

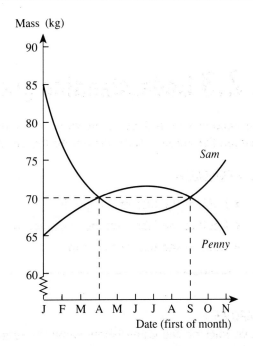

2 Look carefully at this graph.
   **a** Explain in a sentence what information this graph is showing.
   **b** What do you think will happen after the year 2000?
   **c** Copy the graph approximately and mark on it clearly:
   (i) The present time.
   (ii) That part of the curve representing someone born in 1970.
   **d** Calculate to 2 SF the percentage change in the population of 21–24 year olds from:
   (i) 1980 to 1990
   (ii) 1990 to 2000.
   **e** Comment on your answers to part **d**.

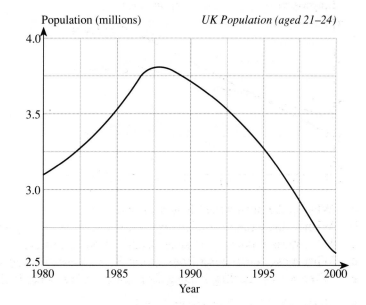

27

**3** An international athlete can run a mile in four minutes. To find out how fast he could run 400 metres, he uses the 'British Milers' Club' conversion graph which is drawn here.

**a** A male runner has a personal best (PB) of 50 s for the 400 m. What would you expect his PB time for the mile to be?

**b** A female runner has a PB time of 4 minutes 10 seconds for the mile. What would you expect her PB time for the 400 m to be?

**c** A male and female runner **both** have PB times of 4 minutes 10 seconds for the mile. If they raced each other over 400 m, who would you expect to win and by how far?

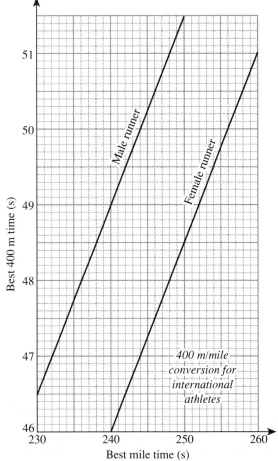

**4** The lower graph shows the amount of petrol in a car's tank monitored during a journey.

**a** What does the dotted line represent?

**b** How much petrol was bought at the first stop?

**c** What was the petrol consumption in miles per gallon: (i) before the first stop   (ii) after the first stop?

**d** The journey involved 'tour driving' and 'motorway driving'. Which part of the graph do you think represents 'motorway driving'? Explain.

**e** What was the average petrol consumption over the 180 miles?

**f** At the **second** stop the tank is filled with 4 gallons of petrol. During the next part of the journey the car encounters a traffic jam and its petrol consumption is reduced to 20 mpg for the next 20 miles. It then continues on a clear motorway for the next 120 miles.

Copy the graph but extend it to show the full 320 miles. Use it to find how many gallons of petrol remain in the tank.

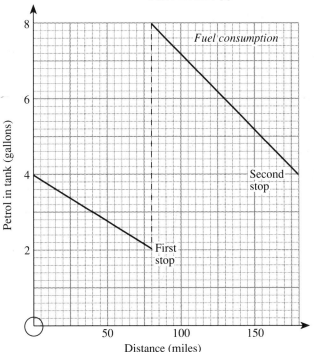

**5** This is a graph relating speed (mph) to traffic flow (vehicles per hour in a single lane) on UK motorways.

**a** What is the traffic flow at 50 mph?

**b** At what speed is there a traffic flow of 5500 vehicles per hour?

**c** At what speed is the traffic flow maximum?

**d** At what speed is there a traffic flow of only 2000 vehicles per hour? Comment.

**e** Estimate the mean spacing of the vehicles in metres at 70 mph.
(1 mile ≈ 1600 m. Average vehicle length ≈ 4 m.)

**f** Compare your answer in part **e** to the mean spacing of the vehicles at maximum traffic flow. Try to explain your answer.

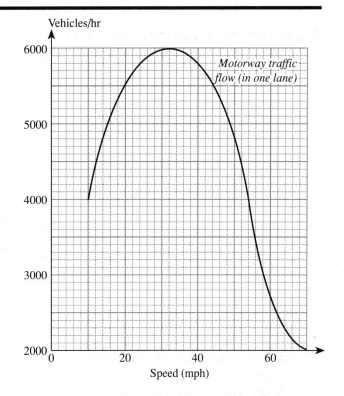

# ___ 2.4 Investigating graphs

In this section you will be investigating the relationship between two variables by means of a graph.

> *REMEMBER*
>
> - First, complete a table of data from the information given.
> - Only then can you draw the graph.

# ___ Exercise 9

**1** Copy and complete the table below showing the area of each square.

| Side of square (cm) | 0 | 2 | 4 | 6 | 8 | 10 |
|---|---|---|---|---|---|---|
| Area of square (cm²) | | | | | | |

**a** Draw the graph of area of square (cm²) against side of square (cm).

**b** From your graph find:

(i) The area of a square of side 5.5 cm.

(ii) The side of a square of area 55 cm².

2 Each of the rectangular windows in this question has an area of $6\,\text{m}^2$ and is of any rectangular shape.

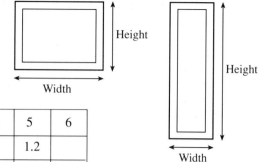

Height

Width

Height

Width

a If the width of a window is 1 m, what is its
(i) height   (ii) perimeter?
b Copy and complete the table:

| Width (m) | 1 | 1.5 | 2 | 3 | 4 | 5 | 6 |
|---|---|---|---|---|---|---|---|
| Height (m) | | | 3 | | | 1.2 | |
| Perimeter (m) | 14 | | 10 | | 11 | | |

c Draw a graph of perimeter (m) against height (m).
d If the cheapest window is the one with the smallest perimeter, find the dimensions of the cheapest window.
e If these windows cost £30 per metre of perimeter length, find the cost of the cheapest window.

3 A small 50 m tunnel is being dug through a hill by two teams.

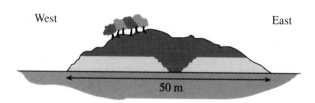

West                    East

50 m

The tables below show the rate at which each team progresses.

| **West Team** | Number of days digging | 0 | 1 | 2 | 3 | 4 |
|---|---|---|---|---|---|---|
| | Tunnel length dug (m) | 0 | 8 | 14 | 18 | 20 |

| **East Team** | Number of days digging | 0 | 1 | 2 | 3 | 4 |
|---|---|---|---|---|---|---|
| | Tunnel length dug (m) | 0 | 9 | 16 | 19 | 22 |

a Copy and complete the table below showing the total length of both tunnels.

| Number of days digging | 0 | 1 | 2 | 3 | 4 |
|---|---|---|---|---|---|
| Tunnel length dug (m) | 0 | | 30 | | |

b Draw the graph of total length (m) against number of days digging.
c Extend your graph to help you estimate when the tunnel will be completed.
d If the digging cost is £25 000 per day, find the total digging cost to complete the tunnel.

4 An observer, at the top of a 50 m cliff, spots a ship 50 m from the harbour at the foot of the cliff when the angle of depression is 45°.
a By accurate scale drawing of a diagram similar to this one, find the distance of the ship from the harbour when the angle of depression is 30°.

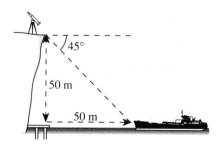

45°

50 m

50 m

**b** Copy and complete the table below, by drawing further angles of depression on your diagram.

| Angle of depression | 30° | 40° | 45° | 50° | 60° | 70° | 80° | 90° |
|---|---|---|---|---|---|---|---|---|
| Distance from harbour (m) | | | 50 | | | | | 0 |

**c** Draw a graph of 'Distance from harbour' against 'Angle of depression'.

**d** Use your graph to estimate the angle of depression when the ship is 70 m from harbour.

**e** If the ship is moving at 18 km/h, use your graph to estimate how long before it docks in harbour from the time when the angle of depression is 35°. Explain why your answer could be **very** inaccurate.

## MASTERMINDER

**5** Copy and complete the table for speed conversions below. (Take 1 mile ≈ 1609 m.)

| Speed (m/s) | 0 | 10 | | 20 | | 50 |
|---|---|---|---|---|---|---|
| Speed (mph) | | | 35 | | 60 | |

**a** Draw the graph of speed (mph) against speed (m/s).

**b** Use this graph to convert: (i) 5 m/s to miles per hour   (ii) 50 mph to metres per second.

**c** Use your graph to help you place the following in order of speed. Write down the speed of each in m/s.

Olympic athlete:
10 km in 30 min

Olympic swimmer:
100 m in 48.42 s

Downhill skier:
2.5 miles in 3 min

Cyclist:
15 miles in 30 min

Racehorse:
40 km in 34 min

Killer Whale:
8 miles in 15 min

**d** Suppose you are travelling at $x$ m/s. Show that this speed in mph ($v$) is given by the equation $v = 2.237x$.

# ___ 2.5 Travel graphs

In this section we first revise travel graphs of distance against time, and then we look at travel graphs of speed against time.

## ___ Distance-time graphs

■ *EXAMPLE 1*

A vintage car takes part in the annual 'London to Brighton Motor Rally' and then returns to London. Here is its distance–time graph.

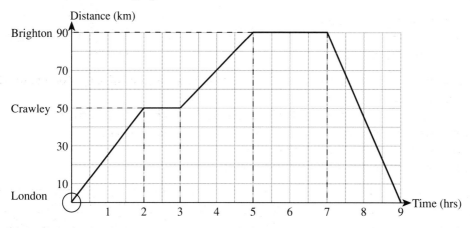

**a**  What is the speed of the car from London to Crawley?
**b**  The car breaks down at Crawley. For how long?
**c**  What is the speed of the car from Crawley to Brighton?
**d**  The car is towed on a trailer back to London from Brighton. At what speed is the car towed?

**a**  [W]  Speed from London to Crawley
 [W]  $= \frac{50}{2}$
 [A]  $= 25\,\text{km/h}$

**b**  The car is at Crawley for 1 hour.

**c**  [W]  Speed from Crawley to Brighton
 [W]  $= \frac{40}{2}$
 [A]  $= 20\,\text{km/h}$

**d**  [W]  Speed from Brighton to London
 [W]  $= \frac{90}{2}$
 [A]  $= 45\,\text{km/h}$

32

# Exercise 10

1 This distance–time graph shows the
journeys of a car and a motorcycle between
Manchester (M) and Birmingham (B).
a When did the car stop and for how long?
b What was the speed of the car up to the
first stop?
c When did the car and the motorcycle
pass each other?
d How far apart were the car and the
motorcycle at 09:30?
e After the motorcycle's first stop, it
increased its speed until it arrived in
Birmingham. The speed limit on the
road was 70 mph. Was the motorcycle
speeding?
f Over the whole journey (excluding
stops), what was the mean speed of
(i) the car   (ii) the motorcycle?

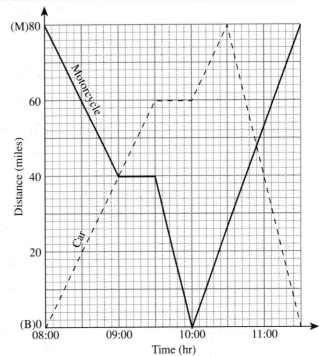

2 Naseem leaves home at 09:00 and drives to Clare's house at a speed of 60 km/h for 1 hour; then
stops at a petrol station for 15 minutes.
She continues on her journey at 40 km/h for 30 minutes, at which point she arrives.
At 13:00 she returns home at a constant speed of 80 km/h without stopping.
a Draw a travel graph to illustrate Naseem's journey.
b Use this graph to estimate when Naseem returns home.

3 Three motorcylists A, B and C
set out on a journey along the
same road. Their journey is
illustrated in this travel graph.
a Place the riders in order (first,
second and third) after:
(i) 0 seconds   (ii) 15 seconds
(iii) 30 seconds.
b When are all riders the same
distance along the road?
c Which rider travels at a
constant speed?
d Which rider's speed gradually
increases?
e Which rider's speed gradually
decreases?

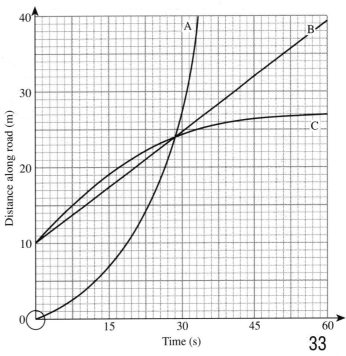

33

**4** The diagram shows distances, in km, between some junctions on a motorway. The junctions are numbered [1], [2], etc. S is the Service Area.

**Driver A** (North bound) joins [5] at 08:00, arrives at S at 09:00, resting for half an hour, then continues his journey passing [1] at 12:00.

**Driver B** (South bound) joins [1] at 08:00, arrives at S at 10:00, resting for one hour, then continues her journey passing [5] at 12:00.

**a** Draw a graph of distance (km) from [1] against time (hours), to illustrate both journeys.

**b** When does driver A pass driver B?

**c** What is A's final speed?

**d** What is B's final speed?

**e** Find the mean speeds of A and B (excluding stops).

## Speed-time graphs

We use travel graphs of speed against time to find out more about accelerations and distances travelled.

A train travels from A to D via B and C. The graph shows details of its speed over time.

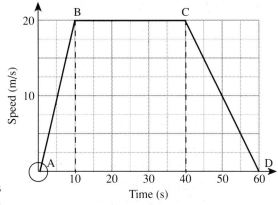

The train's speed is **increasing** between A and B. It is therefore **accelerating**.

The train's speed is **decreasing** between C and D. It is therefore **decelerating** or **retarding**.

The train's speed is **constant** between B and C, at 20 m/s for 30 seconds. Therefore it has travelled 20 × 30 metres (600 m) between B and C. Note that this is the area under the graph between B and C.

> ___ *NOTE*
>
> In a speed-time graph:
>
> • **Acceleration** = Gradient of line = $\dfrac{\text{Change in speed}}{\text{Time}}$
>
> • **Distance travelled** = Area under the graph = Speed × Time

■*EXAMPLE 2*

Look carefully at the graph on page 34.

**a** What is 'acceleration'?

**b** What is the **total** distance travelled by the train?  Hence find the mean speed for the whole journey.

**c** What is the acceleration between (i) A and B   (ii) B and C   (iii) C and D?

**a** Acceleration is a measure of how fast the speed is changing, that is, speed change per second (m/s per second or m/s$^2$).

**b** [W]    Total distance travelled = Area under ABCD

   [W]    $= \frac{1}{2} \times 10 \times 20 + 30 \times 20 + \frac{1}{2} \times 20 \times 20$

   [A]    $= 900\,\text{m}$

   Therefore mean speed $= \dfrac{900}{60} = 15\,\text{m/s}$

**c** (i) [W]    Acceleration = Gradient of line AB

   [W]    $= \dfrac{20}{10}$

   [A]    $= 2\,\text{m/s}^2$

(ii) There is no acceleration between B and C as the speed is constant.

(iii) [W]    Acceleration = Gradient of line CD

   [W]    $= \dfrac{-20}{20}$

   [A]    $= -1\,\text{m/s}^2$   (The minus signs shows a retardation.)

# —— **Exercise 11**

**1** Look carefully at this graph of speed against time for a journey of 15 seconds. Find:
   **a** The initial acceleration.
   **b** The final acceleration.
   **c** The total distance travelled.
   **d** The mean speed.

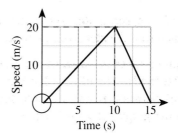

**2** This is the speed–time graph for a three-hour journey. Find:
   **a** The initial acceleration.
   **b** The final acceleration.
   **c** The total distance travelled.
   **d** The mean speed.

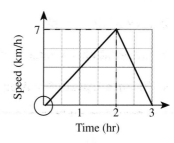

**3** The acceleration of the first part of the journey shown is $3 \text{ m/s}^2$. Find:
  **a** The maximum speed $S$.
  **b** The total distance travelled.
  **c** The mean speed of the whole journey.

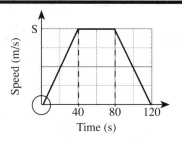

**4** This is the speed–time graph for a 'Sparker' firework.
  **a** What is the maximum speed reached by the firework?
  **b** When does the firework have zero acceleration?
  **c** Estimate the total distance travelled in the 25-second period.
  **d** By calculation, estimate the mean speed of the firework during this time.

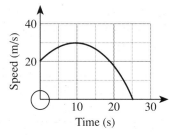

## MASTERMINDER

**5** Look at this travel graph.
  The initial acceleration is $-2 \text{ m/s}^2$. Find:
  **a** The total distance travelled.
  **b** The deceleration after $2t$ seconds.
  **c** The mean speed of the whole journey.

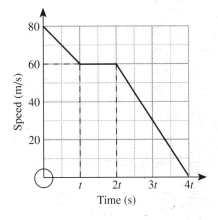

## ── Revision Exercise 2

**1** The diagram shows vertical cross-sections of four containers.

A          B          C          D

Each container is filled from a tap from which the water flows at a constant rate.
Draw graphs of the depth of water against time for each vessel. (Assume the containers are empty at the start.)

**2** A donkey is tethered to a pole at A in the corner of a square field ABCD. The rope is the same length as the side of the field.
The donkey starts at B and trots at a constant speed to corner D keeping the rope taut.
To illustrate this journey, draw graphs of:
**a** Distance from A against time.
**b** Distance from B against time.
**c** Distance from C against time.
**d** Distance from D against time.

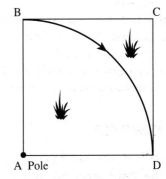

**3** This conversion graph shows 'petrol consumption in km per litre' against 'petrol consumption in miles per gallon' for cars.

**a** A British car travels at 60 mph consuming one gallon of petrol per 30 miles.
(i) Use the graph to convert this petrol consumption to km per litre.
(ii) How many gallons of petrol will this car use if it is driven for 90 minutes at 60 mph?

**b** A foreign car travels at 100 km/h consuming one litre of petrol per 10 km. Use the graph to convert this petrol consumption to mpg.

**c** Why is it **not** possible to say which car has a more economical petrol consumption?

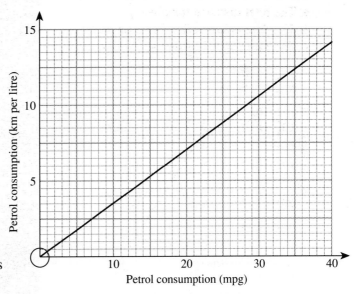

4   Mark and Alex train for a triathlon by swimming 1 km along the coast, cycling 9 km in the same direction along the straight coast road and running directly back to their starting point via the same road. The times of this training session are shown below.

| Mark (min) | | | Alex (min) | |
|---|---|---|---|---|
| Swimming | 20 | | Swimming | 15 |
| Rest | 5 | | Rest | 5 |
| Cycling | 10 | | Cycling | 15 |
| Rest | 10 | | Rest | 5 |
| Running | 35 | | Running | 50 |

a Draw the distance (km) against time (h) graph to illustrate this information, given that Mark and Alex both start at 09:00. (Draw the time axis from 09:00 to 10:30.)
b Use your graph to estimate: (i) when Mark and Alex finish   (ii) when Mark and Alex are equal.
c Calculate the mean speed for both athletes over the whole session, excluding stops.

5   A milkman's van accelerates from rest to 6 m/s in 10 seconds, remains at that speed for 20 seconds and then slows steadily to rest in 12 seconds.
a Draw the speed (m/s) against time (s) graph.
b Use this graph to calculate the milk van's: (i) initial acceleration   (ii) final retardation (iii) mean speed over the 42 seconds.

## MASTERMINDER

6   This graph shows the relationship between the body mass of mammals (kg) and their heart pulse (beats/min).
a Use the graph to complete the table below.

|  | Hare | Dog | Man | Horse |
|---|---|---|---|---|
| Pulse (Beats/min) | | 135 | | 65 |
| Mass (kg) | 3 | | 70 | |

b A 'fringe' theory in Biology states that the hearts of all mammals beat the same number of times in an average lifetime.
(i) If man lives on average for 75 years, calculate the total number of heart beats in an average life-span.
(ii) **Investigate** this theory by calculating the expected life-span of the creatures in the above table.

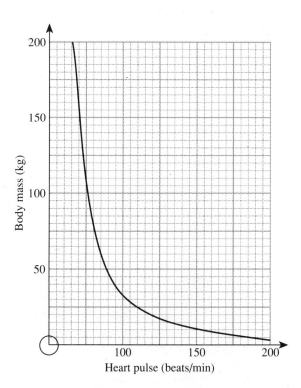

## Basic Algebra Test 1

**Section A**   (1 mark for each correct answer)

**1** $a + a$

**2** $a \times a$

**3** $3e - e$

**4** $\frac{8b}{b}$

**5** $2d + e - d$

**6** $2d \times e \times d$

**7** $2x^2 - x^2$

**8** $2x^2 \times x$

**9** $4 - (x + 1)$

**10** $\frac{x}{3} \times 9$

**11** $c \div (3c)$

**12** $\frac{a + a + a}{a}$

Find the value of each expression when $a = 2$, $b = -1$ and $c = 3$.

**13** $2ab$

**14** $a - b$

**15** $\frac{ac}{b}$

**16** $\frac{c - b}{a}$

Solve for $x$:

**17** $8x = 48$

**18** $\frac{x}{3} = 9$

**19** $14 = 7 + x$

**20** $\frac{24}{x} = 4$

Factorize completely:

**21** $3x + 3$

**22** $4x - x^2$

Solve the inequalities:

**23** $5x > 3$

**24** $5y - 3 \leqslant 2y + 3$

**Section B**   (2 marks for each correct answer)

Simplify if possible:

**25** $\frac{2x}{3} - \frac{x}{5}$

**26** $\frac{2x^3}{3} \div 6x$

**27** $\frac{2x^3}{3} \times \frac{1}{6}$

**28** $(3c)^2 + 2c^2$

Solve for $a$:

**29** $32 + 2a = 6a$

**30** $2(4 - a) = 3$

**31** $\frac{2a - 3}{2a} = 3$

**32** $\frac{2a}{2 - 3a} = 3$

## Puzzlers

**1** **Practical**   Estimate the number of words in the book you are currently reading.

**2** In the addition sum each of eight letters represents a different number. Find the number represented by each letter.

$$
\begin{array}{r}
S\ E\ N\ D \\
M\ O\ R\ E \\
\hline
M\ O\ N\ E\ Y
\end{array}
$$

**3** Quince, quonce and quance are three types of fruit. If seven quince weigh the same as four quonce, and five quonce weigh the same as six quance, which of the following gives the order of heaviness of the fruits (heaviest last)?

**a** Quince, quonce, quance.

**b** Quance, quince, quonce.

**c** Quonce, quance, quince.

**d** Quonce, quince, quance.

**e** Quince, quance, quonce.

# Coursework: World sprint record

This is the photo-finish of one of the the greatest 100 m races in history. It was the final of the World Championships in 1987. The grid, calibrated in hundredths of a second and reading from right to left, shows Johnson (Canada) as he breasts the tape to win followed by Lewis (US), Stewart (Jamaica) and Christie (UK).

10.1      10.0      9.9      9.8

1   Use the figure to work out the finishing times of Lewis, Stewart and Christie, if Johnson finished in a time of 9.83 seconds.

When Johnson crossed the finishing line, the distance $d$ of a competitor in the same race behind Johnson is given by the formula below, where $t$ is the finishing time of that competitor.

$$d = 100\left(1 - \tfrac{9.83}{t}\right) \text{ metres}$$

Use this formula to work out the values of $d$ for Lewis, Stewart and Christie.

2   All members of your class should be timed over 100 m, and, after a 15 minute rest, timed over the 200 m. (Or, your teacher will give you the data.) All the times should be recorded in a table.

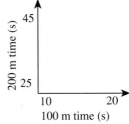

   **a** Use a larger scale to draw the axes shown here. Place a small cross to represent the 100 m and 200 m time for each pupil.

   **b** Explain why the points cannot be joined by a single straight line. Comment on any points which appear to be 'out of place'.

   **c** Calculate the mean time for the 100 m and for the 200 m. Plot this point on your graph and mark it with the letter M. Use a ruler to draw one straight line through M, of 'best fit' for all the points.

3   **a** Suppose you had competed in the final of the 100 m in the 1987 World Championships. How far behind Johnson would you have been?

   **b** If a pupil in your class ran the 200 m in 40 seconds and competed against Johnson in the 100 m, use your graph to help estimate how far behind Johnson that pupil would have finished.

## EXTENSION

4   Show that the formula in part **1** is true.

5   Draw a distance against time graph and a speed against time graph, to illustrate a race between you and Johnson over 100 m.

6   Compare the difference between your school record and the present world record for a number of track and field events. Comment on your results.

# 3 ALGEBRA I

## 3.1 Basic principles

Algebra is the 'language' of mathematics. Read through these Examples to remind yourself of the basic principles of Algebra – simplifying, substituting, factorizing and solving equations – and how these principles are used in expressions.

## Simplifying

■ *EXAMPLE 1*

Simplify the following: (*Answer*)

**a** $3b^2 - b^2 + c$ $= 2b^2 + c$

**b** $3a^2 \times 2$ $= 3 \times a \times a \times 2 = 6a^2$

**c** $(3a)^2$ $= 3a \times 3a = 9a^2$

**d** $4 \div 4f$ $= \frac{4}{4f} = \frac{1}{f}$

**e** $\frac{2a}{3} \times \frac{6}{a}$ $= \frac{12a}{3a} = 4$

**f** $\frac{2a^2}{3} \div \frac{a}{6}$ $= \frac{2a^2}{3} \times \frac{6}{a} = 4a$

**g** $\frac{n}{3} + \frac{n}{4}$ $= \frac{4n}{12} + \frac{3n}{12} = \frac{7n}{12}$

**h** $r - 2(2r - 3)$ $= r - 4r + 6 = 6 - 3r$

REMEMBER

| | |
|---|---|
| Brackets | **B** |
| Indices | **I** |
| Division | **D** |
| Multiplication | **M** |
| Addition | **A** |
| Subtraction | **S** |

## Substituting

When substituting directed numbers into expressions, take great care with the signs. It often helps to put brackets round each term (see Example 2).

■ *EXAMPLE 2*

When $a = 2$, $b = 3$ and $c = -4$, find: **a** $5a - bc$ **b** $\frac{a^2}{c} - b$ **c** $c^2 + 6c$ **d** $a(bc)^2$.

**a** $5a - bc = (5 \times 2) - (3 \times -4)$
$= (10) - (-12)$
$= 10 + 12$
$= 22$

**b** $\frac{a^2}{c} - b = (\frac{2 \times 2}{-4}) - (3)$
$= (-1) - (3)$
$= -4$

**c** $c^2 + 6c = (-4 \times -4) + (6 \times -4)$
$= (16) + (-24)$
$= 16 - 24$
$= -8$

**d** $a(bc)^2 = 2(3 \times -4)^2$
$= 2(-12)^2$
$= 2(144)$
$= 288$

41

# Factors

◾*EXAMPLE 3*

Factorize:         (*Answer*)

**a** $3a^2 - 2a$      $= a(3a - 2)$

**b** $12x + 3y$      $= 3(4x + y)$

**c** $10b^2 - 15ab$    $= 5b(2b - 3a)$

> **REMEMBER**
>
> The **highest common factor** (HCF) of two terms is the highest factor which occurs in both terms.

# Equations

Look carefully at the following simple weighing balance, which illustrates the principles of solving equations.

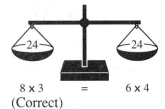

8 x 3   =   6 x 4
(Correct)

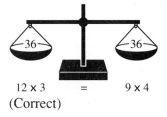

12 x 3   =   9 x 4
(Correct)

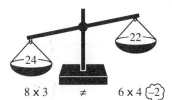

8 x 3  ≠  6 x 4 (−2)
(Subtracting 2 from the righthand side (RHS) unbalances the equation.)

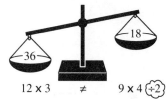

12 x 3  ≠  9 x 4 (÷2)
(Dividing RHS by 2 unbalances the equation.)

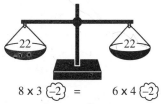

8 x 3 (−2) = 6 x 4 (−2)
(Subtracting 2 from LHS **and** RHS keeps the equation balanced.)

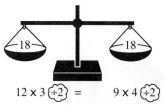

12 x 3 (÷2) = 9 x 4 (÷2)
(Dividing LHS **and** RHS by 2 keeps the equations balanced.)

> **REMEMBER**
>
> When solving equations: you must do the **same operation to both sides**.

Example 4 shows how to solve algebraic equations using this rule. Read carefully through it **before** starting Exercise 12.

■ *EXAMPLE 4*
Solve the algebraic equations:

**a**  $a + 3 = 21$  **b**  $b - 1.5 = 3.2$  **c**  $10.3 = \frac{c}{7}$  **d**  $4.5d = 22.5$  **e**  $18.3 - e = 6.2$  **f**  $3 = \frac{15}{f} - 2$

**a**  $a + 3 = 21$   (Subtract 3 from both sides)  **b**  $b - 1.5 = 3.2$ (Add 1.5 to both sides)
$\qquad a = 18$  $\qquad\qquad\qquad b = 4.7$
(*Check*: $18 + 3 = 21$)  (*Check*: $4.7 - 1.5 = 3.2$)

**c**  $10.3 = \frac{c}{7}$   (Multiply both sides by 7)  **d**  $4.5d = 22.5$ (Divide both sides by 4.5)
$7 \times 10.3 = \frac{c}{7} \times 7$  $\qquad\qquad\qquad \frac{45d}{4.5} = \frac{22.5}{4.5}$
$\qquad 72.1 = c$  $\qquad\qquad\qquad d = 5$
(*Check*: $10.3 = \frac{72.1}{7}$)  (*Check*: $4.5 \times 5 = 22.5$)

**e**  $18.3 - e = 6.2$   (Add $e$ to both sides)  **f**  $\qquad 3 = \frac{15}{f} - 2$ (Add 2 to both sides)
$\qquad 18.3 = 6.2 + e$ (Subtract 6.2 from both sides)  $\qquad 5 = \frac{15}{f}$ (Multiply both sides by $f$)
$\qquad 12.1 = e$  $\qquad 5f = 15$ (Divide both sides by 5)
(*Check*: $18.3 - 12.1 = 6.2$)  $\qquad f = \frac{15}{5}$
$\qquad\qquad\qquad\qquad\qquad\qquad f = 3$
$\qquad\qquad\qquad\qquad\qquad$(*Check*: $3 = \frac{15}{3} - 2$)

# Exercise 12

**1**  Simplify:
    **a** $2b \times b$      **b** $2b + b$      **c** $2b \div b$      **d** $4a \times 2a$      **e** $4a - 2a$
    **f** $4a \div 2a$      **g** $c^2 \div 3c$      **h** $(4e)^2 \div 4e^2$      **i** $(a + a)^2$      **j** $(a + a)^3$

**2**  Find the value of the following, when $r = -4$, $s = -2$, $t = 5$.
    **a** $r + s + t$      **b** $rst$      **c** $2r - 3s$      **d** $r - s$      **e** $st - r$
    **f** $(r + s + t)^2$      **g** $(rst)^2$      **h** $3s^2$      **i** $\frac{rst}{tsr}$      **j** $r^2 + s^2 + t^2$

**3**  Factorize:
    **a** $2x + 2$      **b** $3x^2 + x$      **c** $xy + 2x$      **d** $2xy - 4yz$      **e** $2x^2 - 4x$
    **f** $12b + 4ab$      **g** $ab^2 - 3abc$      **h** $3abc - ab^2$      **i** $3a^2 - 12a$      **j** $3a^3 - 12a^2$

**4**  Solve for $a$:
    **a** $a + 7 = 25$      **b** $1.6 + a = 9.5$      **c** $2a + 3 = 7$      **d** $5a + 1.5 = 36.5$

**5**  Solve for $b$:
    **a** $b - 4 = 7$      **b** $b - 1.1 = 3.3$      **c** $2b - 5 = 11$      **d** $3b - 2.5 = 24.5$

**6**  Solve for $c$:
    **a** $5 - c = 6$      **b** $9.3 - c = 1.2$      **c** $12 - 3c = 9$      **d** $7.5 - 2c = 1.5$

7 Solve for $d$:

   **a** $5d = 125$        **b** $1.1d = 121$        **c** $3.25d = 52$        **d** $1.25d = 156.25$

8 Solve for $e$:

   **a** $9.4 = \frac{e}{5}$        **b** $1.4 = \frac{e}{3}$        **c** $0.1 = \frac{e}{110}$        **d** $120 = \frac{e}{0.05}$

9 Solve for $f$:

   **a** $4 = \frac{12}{f}$        **b** $1.2 = \frac{15}{f}$        **c** $1.3 = \frac{169}{f}$        **d** $140 = \frac{1120}{f}$

10 Solve for $g$:

   **a** $\frac{4}{g} + 5 = 7$        **b** $7 = \frac{10}{g} - 3$        **c** $5 = 1 - \frac{8}{g}$        **d** $1.5 = \frac{8}{g} - 22.5$

## ___ Sequences

A series of numbers which follows a definite pattern is called a 'sequence'. Many problems in mathematics can be solved by using sequences.

---
### REMEMBER

- To continue a sequence, look at the **difference** between the numbers.
- To find the rule for a sequence, use a 'sequence table'.
- Use the rule to find the sequence.
---

■ *EXAMPLE 5*

In the sequence 5, 7, 9, 11, ..., find **a** the fifth term    **b** the rule for the $n$th term    **c** the fortieth term.

**a**    The fifth term is 13.

**b**

| Term number $(n)$ | 1 | 2 | 3 | 4 |
|---|---|---|---|---|
| Sequence | 5 | 7 | 9 | 11 |

From the sequence table you will notice that each term in the sequence is 'Twice the term number plus 3'.

Therefore the $n$th term is $2n + 3$ (this is the rule for the sequence).

**c**    The fortieth term is given when $n = 40$.

Therefore the fortieth term is $2 \times 40 + 3 = 83$.

■ *EXAMPLE 6*

Find the sum of the first 100 odd counting numbers.

First construct a sequence table:

| Term number ($n$) | 1 | 2 | 3 | 4 |
|---|---|---|---|---|
| Sequence | 1 | 1+3 = 4 | 1+3+5 = 9 | 1+3+5+7 = 16 |

From the sequence table you will see that each term in the sequence is the square of the term number.

Therefore the $n$th term is $n^2$.

Therefore the 100th term is $100 \times 100 = 10\,000$.

# ___ Exercise 13

**1**  Copy and complete the table:

| | Term number ($n$) | | | | Rule for nth term |
|---|---|---|---|---|---|
| | *1* | *2* | *3* | *4* | |
| **a** | 6 | 12 | 18 | 24 | |
| **b** | 6 | 7 | 8 | 9 | |
| **c** | | | | | $4n$ |
| **d** | | | | | $n + 7$ |
| **e** | 19 | 18 | 17 | 16 | |
| **f** | −2 | −1 | 0 | 1 | |
| **g** | | | | | $4n + 3$ |
| **h** | 4 | 9 | 14 | 19 | |
| **i** | | | | | $n^2 + 2$ |
| **j** | $1\frac{1}{2}$ | 3 | $5\frac{1}{2}$ | 9 | |

**2**  Look at this pattern of circles:

**a** Copy and complete the table:

| Number of circles ($n$) | 1 | 2 | 3 | 4 | 5 | 6 |
|---|---|---|---|---|---|---|
| Number of dots | 0 | 2 | 4 | | | |

**b** Write down the rule to give the number of dots with $n$ circles.
**c** How many dots would there be in a pattern of 750 circles.
**d** A pattern has 1000 dots. How many circles are there?

**3**  How many squares are there in the fiftieth cross of the sequence?

 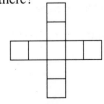 

# __ 3.2 Brackets

A term outside a bracket operates on each of the terms inside the bracket. Therefore:

$3(b + 2) = 3 \times b + 3 \times 2 = 3b + 6$

(This is called 'expanding out' the bracket.)

■ *EXAMPLE 1*

Solve the equation $3(x - 2) = x$.

$$\begin{aligned}
3(x - 2) &= x \quad &&\text{(Expand out the bracket)} \\
3x - 6 &= x \quad &&\text{(Subtract } x \text{ from both sides)} \\
2x - 6 &= 0 \quad &&\text{(Add 6 to both sides)} \\
2x &= 6 \quad &&\text{(Divide both sides by 2)} \\
x &= 3
\end{aligned}$$

(*Check*: $3(3 - 2) = 3$)

■ *EXAMPLE 2*

Solve the equation $y - 2(y - 1) = -4(y + 1)$ .

$$\begin{aligned}
y - 2(y - 1) &= -4(y + 1) \quad &&\text{(Expand out the brackets)} \\
y - 2y + 2 &= -4y - 4 \quad &&\text{(Simplify)} \\
-y + 2 &= -4y - 4 \quad &&\text{(Add } 4y \text{ to both sides)} \\
3y + 2 &= -4 \quad &&\text{(Subtract 2 from both sides)} \\
3y &= -6 \quad &&\text{(Divide both sides by 3)} \\
y &= -2
\end{aligned}$$

(*Check*: $-2 - 2(-2 - 1) = -4(-2 + 1)$)

# __ Exercise 14

Solve the following equations:

1  $x + 5(x + 1) = x$

2  $2y - 5(y + 1) = y$

3  $4z = z - (z - 2)$

4  $3(p - 1) = 2(1 - p)$

5  $3(2a - 1) = 2(1 - 3a)$

6  $b - 4 = 7(2 - b)$

7  $3(2c + 1) = 2(c - 1)$

8  $-2(3d - 1) = -(1 - 3d)$

9  $4(t - 1) + 3(t + 2) = 5(t - 4)$

10  $7(w + 4) - 5(w + 3) + (4 - w) = 0$

# — 3.3 Symbolic expression

'Symbolic expression' is the process of writing a mathematical statement which includes a letter or a number of letters.

For example, if John is $x$ years old and Jill is three years younger, we can write

Jill's age = $(x - 3)$ years

## ■ EXAMPLE 1

Find the cost of $x$ pens at **a** 20p each   **b** $y$p each.

**a**   The cost of $x$ pens at 20p each = $20x$ p.

**b**   The cost of $x$ pens at $y$p each = $xy$ p, or £$\dfrac{xy}{100}$.

## — REMEMBER

- Speed $(v)$ = $\dfrac{\text{Distance}}{\text{Time}}$
- Area of rectangle = Length × Breadth
- Volume of cuboid = Base area × Height
- Area of triangle = $\dfrac{b \times h}{2}$
- Area of parallelogram = $b \times h$
- Area of trapezium = $\dfrac{h}{2}(a + b)$

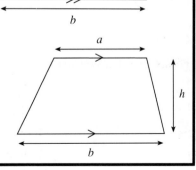

---

┌─── REMEMBER

**1** Write down the **facts**, if necessary on a diagram.    [F]

**2** Write down the correct **equation**.    [E]

**3** **Substitute** the facts into the equation.    [S]

**4** Show all the **working**.    [W]

---

■ *EXAMPLE 2*

The highest speed ever achieved on a bicycle is 245 km/h (John Howard, USA, 1985). How long did it take him to travel 100 m?

[F]        $v = 245$ km/h, $d = 100$ m $= 0.1$ km

[E] and [S]    $245 = \frac{0.1}{t}$

[W]        $t = \frac{0.1}{245} \times 60 \times 60$ seconds

            $= 1.5$ seconds (1 DP)

■ *EXAMPLE 3*

Find the value of $b$ for this trapezium if $a = 8$ cm, $h = 3$ cm and the area $A = 19.5$ cm$^2$.

[F]        $a = 8$ cm, $h = 3$ cm, $A = 19.5$ cm$^2$

[E] and [S]        $19.5 = \frac{3}{2}(8 + b)$

[W]        $\frac{19.5 \times 2}{3} - 8 = b$

            $b = 5$ cm

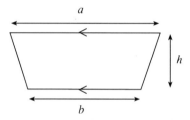

## ─── Exercise 15

**1**  **a** How many mm are there in $q$ cm?

   **b** How many hours are there in $k$ days?

   **c** Make $d$ twelve times smaller.

   **d** Increase $d$ cm by $e$ cm.

   **e** Make $x$ kg $y$ times heavier.

**2**  Richard Noble in 'Thrust 2' set a new world land speed record of 636 mph. How far did he travel in 30 seconds?

**3**  The fastest speed of a ball served in tennis is 222 km/h. How long would it have taken for the ball to travel 24 m, the length of a tennis court?

4   The largest hangar in the world is
    the Boeing 747 manufacturing plant
    at Everett, Washington USA. It has a
    volume of $5.7 \times 10^6 \, \text{m}^3$, a length of
    492 m and a width of 630 m.
    Find its height to 3 SF.
    (Assume the building to be a
    rectangular block.)

5   One diagonal of a rhombus is 24 cm long. If the area is $192 \, \text{cm}^2$, find the length of the other
    diagonal.

6   This diagram is an arrowhead. Find the length $x$.

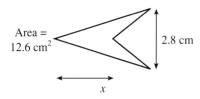

7   This diagram is a kite. Find the length $x$.

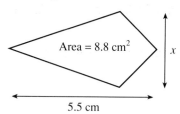

# — 3.4 Problem solving

■ *EXAMPLE 1*

The sum of three consecutive whole numbers is 105. Find the numbers.

Let the smallest number be $x$.
Therefore the other numbers are $(x + 1)$ and $(x + 2)$.
The sum of the three numbers is 105, therefore:

$$x + (x + 1) + (x + 2) = 105$$
$$3x + 3 = 105$$
$$3x = 102$$
$$x = 34$$

Therefore the three numbers are 34, 35 and 36.

(*Check*: $34 + 35 + 36 = 105$)

■ *EXAMPLE 2*

The length of a rectangle is 5 cm greater than its width. If its perimeter is 24 cm, find its width.

Let the width be $x$ cm.
Therefore the length is $(x + 5)$ cm.
The perimeter is 24 cm, therefore:

$$x + (x + 5) + x + (x + 5) = 24$$
$$4x + 10 = 24$$
$$4x = 14$$
$$x = 3.5$$

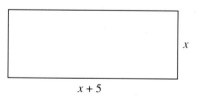

Therefore the width is 3.5 cm and the length is 8.5 cm.

(*Check*: $3.5 \text{ cm} + 8.5 \text{ cm} + 3.5 \text{ cm} + 8.5 \text{ cm} = 24 \text{ cm}$)

# — Exercise 16

**1** The sum of three consecutive numbers is 78. Find the numbers.

**2** The sum of four consecutive numbers is 78. Find the numbers.

**3** Find three consecutive numbers which add up to 114.

**4** When a number is doubled and then added to 47, the result is 73. Find the number.

**5** When 9 is subtracted from four times a certain number the result is 21. Find the number.

**6** I think of a number, multiply it by 7 and then add 5. If the result is 61, what was the number?

**7** I think of a number, divide it by 8 and then subtract 3. If the result is 6, what was the number?

**8** The length of a rectangle is three times its width. If the perimeter is 104 cm, find the width.

**9** The perimeter of the rectangular field is 196 m. Find its width and length.

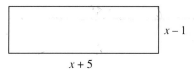

$x - 1$

$x + 5$

**10** The difference between two numbers is 14. Find the numbers if their sum is 40.

**11** In twelve years time Cathy will be three times as old as she is now. How old is she now?

**12** David is three years older than Tariq who is five years older than Carl. If their combined age is 40, find the age of each person.

**13** Linda weighs 7 kg less than Ann, who in turn is 9 kg lighter than Justine. If their total mass is 167 kg, how heavy is each person?

**14** A sweater costs £18 more than a blouse. If the price of the two is £41, find the cost of the sweater.

**15** Find the area of the rectangle if the perimeter is 42 cm.

$2x - 1$

$3x + 2$

## MASTERMINDER

**16** Jake takes part in a bicycle race which starts at Leeds and passes through Sheffield, Nottingham and finishes at Rugby. The details of Jake's race are shown on this diagram.
Find each of the following in terms of the appropriate letter or letters.
**a** The total distance cycled.
**b** The total time taken in hours.
**c** His overall mean speed in km/h.

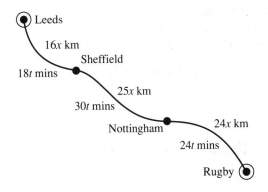

Leeds

16x km

Sheffield

18t mins

25x km

30t mins

Nottingham

24x km

24t mins

Rugby

# ___ 3.5 Simplifying algebraic fractions

The operations of multiplying and dividing, adding and subtracting algebraic fractions are performed in the same way as for numbers. Make sure that you understand these Examples before starting Exercise 17.

■ *EXAMPLE 1*

Simplify as far as possible:

**a** $\frac{2a^2}{a} \times \frac{3b}{b^2}$   **b** $\frac{3a^2}{bc} \div \frac{2a}{b^2}$   **c** $\frac{3}{a} + \frac{4}{b}$   **d** $\frac{2a-1}{3} - \frac{a+3}{4}$.

**a** $\quad \dfrac{2a^2}{a} \times \dfrac{3b}{b^2} = \dfrac{2 \times a \times a}{a} \times \dfrac{3 \times b}{b \times b} = \dfrac{6a}{b}$

**b** $\quad \dfrac{3a^2}{bc} \div \dfrac{2a}{b^2} = \dfrac{3a^2}{bc} \times \dfrac{b^2}{2a}$

$\qquad = \dfrac{3 \times a \times a}{b \times c} \times \dfrac{b \times b}{2 \times a}$

$\qquad = \dfrac{3ab}{2c}$

**c** $\quad \dfrac{3}{a} + \dfrac{4}{b} = \dfrac{3b}{ab} + \dfrac{4a}{ab} = \dfrac{3b + 4a}{ab}$

**d** $\quad \dfrac{2a-1}{3} - \dfrac{a+3}{4} = \dfrac{4(2a-1)}{12} - \dfrac{3(a+3)}{12}$

$\qquad = \dfrac{4(2a-1) - 3(a+3)}{12} = \dfrac{8a - 4 - 3a - 9}{12}$

$\qquad = \dfrac{5a - 13}{12}$

## ___ Exercise 17

Simplify the following:

**1** $\frac{2}{5} \times \frac{3}{4}$   **2** $\frac{2a}{3} \times \frac{3a}{4}$   **3** $\frac{2a}{b} \times \frac{b^2}{a}$   **4** $\frac{a^2b}{c} \times \frac{ac^3}{b^2}$

**5** $\frac{3}{4} \div \frac{2}{9}$   **6** $\frac{2a}{3} \div \frac{5a}{6}$   **7** $\frac{ab}{c} \div \frac{a}{b}$   **8** $\frac{15a^2b}{c} \div \frac{5ac}{b^3}$

**9** $\frac{2}{5} + \frac{3}{4}$   **10** $\frac{2a}{3} + \frac{a}{4}$   **11** $\frac{3a}{5} + \frac{4a}{3}$   **12** $\frac{a}{2} + \frac{a+1}{3}$

**13** $\frac{4}{5} - \frac{3}{10}$

**14** $\frac{2a}{3} - \frac{a}{5}$

**15** $\frac{a}{b} - \frac{c}{d}$

**16** $\frac{a-3}{2} - \frac{a}{4}$

**17** $\frac{3}{a} + \frac{2}{3a}$

**18** $\frac{a+2}{2} + \frac{3a-2}{3}$

**19** $\frac{2a+1}{3} - \frac{3a-1}{2}$

**20** $\frac{a-1}{3} - \frac{a+2}{4}$

**21** $\frac{8ab^2}{12ab}$

**22** $\frac{24a^2bc^2}{12ab^2c}$

**23** $\frac{(2a)^3}{4a}$

**24** $\frac{(2a)^2(3b)^2}{6abc}$

**25** $\frac{9a-a^2}{a}$

**26** $\frac{2a+3a^2}{2a}$

**27** $\frac{5a+10b}{15ab}$

**28** $\frac{(2a)^2-8a}{4a}$

MASTERMINDERS

**29** $\frac{2}{a+3} + \frac{3}{a-2}$

**30** $\frac{3}{2a-1} - \frac{4}{3a+1}$

# 3.6 Solving algebraic fractions

When solving equations with fractions, both sides of the equation should be multiplied by the **lowest common multiple of the denominators** to eliminate the fractions.

■*EXAMPLE 1*
Solve: **a** $\frac{a}{5} = \frac{a-2}{3}$  **b** $\frac{a+2}{3} = \frac{2a-1}{4} - 1$.

**a**   First, multiply both sides by 15 (the lowest common multiple of the denominators):

$$15 \times \frac{a}{5} = 15 \times \frac{(a-2)}{3}$$
$$3a = 5(a-2)$$
$$3a = 5a - 10$$
$$10 = 2a$$
$$5 = a$$
(*Check*: $\frac{5}{5} = \frac{5-2}{3}$)

**b**   Multiply both sides by 12 (the lowest common multiple of the denominators):

$$12 \times \frac{a+2}{3} = 12 \times \left(\frac{2a-1}{4} - 1\right)$$
$$4(a+2) = 3(2a-1) - 12$$
$$4a + 8 = 6a - 3 - 12$$
$$23 = 2a$$
$$\frac{23}{2} = a$$
$$a = 11\tfrac{1}{2}$$
(*Check*: $\frac{11\frac{1}{2}+2}{3} = \frac{23-1}{4} - 1$)

## ___ Exercise 18

Solve the following equations:

**1** $\frac{x}{9} = \frac{2}{3}$   **2** $12 = \frac{x}{5}$   **3** $\frac{5}{x} = 2$   **4** $7 = \frac{-3}{x}$

**5** $\frac{4}{x} = \frac{1}{5}$   **6** $\frac{-2}{3} = \frac{5}{x}$   **7** $\frac{x}{2} = \frac{x-1}{3}$   **8** $\frac{2x+1}{3} = \frac{x}{4}$

**9** $\frac{x+2}{4} = \frac{x+1}{5}$   **10** $\frac{x-1}{2} = \frac{3x+1}{5}$   **11** $\frac{x}{2} + \frac{x}{3} = 6$   **12** $\frac{2x}{3} - \frac{x}{4} = 5$

**13** $\frac{4x-3}{3} + 2 = x$   **14** $10 = 1 - \frac{x-3}{2}$   **15** $\frac{3}{x+3} = \frac{10}{x}$   **16** $\frac{-5}{x} = \frac{3}{2x-1}$

**17** $\frac{4}{x-5} = \frac{7}{x+3}$   **18** $\frac{3}{x+3} = \frac{-6}{2x-5}$   **19** $\frac{x-3}{2} + \frac{2x}{3} + 2 = 0$   **20** $\frac{x-1}{2} + \frac{2x+1}{5} + 5 = 0$

**21** $\frac{1}{2}(x+4) + \frac{1}{3}(3x+1) = 0$   **22** $\frac{1}{4}(7x-3) - \frac{1}{5}(2x+1) = 0$

### MASTERMINDERS

**23** $\frac{x+1}{2} + \frac{3x+2}{5} + 1 = \frac{1-x}{2}$   **24** $\frac{2x+5}{3} - \frac{5-2x}{4} - 2 = 3x$   **25** $-7 - \frac{x-1}{3} = -\frac{1-3x}{2}$

## ___ 3.7 Simultaneous equations

We are going to look at equations with **two** variables, say $x$ and $y$. For example, in the equation $y = 2x + 3$, when $x = 3$, $y = 9$, and when $x = 4$, $y = 11$. We can write the solutions like this:

$x$   ... 3   4   5   ...
$y$   ... 9   11   13   ...

There is no one answer for the values of $x$ and $y$. It is impossible to solve this equation on its own. However, if we are given a second equation in which $x$ and $y$ represent the same numbers as in the first equation, we can solve these two equations **simultaneously** (at the same time).

■ *EXAMPLE 1*
Solve the simultaneous equations:   $y = 2x + 3$   [1]
$y = 4x - 3$   [2]

Since $y$ has the same value in each equation, we can write:
$$2x + 3 = 4x - 3$$
$$3 + 3 = 4x - 2x$$
$$6 = 2x$$
$$x = 3$$
(Substitute $x = 3$ in equation [1].)
$$y = 2 \times 3 + 3$$
$$y = 9$$

(Check these answers by substituting them in equation [2].)
$$9 = 4 \times 3 - 3 = 9$$

## Exercise 19

Solve the simultaneous equations:

**1** $y = x + 1$
$y = 3x - 1$

**2** $y = x + 3$
$y = 2x + 1$

**3** $y = 2x + 3$
$y = 3x - 1$

**4** $y = 6x - 5$
$y = 5x + 1$

**5** $y = 4x + 3$
$y = 2x + 8$

**6** $y = 7 - 2x$
$y = 2x + 1$

**7** $y = 10 - 3x$
$y = 12 - 2x$

**8** $y = 2x + 7$
$y = 1 - 2x$

**8** $y = 2x + 7$
$y = 6x - 21$

MASTERMINDERS

**10** $4y = x + 20$
$2y = 16 + x$

**11** $2x + 3y = -6$
$3x - 2y = 17$

**12** $6x - 5 = 2y$
$14x - 17 = 6y$

## Activity 4

There is a definite procedure in solving simultaneous equations, hence a computer can be used in their solution.    Consider the following simultaneous equations:

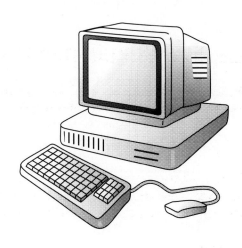

$$ax + by = c \qquad [1]$$
$$dx + ey = f \qquad [2]$$

From equation [1]:

$$y = \frac{c - ax}{b} \qquad [1]$$

Substitute in [2]:

$$dx + \frac{e(c - ax)}{b} = f \qquad [2] \quad \text{(Multiply by } b)$$
$$dxb + e(c - ax) = fb \qquad [2]$$
$$dxb + ec - axe = fb$$
$$x(db - ae) = fb - ec$$
$$x = \frac{fb - ec}{db - ae}$$

Substituting in [1] gives:

$$y = \frac{dc - af}{db - ae}$$

In the program on the next page, simply enter the values of $a$, $b$, $c$, $d$, $e$ and $f$ when the equations are in the form of [1] and [2] above.

*Note*: if $db - ae = 0$ the division is impossible!  Can you explain when this would occur?  (The program does check this.)

```
10  REM SOLVING SIM EQNS
20  PRINT "ENTER a, b, c, d, e, and f FOR EACH EQUATION
        ax + by + c : dx + ey = f"
30  INPUT "FIRST EQUATION a, b, c", A, B, C
40  INPUT "SECOND EQUATION d, e, f", D, E, F
50  DET = D*B - A*E
60  IF DET = 0 PRINT "INFINITE SOLUTIONS" : END
70  X = (F*B - E*C)/DET : Y = (D*C - A*F)/DET
80  PRINT "X =   "; X;   ": Y =   "; Y
90  END
```

Use the program to check some of your answers to Exercise 19.

# 3.8 Inequalities

## REMEMBER

- $A < 3$ means '$A$ is less than 3'.
- $B > 5$ means '$B$ is greater than 5'.
- $C \leqslant -7$ means '$C$ is less than or equal to $-7$'.
- $D \geqslant -9$ means '$D$ is greater than or equal to $-9$'.

## Number lines

When $x > 3$, $x$ can be any number as long as it is greater than 3. Its 'number line' looks like this:

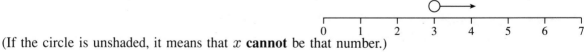

(If the circle is unshaded, it means that $x$ **cannot** be that number.)

When $x \leqslant 4$, but greater than 0, $x$ can be any number as long as it is less than or equal to 4 but greater than 0. Its number line looks like this:

(If the circle is shaded, it means that $x$ **can** be that number.)

A more complicated inequality such as $-2 < x < 5$ has a number line like this:

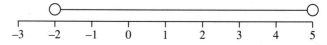

## Solving inequalities

To solve an inequality, we follow the same method as used for solving algebraic equations **except** when multiplying or dividing by a negative number. In this case the inequality sign is 'reversed'.

Look at the inequality '$10 > 5$'. What happens if both sides are multiplied by $-2$?

$10 > 5$      (Multiply both sides by $-2$)
$-20 > -10$      (This is incorrect so the inequality is 'reversed')
$-20 < -10$

**■EXAMPLE 1**
Solve the inequalities **a** $3x - 4 \geqslant 2$    **b** $5 - 3x < 1$

**a**   $3x - 4 \geqslant 2$      (Add 4 to both sides.)
     $3x \geqslant 6$      (Divide both sides by 3)
     $x \geqslant 2$

**b**   $5 - 3x < 1$      (Subtract 5 from both sides)
     $-3x < -4$      (Divide both sides by $-3$, and **reverse the inequality sign**)
     $x > \frac{4}{3}$

*REMEMBER*

- Collect up the lettered terms on the lefthand side.
- When dividing or multiplying both sides by a negative number, you must **reverse** the inequality sign.

## Exercise 20

**1** Put either $>$ or $<$ between each of the following:
   **a** $-3, -6$      **b** $(-2)^3, 1$      **c** $0.15, \frac{1}{6}$      **d** $\pi^2, 10$

**2** Solve the inequalities and show the result on a number line.
   **a** $2x - 3 > 5$      **b** $10 \leqslant 4x - 14$      **c** $2(x + 1) \geqslant 8$      **d** $2(x - 1) < 3(1 - x)$

**3** Solve the inequalities and state the first three integers of the solution set (the group of all possible answers).
   **a** $2x - 9 \geqslant -1$      **b** $\frac{x}{3} - 4 < 5$      **c** $2 + \frac{x}{3} > 5$      **d** $4(x + 1) \leqslant 5(x - 1)$

MASTERMINDER

**4** Show on a number line the solution set of each pair of simultaneous inequalities.
   **a** $x < 4; -1 \leqslant x \leqslant 6$      **b** $x \geqslant -5; -3 < x \leqslant 1$
   **c** $2x - 1 \leqslant 15; -10 < 3x + 5$      **d** $3x - 1 < 20; 2(x + 3) \geqslant 3(x - 3)$

## Revision Exercise 3

**1** Simplify:

**a** $2a - 3b - 4 + a$  **b** $xy - x + 3xy - x$  **c** $y \times y^2 \times y^3$

**d** $3pq + 2p^2 + 5pq - q^2$  **e** $\dfrac{h + h + h + h}{h}$  **f** $(2y)^3 \times (2y)^2$

**2** Remove the brackets from these expressions, and simplify:

**a** $2x + (3 - x)$  **b** $10 - (2y - 1)$  **c** $3p - (1 - 2p)$

**d** $x^2 - x(y - x)$  **e** $2(3a - 1) - 3(a + 1)$  **f** $5(x^2 - 1) - 3(1 - x - x^2)$

**3** If $a = 3$, $b = -2$ and $c = 4$, calculate:

**a** $a - bc$  **b** $a(b - c)$  **c** $a^2 + b^2 + c^2$

**d** $\dfrac{a}{b+2c}$  **e** $(a + b)(b + c)$  **f** $b^3 + 2c$

**4** If $x = 1.2 \times 10^3$, $y = 2.5 \times 10^{-2}$ and $z = 6.2 \times 10^{-3}$, calculate the value of the following, expressing your answers in standard form to 2 SF:

**a** $xy$  **b** $2yz$  **c** $y^2$

**d** $y(y - z)$  **e** $\dfrac{x}{(5xy)^2}$  **f** $xyz(x + y + z)$

**5** Mary copied down some answers to a test. She did not include the brackets! In each question $a = 1$, $b = 2$ and $c = -3$. Re-write the expressions, replacing the brackets.

**a** $ab + c = -1$  **b** $a + bc^2 = 27$  **c** $3b^2 + a = 15$

**d** $abc + a = -4$  **e** $2b - ac^2 = 18$  **f** $3a - cb^2 = 24$

**6** Factorize:

**a** $2x + 6y$  **b** $xy - 3x$  **c** $pq^2 - 2pq$

**d** $4ab - 8a^2$  **e** $u^2v - v^2u$  **f** $2ab^2 + 6a^2b$

**7** Solve:

**a** $2p - 3 = 11$  **b** $3 - 2p = 11$  **c** $\dfrac{q}{6} = 12.5$

**d** $\dfrac{120}{q} = 8$  **e** $\dfrac{3}{r} - 1 = 7$  **f** $14 = 2 + \dfrac{6}{r}$

**8** Solve:

**a** $a + 2(a + 1) = 3$  **b** $2a - 3(a + 1) = a$  **c** $3x = x + (1 - 2x)$

**d** $2x = x - (x - 2)$  **e** $3(t - 1) = 2(t - 2)$  **f** $-2(3t + 1) = -3(1 - 4t)$

**9** Solve:

**a** $\dfrac{w}{2} = \dfrac{3}{4}$  **b** $4 = \dfrac{36}{w}$  **c** $\dfrac{a}{2} = \dfrac{a - 2}{3}$

**d** $\dfrac{2a - 1}{5} = a$  **e** $\dfrac{e - 1}{3} = \dfrac{3e + 1}{4}$  **f** $\dfrac{1 - 2e}{2} = \dfrac{2 + 5e}{5}$

**10** XY is a straight line. Find angle $z$.

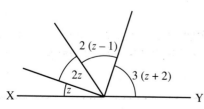

11  The perimeter of the triangle ABC is 36 cm. Find the length of the shortest side.

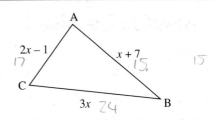

12  Three angles of a triangle are in the ratio 3 : 6 : 9. Find the angles.

13  Solve the simultaneous equations:
$y = 2x - 7$
$y = 3x - 10$

14  The sum of three consecutive odd numbers is 39. Find the numbers.

15  The result of trebling a number is the same as adding 10 to it. Find the number.

16  Alice is four years older than Rupinder who is three years older than Julia. Their combined age is 28 years. Find the age of each girl.

17  Solve the inequalities and show the result on a number line.

**a** $3x - 1 > 8$
**d** $1 + 3(2x - 1) < x$

**b** $12 \leq 3(x - 1)$
**e** $\frac{x}{3} \leq 1 - (3 - 2x)$

**c** $4(x - 2) \leq 3(x - 1)$
**f** $2(3 - x) > \frac{x}{2} + 1$

## MASTERMINDERS

18  Simplify:

**a** $\dfrac{a - \frac{b}{2}}{a - 2b}$

**b** $\dfrac{\frac{1}{ab} - \frac{1}{cd}}{\frac{1}{ac} + \frac{1}{bd}}$

19  Solve:

**a** $\frac{x + 2}{2} + \frac{2x - 1}{3} + 3 = \frac{3 - x}{4}$

**b** $\frac{x - 1}{4} - \frac{x - 2}{5} - \frac{x - 3}{6} = 0$

20  A bus completes a journey in 20 minutes. It travels at 40 km/h for the first half of the distance and at 60 km/h for the second half. Calculate the distance travelled by the bus.

21  If $a = -1$, $b = 2$ and $c = -3$, evaluate:
**a** $xy$ if $4ax = 5b$ and $y + c = ab$.
**b** $mn$ if $\frac{2b}{m} = 3c$ and $n - \frac{3}{b} = \frac{3}{a}$.

22  The length of a rectangular room is twice its width. A carpet, which is three times as long as it is wide, is placed in the centre of the room leaving a 1 metre border all around the room. Calculate the area of the carpet.

## Aural Test 1

Twenty questions will be read out to you. You may do any workings on a piece of paper. You will need the following information to answer Questions 11 to 20.

**11** and **12**

Thousands

Hundreds

Tens

Units

**13**  **a** 5600     **b** 6600     **c** 560     **d** 660     **e** 6500

**14**  **a** 500 m     **b** 5000 m     **c** 1000 m     **d** 3000 m     **e** 2000 m

**15, 16** and **17**

**18** and **19**

| MUSEUM |
| --- |
| Admission Charges |
| ADULT   180p |
| CHILD   90p |

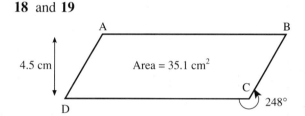

**20** Wesley's time-sheet for a week in July is shown below.

|  | Mon | Tues | Wed | Thurs | Fri | Sat | Sun |
| --- | --- | --- | --- | --- | --- | --- | --- |
| Basic rate (hours) | 6 | 6 | 6 | 6 | 6 |  |  |
| Overtime (hours) |  |  | 0.5 | 1.5 | 2 | 5 | 5 |

## Puzzlers

This is a puzzle from Thomas Thomas (1790) *Reading, poetry, writing and Arithmetic.*

A Man Lying upon his Death Bed bequeathed his Goods which were worth 3600 Crowns in this sort because his Wife being with Child and he uncertain whether the Child were a Male or a Female he made this bequest. That if the Wife bear a Daughter then shou'd the Wife have ½ and the Daughter ⅓. But if she were deliver'd of a Son then the Son shou'd have ⅔ and the Wife ⅓ now it chanc'd that she brought forth a Son and Daughter. Now the Question is how they shall part the Crowns according to the Testators will.

# Coursework: Motoring costs

Rachel is 20 years old and she buys a new sports car. Because the car's fuel consumption is 36 mpg she thinks it will be cheap motoring. She could be wrong! Apart from the cost of fuel, each year she has to pay the road tax, insurance and the maintenance, and she also has to take into account the depreciation of the car.

1   Each of the graphs below corresponds to one of the items of expenditure. Copy each of these graphs and indicate which graph illustrates each expenditure. For each graph, try to explain its shape and why you think your labelling is correct.

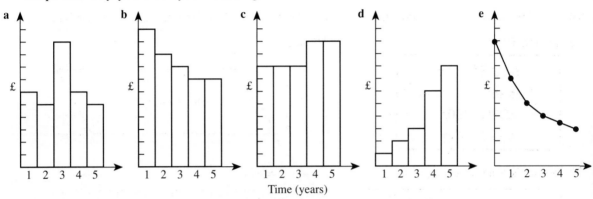

Time (years)

2   Use the following information to calibrate the cost axis on each graph.

In five years, Rachel's car depreciated by £7000 and she had to spend a total of £900 on maintenance. When she was 23 years old, the road tax went up by £20. The average cost per year for her to be insured was £420 and the most she had to spend on fuel in any one year was £500.

3   a Make a table using these headings and complete it for years 1 to 5.

| Year | Annual cost (£) | | | | |
|---|---|---|---|---|---|
| | Maintenance | Road Tax | Depreciation | Insurance | Fuel |
| 1 | | | | | |

  b Work out the mean total cost per week.

4   Devise a sensible **practical** method which Rachel could use to work out the mpg of her car.

5   Show that the total distance Rachel travelled in her car was 23 040 miles and hence work out the mean total cost per mile over the five years. (Assume 1 gallon of petrol costs £2.50.)

## EXTENSION

6   **Investigate** another hidden cost of Rachel's motoring: the interest payable on £7000 over five years. Her monthly repayment to a Bank would be £165 but to a Hire Purchase Company would be £240.

# Fact Finders: The UK hurricane

In the early hours of Friday 16th October 1987 the South East of Britain was battered by a hurricane. It brought awe of the forces of nature to a community that had come to forget them.

The wind speed in London was recorded at 97 mph (the highest since records began in 1940) while gusts along the South coast exceeded measurement capacity! The pressure rose from 959 millibars to 1004 millibars between 2 am and 7 am, causing powerful gusts of wind to sweep across Britain. It was the worst storm in Britain since 1703 when 8000 people were killed.

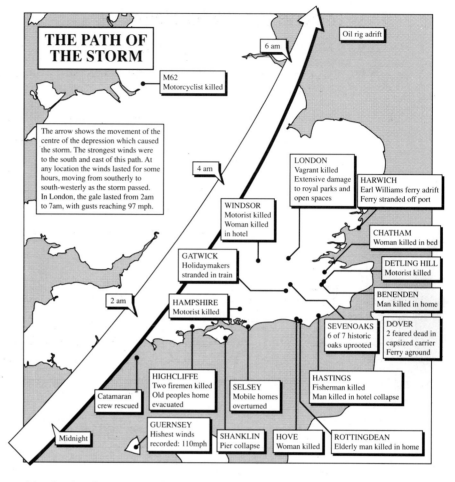

**THE PATH OF THE STORM**

The arrow shows the movement of the centre of the depression which caused the storm. The strongest winds were to the south and east of this path. At any location the winds lasted for some hours, moving from southerly to south-westerly as the storm passed. In London, the gale lasted from 2am to 7am, with gusts reaching 97 mph.

Oil rig adrift

6 am

M62
Motorcyclist killed

4 am

LONDON
Vagrant killed
Extensive damage to royal parks and open spaces

HARWICH
Earl Williams ferry adrift
Ferry stranded off port

WINDSOR
Motorist killed
Woman killed in hotel

CHATHAM
Woman killed in bed

DETLING HILL
Motorist killed

GATWICK
Holidaymakers stranded in train

BENENDEN
Man killed in home

2 am

HAMPSHIRE
Motorist killed

SEVENOAKS
6 of 7 historic oaks uprooted

DOVER
2 feared dead in capsized carrier
Ferry aground

HIGHCLIFFE
Two firemen killed
Old peoples home evacuated

SELSEY
Mobile homes overturned

HASTINGS
Fisherman killed
Man killed in hotel collapse

Catamaran crew rescued

GUERNSEY
Hishest winds recorded: 110mph

Midnight

SHANKLIN
Pier collapse

HOVE
Woman killed

ROTTINGDEAN
Elderly man killed in home

The devastation was catastrophic; in the five hours of the storm 3000 miles of telephone lines and 3000 telephone poles were brought down, 3 million homes were without electricity (250 000 of these in East Anglia), 15 million trees were blown down and 19 people were killed.

Insurance claims amounted to £500 million as a result of the destruction, with £40 million claimed on motor vehicles alone. This caused premiums to increase by 15% in 1988.

The chain-store Woolworths benefited from the storm, as in the three days after the hurricane they sold 25 000 brooms and 25 000 candles.

Emergency services were stretched to their limit, being inundated with calls; Essex firemen had to cope with 1800 calls before 8 am compared to their normal daily total of 50 calls for help.

Brighton was one of the worst hit towns in the country. It was described as looking like 'the scene of a major war' and the Palace Parade 'looked as if an airliner had made a forced landing on the sea front, scattering debris by the ton'.

Despite the extent and power of the storm, the BBC weather forecaster Michael Fish announced on Thursday night that 'There was no possibility of unusual weather...'.

## ▃▃ Questions on the UK hurricane

1 How many years ago was the previous 'worst' storm to hit Britain?

2 During the storm in London, what was the highest recorded wind speed in metres per second to 3 SF? (1 mile ≈ 1600 m)

3 Calculate the rate of pressure increase during the hurricane in millibars per hour.

4 Given that there are about 22 million homes in the UK, estimate the percentage of homes that were without electricity due to the storm.

5 Given that the average tree yields $9 \, m^3$ of wood, estimate the total volume of wood felled by the hurricane. Compare this to the volume of your classroom.

6 Approximately, how many telephone poles were blown down per minute by the storm?

7 A man paid £230 home insurance in 1988. What premium did he pay for his home insurance in 1987?

8 How much did Woolworths receive from their sales of brooms and candles (three days after the storm) if a broom retails at £4.75 and candles at £2.25 per dozen?

9 The direction of the hurricane is shown on the map. This route across England is approximately 432 km. Calculate the mean speed at which the hurricane moved across the country in miles per hour.

10 **Investigate** the 'Beaufort Scale' for wind forces to find out how it classifies the minimum wind speed in mph in order for the wind to be classed as a hurricane.

| Beaufort number | Description of wind | Wind speed | |
|---|---|---|---|
| | | knots | m per s |
| 0 | calm | < 1 | 0.0–0.2 |
| 1 | light air | 1–3 | 0.3–1.5 |
| 2 | light breeze | 4–6 | 1.6–3.3 |
| 3 | gentle breeze | 7–10 | 3.4–5.4 |
| 4 | moderate breeze | 11–16 | 5.5–7.9 |
| 5 | fresh breeze | 17–21 | 8.0–10.7 |
| 6 | strong breeze | 22–27 | 10.8–13.8 |
| 7 | near gale | 28–33 | 13.9–17.1 |
| 8 | gale | 34–40 | 17.2–20.7 |
| 9 | strong gale | 41–47 | 20.8–24.4 |
| 10 | storm | 48–55 | 24.5–28.4 |
| 11 | violent storm | 56–63 | 28.5–32.6 |
| 12 | hurricane | ≥ 64 | ≥ 32.7 |

# 4 GEOMETRY I

## 4.1 Basic principles

### Triangle properties

(A broken line indicates an axis of symmetry.)

**Isosceles triangle**

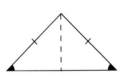

(Acute, obtuse, or right-angled)

**Equilateral triangle**

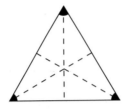

(Rotational symmetry order 3)

### Angle properties

(Notice we write down the statement and give the reason in brackets.)

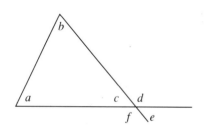

$a + b + c = 180°$      (Angle sum of triangle)

$c + d = 180°$      (Angles on straight line)

$d = a + b$      (Exterior angle of triangle)

$c = e$      (Vertically opposite angles)

$c + d + e + f = 360°$      (Angles at a point)

### Parallel lines

Alternate angles are equal.

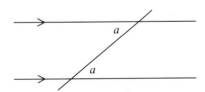

Corresponding angles are equal.

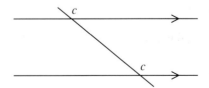

## ▬ Quadrilateral properties

**Arrowhead**

**Kite**

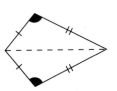

Right-angled, acute
or obtuse

**Isosceles trapezium**

(An irregular trapezium
does not have an axis of
symmetry, but it could
have a right angle.)

**Square**

Rotational symmetry
order 4

**Rhombus**

Rotational symmetry
order 2

**Rectangle**

Rotational symmetry
order 2

**Parallelogram**

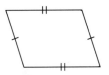

Rotational symmetry
order 2

## ▬ Angles of a polygon

> *REMEMBER*
>
> Angle sum of $n$-sided figure = $(2n - 4)$ right angles

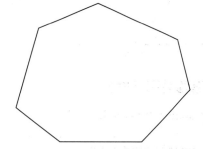

■*EXAMPLE 1*

Find the angle sum of a figure with seven sides.

    [F]       $n = 7$

    [E]       Angle sum = $(2n - 4)$ right angles

    [S]       = $(2 \times 7 - 4) \times 90°$

    [W]      = $900°$

If the polygon is 'regular', then all the interior angles are equal.

> *REMEMBER*
>
> Each interior angle of a regular polygon = $\dfrac{(2n - 4) \text{ right angles}}{n}$

## ■ EXAMPLE 2

A regular figure has ten sides. Find the size of one interior angle.

[F]     $n = 10$

[E]     Each angle $= \dfrac{(2n - 4) \text{ right angles}}{n}$

[S]     $= \dfrac{(20 - 4) \times 90}{10}$

[W]     $= 144°$

# ▬ Exercise 21

In Questions 1 to 13, find, in alphabetical order, the lettered angles.

**1**            **2**            **3** Rectangle     **4** Rhombus     **5** Kite

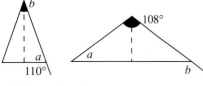   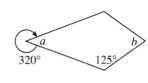

**6** Rotational symmetry order 2     **7**     **8** Rectangle     **9**

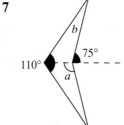 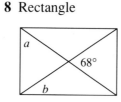 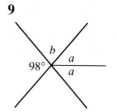

**10** Rotational symmetry order 6     **11**     **12** Kite     **13** Regular pentagon

 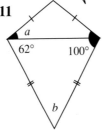 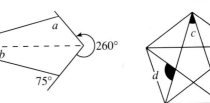

For Questions 14 to 17, work out each of the angles, giving reasons.

**14** ABDC is an arrowhead.
Find angles ADB, DBC, ABD, ACB.

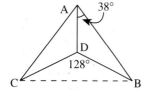

**15** ABCD is an isosceles trapezium.
Find angles ADE, AED, BEC, EAB.

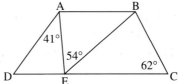

**16** ABCDEFGH is a regular octagon. Find angles CDE, ABG, BFE, FBG.

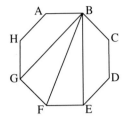

**17** ABCD is a parallelogram and BAE and EDF are straight lines. Find angles ABC, ADC, ADE, AED.

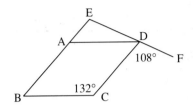

# __ 4.2 Angles of a circle

- A dot indicates the centre of the circle.

- A line which touches a circle is called a **tangent**.

- The straight line XY is called a **chord**.

# __ *Activity 5*

Copy this figure (larger) and measure the angles ACB, ADB and AEB. What do you notice?

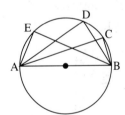

# __ *Activity 6*

Draw a circle and mark the centre O. Draw any tangent to the circle. Join O to where the tangent touches the circle. What do you notice?

> ### REMEMBER
>
> - Angle subtended at the circumference off the diameter of a semicircle = 90°.
> - Angle between radius and tangent = 90°.

Look at this circle and the triangle inside it. Because two of its sides are radii (therefore OA = OB), a triangle like this is isosceles; except for the special case when AB is equal to the radius, when the triangle is equilateral.

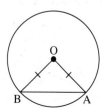

## — Exercise 22

Work out, in alphabetical order, each of the lettered angles in Questions 1 to 12.

**1**
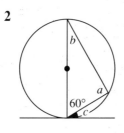

**2**
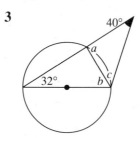

**3**
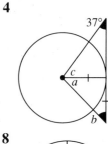

**4**

**5**
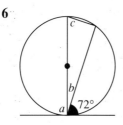

**6**
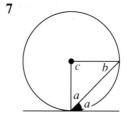

**7**

**8**
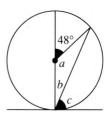

**9**
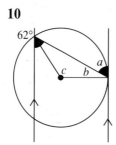

**10**

**11**
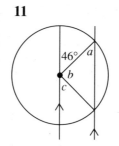

**12**

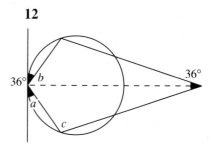

**13** Find angles ABE and BED.
What can you say about AB and CD?

**14** Find angles ACD and BCX.
Name the quadrilateral ABCD.

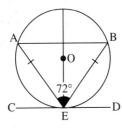

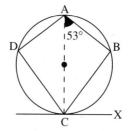

**15** **Investigate** all the different types of quadrilateral which can be drawn inside a circle so that each vertex (corner) lies on the circumference. (These quadrilaterals are called 'cyclic quadrilaterals'.)

**16** ABCD is a quadrilateral and FH is a straight line. Find angles FBG and GCH and name the quadrilateral.

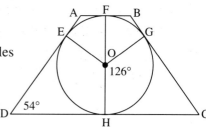

**17** Find angles ADE and ECF.
Name the quadrilateral ABCD.

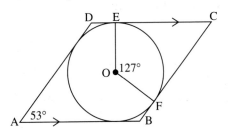

**18** AC and EC are straight lines.
Find all the missing angles.

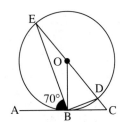

**19** There are many objects in the world around us that are circular or have circular cross-sections. Name ten circular objects.

For Questions 20 to 25, write down, in terms of $x$, the size of each of the angles listed. If necessary simplify your answer.

**20** AB̂O, AÔB, AB̂D

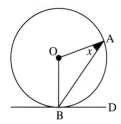

**21** CÂD, BĈA, BĈD

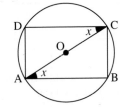

**22** OB̂A, AÔB, CÔB

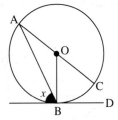

**23** BĈA, AB̂C, BÔC

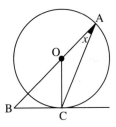

**24** OÂC, OB̂C, AĈB

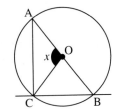

**25** CÔB, BÔA, AÔC

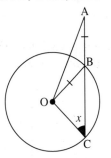

## MASTERMINDERS

**26** O is the centre of a circle and PR is a chord. If the tangents at P and R meet at T, prove that PT̂R = 2 × OP̂R. (Let OP̂R = $x$).

**27** AB is a diameter of a circle and AP is any chord. The tangent at B to the circle cuts AP produced at T. Prove that AT̂B = PB̂A.

**28** AB is a chord of a circle whose centre is O. AN is drawn perpendicular to the tangent at B to the circle. Prove that OB̂A = BÂN.

# ▬ **4.3** Similar triangles

## ▬ *Activity 7*

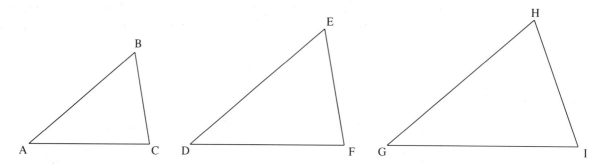

1 Measure each of the angles in the three triangles drawn above. You should find that the **corresponding** angles in triangles ABC and DEF are equal. This is because these two triangles are **similar** in shape.

2 Now measure each of the nine sides and use your measurements to work out the following ratios:

$$\frac{AC}{DF}, \quad \frac{AB}{DE}, \quad \frac{BC}{EF}, \quad \frac{AB}{GH}, \quad \frac{AC}{GI}, \quad \frac{EF}{HI}$$

You should find that only the first three ratios give the same result. This is because only triangles ABC and DEF are **similar** in shape.

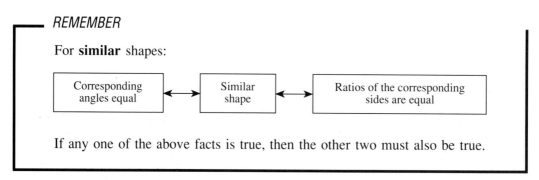

*REMEMBER*

For **similar** shapes:

| Corresponding angles equal | ⟷ | Similar shape | ⟷ | Ratios of the corresponding sides are equal |

If any one of the above facts is true, then the other two must also be true.

## ■ EXAMPLE 1
Which of the following triangles are similar to each other?

**a** 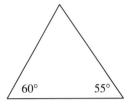  **b** 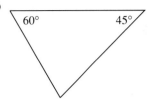  **c**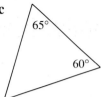

The angle sum of a triangle is 180°. So in **a** the angles are 55°, 60° and 65°, in **b** the angles are 45°, 60° and 75° and in **c** the angles are 55°, 60° and 65°. Therefore the triangles in **a** and **c** are similar in shape.

## ── Exercise 23

For each question, find which of the three triangles are similar in shape.

**1 a**  **b** 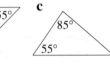 **c**   **2 a**  **b**  **c**

**3 a**  **b**  **c**   **4 a**  **b**  **c**

MASTERMINDER

**5 a** 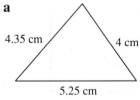 **b** 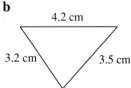 **c**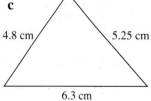

## ▬ Finding heights

The ancient Egyptians used similar triangles to work out the height of their pyramids. The unit they used was the 'cubit', which was the length from the elbow to the finger tips.

### ■ EXAMPLE 2

The shadow of the pyramid reached C, which was 500 cubits from B. The Egyptian surveyor found that a pole, of length 4 cubits, had to be placed at Y, 20 cubits from C, for its shadow to reach C. What is the height of the pyramid AB?

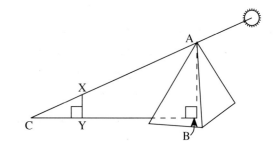

(Since XY and AB are both vertical, the triangles CXY and CAB are similar in shape. Therefore the ratio of their corresponding sides are equal.)

[F]

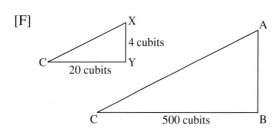

[E] $\dfrac{AB}{XY} = \dfrac{CB}{CY}$

[S] $\dfrac{AB}{4} = \dfrac{500}{20}$

[W] $AB = \dfrac{500}{20} \times 4$

$AB = 100\,\text{cubits}$

(Always redraw the two similar triangles in correspondingly similar positions.)

Use this method to estimate the height of a suitable building near your classroom.

## ▬ *Activity 8*

This is another method to work out the height of a building or a room, again using similar triangles.

Look at the diagram. To find the height of the room AB, place a mirror on the ground at any point R. An observer stands in line with the room at point Y where the top of the room can be seen in the mirror.

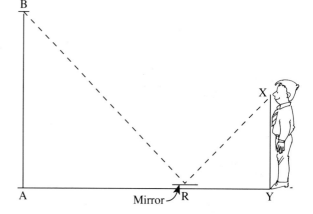

1   Explain why the triangles ABR and YXR are similar in shape.

2   Show that the ratio of the corresponding sides is given by

$$\frac{AB}{XY} = \frac{AR}{RY}$$

**3**  Use this method to find the height of your classroom or some other building.

**4**  Repeat the experiment by placing the mirror in a different position. Describe your method and comment on the accuracy of your results.

---
*REMEMBER*

When using similar triangles:

**1** Show that the two triangles are similar in shape.

**2** If necessary, redraw the triangles in a corresponding position.

**3** Write down the ratio of the corresponding sides.

---

# ___ Exercise 24

**1**  Find AC.

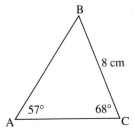

**2**  Find XZ.

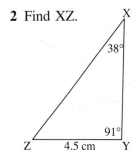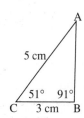

**3**  Find HK.

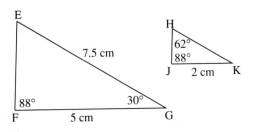

**4**  Find DE.

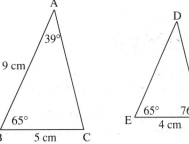

**5**  Find XY.

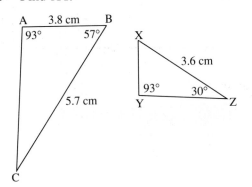

**6**  Find LM.

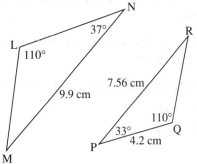

**7** Find OP.

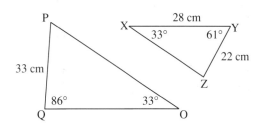

**8** Find AC.

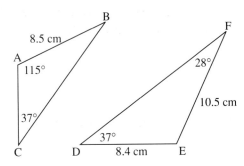

Questions 9 to 11 refer to the diagram below, where ABC and EDC are straight lines.

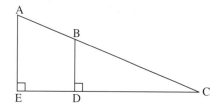

**9** Find BD when DC = 7 m, EC = 10.5 m and AE = 4.5 m.

**10** Find ED when BD = 4 m, AE = 6 m and DC = 6 m.

**11** Find AE when AC = 12 m, BD = 5 m and AB = 4 m.

**12** A house of height 5.6 m casts a shadow of 8 m. Find the height of a building casting a shadow of 28 m.

**13** A tree of height 4.5 m casts a shadow of 4 m. Find the length of Gill's shadow if she is 180 cm tall.

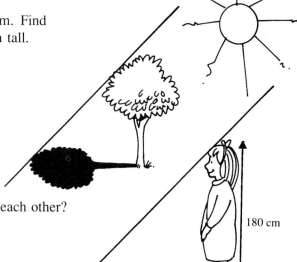

**14** Which of the following **must** be similar to each other?
   **a** Two squares.
   **b** Two rhombuses.
   **c** Two rectangles.
   **d** Two regular octagons.
   **e** Two circles.

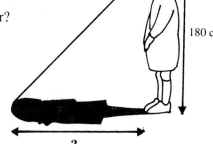

**15** The diagram shows a rectangular lawn 12 m
by 6 m surrounded by a path of width 1 m.
Are the two rectangles similar?

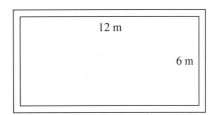

**16** Which slope is the odd one out?

**a**      **b**      **c**

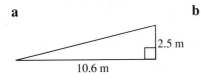  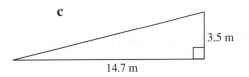

**17** Which slope is the odd one out?

**a**      **b**      **c**

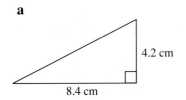  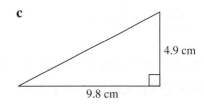

## MASTERMINDERS

**18** In the diagram, AB = 3 cm, BC = 6 cm, CD = 5 cm.
Calculate BE.

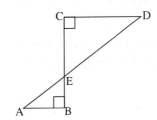

**19** ABC is a triangle in which AB = AC. D is a point on AB such that CB = CD. If AC = 9 cm
and BC = 3 cm, find AD.

**20** Nadia is 170 cm tall and is standing 15.4 m from the base of a lamp post whose bulb is 6.46 m
above the ground. How long is Nadia's shadow?

**21** In this diagram ABCD is a rectangle. Calculate the
sum of angles AED and BEF.

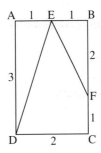

# — **4.4 Gradients**

In Questions 16 and 17 on page 75 we compared the 'slope' of different lines. If the ratio of the corresponding sides was the same, then the slope of the line was the same. The 'gradient' (another word for slope) is defined as the ratio of height to distance, that is:

$$\text{Gradient} = \frac{\text{Vertical height}}{\text{Horizontal distance}}$$

The gradient of this hill is 0.2.

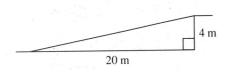

The gradient of this ladder is 2.5.

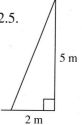

$$\text{Gradient} = \frac{\text{Vertical height}}{\text{Horizontal distance}} = \frac{4}{20} = 0.2$$

$$\text{Gradient} = \frac{\text{Vertical height}}{\text{Horizontal distance}} = \frac{5}{2} = 2.5$$

> *REMEMBER*
>
> For a slope of vertical height $y$ over a horizontal distance $x$:
>
> $$\text{Gradient of slope} = \frac{y}{x}$$
>
>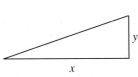

■ *EXAMPLE 1*

In the diagram, the gradient of the hill is 0.3. Find $x$.

[F]

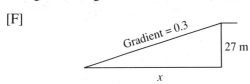

[E] and [S]     $0.3 = \frac{27}{x}$

[W]          $0.3x = 27$

            $x = \dfrac{27}{0.3}$

            $x = 90\,\text{m}$

## Contours

A contour is a line on a map joining points of the same height above sea-level. A cross-section through a hill including the contours is shown alongside.

A map of the same hill including a foot-path (A to E) up the hill is shown below.

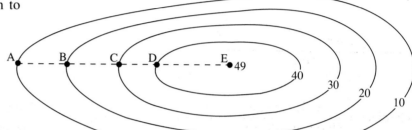

The **horizontal distances** between A, B, C, D and E can be found by scaling from the map. In this case the scale is 1 cm to 10 m.
Hence the distances are:
AB = 13 m, BC = 14 m,
CD = 10 m, DE = 20 m.

Scale: 1 cm to 10 m

The **profile** of the path can now be drawn and the gradients of each part can be calculated.

Gradient AB = $\frac{10}{13} \approx 0.77$

Gradient BC = $\frac{10}{14} \approx 0.71$

Gradient CD = $\frac{10}{10} = 1.00$

Gradient DE = $\frac{9}{20} = 0.45$

Why is the profile of the path AE **not** exact?

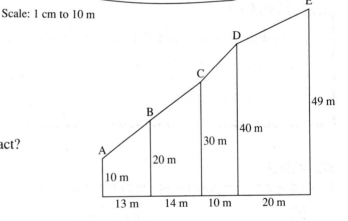

## Exercise 25

**1** Calculate the gradients of:

**a** A ladder    **b** A railway    **c** Line AB    **d** Road XY

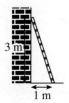

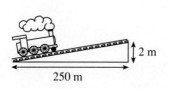

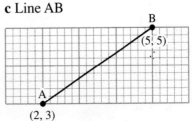

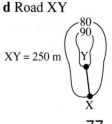

XY = 250 m

In Questions 2 to 6, find the value of $x$.

**2**
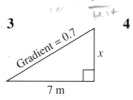
Gradient = 0.5
$x$
15 m

**3**

Gradient = 0.7
$x$
7 m

**4**

Gradient = 2.6
9.1 m
$x$

**5**

Gradient = 1.5
$x$
1.6 m

**6**
Gradient = 2.1
4.2 m
$x$

**7** Which of these two hills has the greater gradient?

**a**
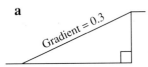
Gradient = 0.3

**b**
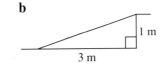
1 m
3 m

**8** This diagram shows a cross-section through a mountain path. How high is A above B?

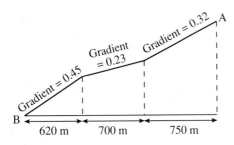

Gradient = 0.32  A
Gradient = 0.23
Gradient = 0.45
B
620 m    700 m    750 m

**9 a** From the map below, draw the profile of road (i) ABCDE  (ii) EFGHI.
**b** Calculate the gradient of each part of both roads.

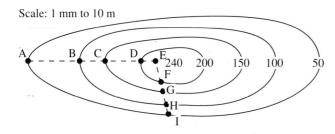

Scale: 1 mm to 10 m

A    B  C  D  E
240  200  150  100  50
F
G
H
I

**10** The roof on a house has a gradient of 1. Comment.

## ____ Revision Exercise 4

**1** Calculate the lettered angles:

**a**   **b** 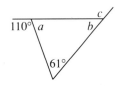  **c** 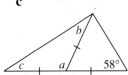  **d**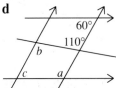

**2** Calculate the size of each exterior angle of a regular polygon of: **a** 6 sides  **b** 8 sides  **c** 20 sides  **d** $n$ sides.

**3** Calculate the lettered angles:

**a** 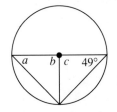  **b** 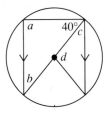  **c** 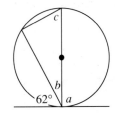  **d**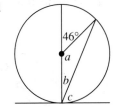

**4** Calculate the lettered lengths:

**a** 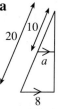  **b** 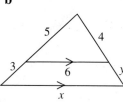  **c** 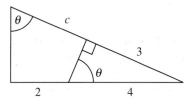  **d**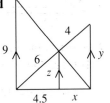

**5** The design brief for a new road states that a straight section XY must have a gradient of not greater than 0.3 and not less than 0.1. Which of these are possible choices?

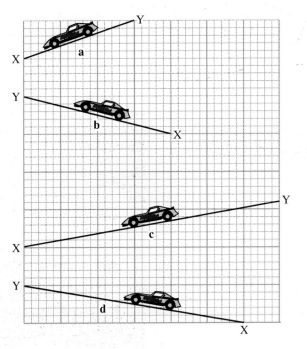

79

**6**

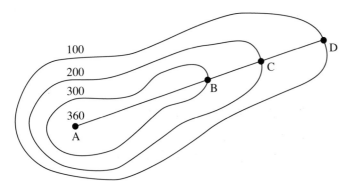

If AB = 300 m, BC = 80 m and CD = 110 m:
**a** Calculate the gradients of: (i) AB   (ii) BC   (iii) CD.
**b** What is the mean gradient between A and D?

**7 a** From this map, draw the profile of road
   (i) ABCDE
   (ii) AQRST
**b** Calculate the gradient of each part of both roads.

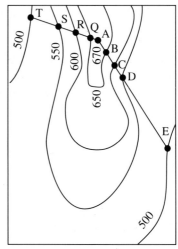

Scale: 1 mm to 10 m

## MASTERMINDERS

**8** WXYZ is a square and point A is a point inside the square, such that triangle WAZ is equilateral. Calculate angle AXZ.

**9** Two ships' masts are of height 6 m and 4 m respectively. Guy wires are stretched from the top of each to the base of the other as shown here. AB, EF and DC are perpendicular to BC. Calculate height $h$.

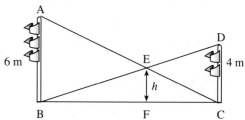

**10** Calculate the number of sides of each regular polygon of interior angle: **a** 144°   **b** 150°
   **c** 156°   **d** $x°$.

## ___ Basics Test 2

**A** Calculator
Give all your answers to 3 SF.

**1** $(2.9 \times 10^{-3}) + (3.8 \times 10^{-1})$    **2** $(2.9 \times 10^{-3}) \times (3.8 \times 10^{-1})$

**3** $10^4 - 398 \times 3.01$    **4** $\sqrt[3]{700}$

**5** Solve for $a$: $\frac{7.83}{a} = 5.097$    **6** Solve for $b$: $5.097 - b = 7.83$

**B** Paper and pencil

**7** $\frac{0.32}{0.8}$    **8** $1\frac{3}{8} \div \frac{1}{6}$

**9** A cube has a volume of $216\,\text{cm}^3$. What is the area of one of its faces?

**10** If Ptas 240 can be exchanged for £1, how many pounds could be exchanged for Ptas 1680?

**11** $(1.3 \times 10^3)^2$    **12** $\frac{1}{3} + \frac{1}{4} + \frac{1}{5}$

**13** A house was valued at £125 000. What is its value now if it has increased by 10%?

**14** The total thickness of 1500 sheets of paper is 12 mm. What is the thickness of one sheet?

**15** What is the average mass of three boys each weighing 60 kg and two girls each weighing 55 kg?

**C** Mental
Ten questions will be read out to you. You need the following information for Questions 16–20:

$$a = -2, \quad b = -3, \quad c = 0, \quad d = 4$$

## ___ Puzzlers

**1** **Practical**    With the use of a stop watch and tape measure, devise a method, and use it, to work out the speed of a passing car in miles per hour.

**2** In the multiplication sum each letter represents a different number. Find the number which each letter represents. (There are two possibilities.)

$$\begin{array}{r} \text{T H I N G} \\ \underline{\text{H}} \\ \text{S H A W L} \end{array}$$

**3** The five wheels shown all rotate in contact with each other, without slipping. The right-hand wheel is 40 cm in diameter and rotates 12 times per minute. The left-hand wheel is 30 cm in diameter. What is the diameter of the smallest wheel if it rotates once every second?

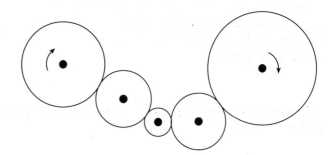

# Coursework: The Cross-staff

In the sixteenth century the 'Cross-staff' was invented to find the width of buildings from a distance.

It consisted of a staff – a straight piece of wood about a metre long – which was pointed at the centre of the building, and a cross-piece, which was moved at right angles along the staff until its ends lined up with the ends of the building.

1  Figure 1 shows a Cross-staff PZXY pointing at a building AB. The user is standing at P, which is 25 m from the wall at D. He adjusts the cross-piece XY and notes that PZ = 20 cm. If the cross-piece is 24 cm long, calculate the width of the building AB.

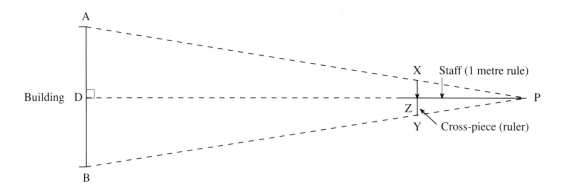

**Figure 1**

2  Use a metre rule and a 30 cm ruler to make a Cross-staff. Use it in the practical work described below.
   **a** Stand facing the middle of your chosen building. Measure your distance from it and mark your position on the ground.
   **b** Line up the ends of your ruler with the ends of the building, and note the distance the ruler is from your eye.
   **c** Draw a diagram and on it show the measurements of DP, XY and ZP. Use your measurements to calculate the width of the building.
   **d** Now measure the actual width of the building and work out the percentage error in your calculation.

3   This part shows how it is possible to measure the width of a building from a distance. The following instructions refer to Figure 2.

Return to your position P on the ground marked in part 2 **a**. Adjust your 30 cm ruler XY to line up with the ends of the building again.

**a** Move your ruler away from your eye by the distance equal to the ruler's length. Walk backwards at right angles to the building to the point P′ until the ends of your ruler line up again with the ends of the building. The new position of your ruler is shown at X′Z′Y′.

**b** Measure P′Z′ and PP′. (Remember: ZX = ZY = Z′X′ = Z′Y′.)

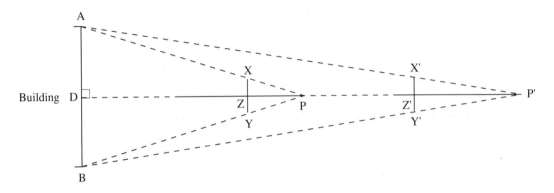

**Figure 2**

**c** Copy the table below and write down your measurements on the first line.

|   | XY | PZ | P′Z′ | P′P |
|---|----|----|------|-----|
| 1 |    |    |      |     |
| 2 |    |    |      |     |
| 3 |    |    |      |     |

**d** Facing the same building, but standing in a different position to P, repeat the above twice more. Complete your table.

**e** Work out the average of your three P′P distances and compare your answer to the actual width of the building. Explain how, in the sixteenth century, the Cross-staff would have been used to find the width of a building, **from a distance** (that is, without measuring PD.)

## EXTENSION

4   **a Investigate** how your Cross-staff could be used to measure the **height** of a building from a distance.

**b** In Figure 2, when PZ = 40 cm, PD = 20 m and XY = 30 cm, find lengths AB, P′Z′, DP′, PP′.

**c** In Figure 2, when PZ = 20 cm, XY = 30 cm and PD = $q$ cm, find, in terms of $q$, the lengths AB, DP′, PP′. Comment on your answers to **b** and **c**.

**d** When AB = $x$, PP′ = $y$, DP = $q$, XY = $c$, ZP = $a$ and Z′P′ = $b$, use algebra to prove that the Cross-staff, as used in part 3, actually works.

# 5 TRIGONOMETRY

## 5.1 Basic principles

How can you find the height of this tower? (Scale drawing, the Cross-staff method, the mirror method, ...)

Suppose you stand at A and measure the angle of elevation and the distance to the base of the tower. One way to find the height is to make a scale drawing of the tower using these measurements. A quicker and more accurate method, however, is to use Trigonometry.

At this stage in Trigonometry, we only use **right-angled triangles**. If there is no right-angled triangle in the problem we are investigating, we have to construct one. Look at the following.

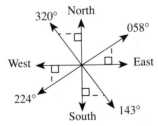

**NOTE**

'Trigonometry' means 'triangle measurement'.

**Isosceles triangle**
(Construct the 'altitude' AD)

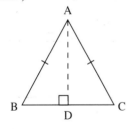

**Circle** (centre O)
(Construct OC)

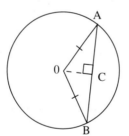

**Bearings** (measured clockwise from North). (Drop a perpendicular onto an adjacent North, East, South or West line.)

The sides of a right-angled triangle are given special names, used all the way through the rest of this chapter.

**REMEMBER**

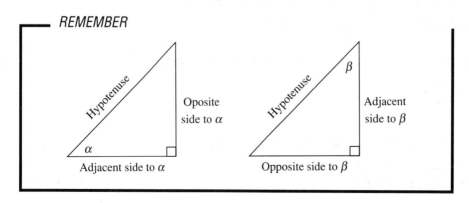

# __ 5.2 Tangent ratio

## __ Calculating sides

## __ *Activity 9*

1   This is a rocket's flight-path, with an angle of elevation of 30°.

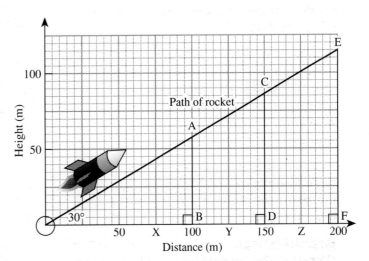

Copy and complete the table to find the gradient of the hypotenuse of each right-angled triangle.

| Triangle | Length of side 'opp' to 30° (m) | Length of side 'adj' to 30° (m) | Gradient = $\dfrac{opposite}{adjacent}$ |
|---|---|---|---|
| OAB OCD OEF | | | |

What do you notice?

2   You should have found that the ratio 'opp : adj' for an angle of 30° is the same for all three triangles. In fact, it is the same for any **similar** right-angled triangle with an angle of 30°. This is because we are calculating the **gradient** of the same line each time.

The actual value of $\dfrac{\text{opp}}{\text{adj}}$ for 30° = 0.577 350 to 6 DP.

The rocket's height ($h$) can now be calculated at any point, for example at Y.

$$0.577\,350 = \frac{\text{opp}}{\text{adj}} = \frac{h}{125}$$

$$125 \times 0.577\,350 = h$$

$$h = 72.2\,\text{m to 3 SF}\quad \text{(Check this on the graph.)}$$

Calculate the rocket's height vertically above **a** X   **b** Z.
Check both your answers on the graph.

(*Continued*)

**3**   The ratio of 'opp : adj' for an angle $\theta$ is called the **tangent ratio** of $\theta$, or $\tan \theta$.

---
**REMEMBER**

$$\tan \theta = \frac{\text{Opposite side}}{\text{Adjacent side}} = \frac{\text{opp}}{\text{adj}}$$

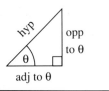

---

You can find the tangent ratio very easily using your calculator. (Make sure your calculator is showing degrees.) You enter the value of $\theta$, say 73°, and press the `tan` button:

73 `tan` = 3.271 (to 4 SF)

Copy and complete the table to 4 SF.

| $\theta°$ | 0° | 15° | 30° | 45° | 60° | 75° | 89° |
|---|---|---|---|---|---|---|---|
| $\tan \theta°$ | | | | 1.000 | | | |

Why is $\tan 89°$ so large?

■ *EXAMPLE 1*

In this triangle, find side $x$ to 3 SF.

[F]          See diagram.

[E] and [S]          $\tan 30° = \dfrac{x}{10}$

[W]          $10 \times \tan 30° = x$

Calculator instructions: 10 ✕ 30 `tan` = 5.773 503 to 7 SF

Therefore $x = 5.77$ cm to 3 SF.

■ *EXAMPLE 2*

How far is the foot of the ladder from the base of the wall?

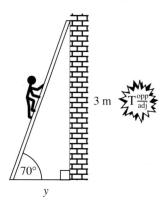

[F]          See diagram.

[E] and [S]          $\tan 70° = \dfrac{3}{y}$

[W]          $y \times \tan 70° = 3$

$$y = \frac{3}{\tan 70°}$$

Calculator instructions: 3 ÷ 70 `tan` = 1.091 911 to 7 SF

Therefore $y = 1.09$ m to 3 SF.

## — Exercise 26

Give all your answers to 3 SF.

**1** State which sides are the hypotenuse, opposite and adjacent to the given angle $\theta$:

**a** 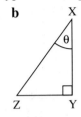  **b** 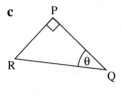  **c** 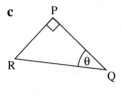  **d**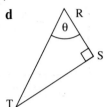

**2** Find each side $x$.

**a**   **b** 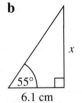  **c** 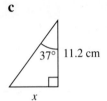  **d**

**3** Find each side $y$.

**a**   **b**   **c** 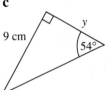  **d**

**4** The angle of elevation of the top of a cliff from a boat 125 m away from its foot is 35°. Find the height of the cliff.

**5** The angle of depression from a window 10 m above the ground, to an object on the ground, is 15°. Find the distance of the object from the base of the building.

**6** Calculate length $x$.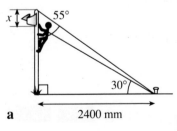

**a** 2400 mm     **b** 280 cm

**7** Find the area of the side of this building: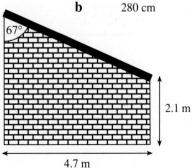

MASTERMINDERS

**8**  In triangle ABC, angle B = 62°, angle C = 75° and the altitude AX = 8 cm. Calculate BX and CX.

**9**  A regular pentagon has sides of 11 cm. Calculate the radius of the largest circle which can be drawn inside the pentagon.

## ⎯⎯ Calculating angles

So far we have found one side of a right-angled triangle, given an angle and an adjacent or opposite side. Now we will find the angle, given the adjacent and opposite sides. This is the 'inverse' operation and therefore we use the ▮INV▮ ▮tan▮ buttons on the calculator to find the angles, as in Example 3.

▮*EXAMPLE 3*

Find $\alpha$ and $\beta$ to the nearest degree.

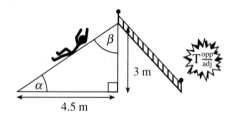

|   |   |
|---|---|
| [F] | See diagram. |
| [E] and [S] | $\tan \alpha = \frac{3}{4.5}$, $\tan \beta = \frac{4.5}{3}$ |
| [W] | Calculator operations: |

3 ▮÷▮ 4.5 ▮=▮ ▮INV▮ ▮tan▮ 33.690 07 to 7 SF

4.5 ▮÷▮ 3 ▮=▮ ▮INV▮ ▮tan▮ 56.309 93 to 7 SF

$\alpha = 34°$ to the nearest degree.

$\beta = 56°$ to the nearest degree.

⎯ *REMEMBER*

To calculate an angle from a tangent ratio, use the ▮INV▮ ▮tan▮ buttons.

## Exercise 27

**1** Find the angles which have the following tangents, to 2 SF:
**a** 0.268    **b** 0.577    **c** 1.000    **d** 1.732    **e** 2.747    **f** 3.732

**2** Find the angle marked $\alpha$ to 1 DP.

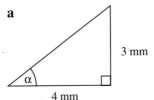  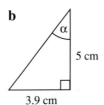  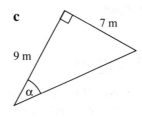  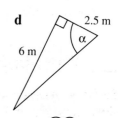

**3** Calculate the angles of the pitched roof to 1 DP.

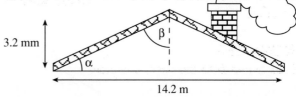

**4** A tower is 65 m high. Find the angle of elevation, to 1 DP, of its top from a point 150 m away on level ground.

**5** ABCD is a rectangle. Find $\alpha$ and $\beta$ to the nearest degree.

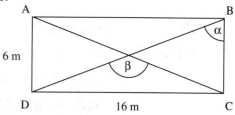

**6** The diagonals of a rhombus are 14 cm and 21 cm. Find, to 2 SF, the acute angle of the rhombus.

## MASTERMINDERS

**7** In the quadrilateral ABCD, AB = 3 cm, BC = 5.5 cm, CD = 4 cm, AD = 5 cm, angle B = angle D = 90°. Calculate angle A to 1 DP.

**8** A church C is 8.6 km North and 12.5 km West of a school S. Calculate to 3 SF the bearing of:
**a** S from C   **b** C from S.

**9** The area of the kite ABCD is 38 cm². 
BE = ED = 4 cm and EC = 6 cm. 
Find the angle BAD to 2 SF .

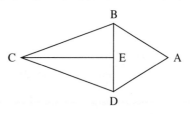

# — 5.3 Sine and cosine ratios

## — Calculating sides

## — *Activity 10*

1  The slope of a skier's run down a mountain is shown below. Copy and complete the table.

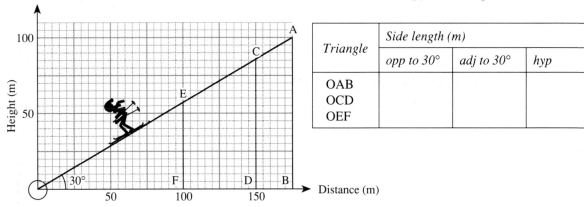

| Triangle | Side length (m) | | |
|---|---|---|---|
| | opp to 30° | adj to 30° | hyp |
| OAB | | | |
| OCD | | | |
| OEF | | | |

   **a** Work out the 'opp : hyp' ratio for each triangle. This ratio is the same for any similar triangle. The actual ratio of 'opp : hyp' = 0.5. This is called the **sine ratio** of 30°, or sin 30°.
   **b** Use your calculator to work out to 3 DP: sin 0°, sin 15°, sin 30°, sin 45°, sin 60°, sin 90°.

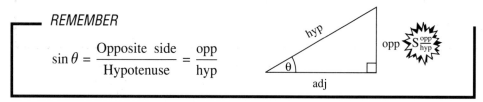

REMEMBER

$$\sin \theta = \frac{\text{Opposite side}}{\text{Hypotenuse}} = \frac{\text{opp}}{\text{hyp}}$$

2  **a** Work out the 'adj : hyp' ratio for each triangle. This ratio is the same for any similar triangle. The actual ratio of 'adj : hyp' = 0.866 25 to 6 DP. This is called the **cosine ratio** of 30° or cos 30°.
   **b** Use your calculator to work out to 3 DP: cos 0°, cos 15°, cos 30°, cos 45°, cos 60°, cos 90°.

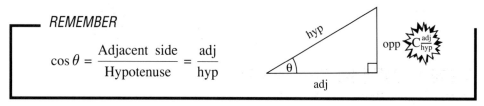

REMEMBER

$$\cos \theta = \frac{\text{Adjacent side}}{\text{Hypotenuse}} = \frac{\text{adj}}{\text{hyp}}$$

## ■ EXAMPLE 1

Find side $x$ to 2 SF in this triangle.

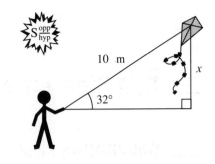

| [F] | See diagram. |
| --- | --- |
| [E] and [S] | $\sin 32° = \dfrac{x}{10}$ |
| [W] | $10 \times \sin 32° = x$ |

$10 \boxed{\times} 32 \boxed{\text{sin}} \boxed{=} 5.299\,193$ to 7 SF

Therefore $x = 5.3$ m to 2 SF.

## ■ EXAMPLE 2

Find side $y$ to 3 SF in this triangle.

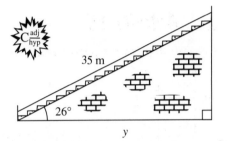

| [F] | See diagram. |
| --- | --- |
| [E] and [S] | $\cos 26° = \dfrac{y}{35}$ |
| [W] | $35 \times \cos 26° = y$ |

$35 \boxed{\times} 26 \boxed{\text{cos}} \boxed{=} 31.457\,79$ to 7 SF

Therefore $y = 31.5$ m to 3 SF.

---

### REMEMBER

When using the three trigonometrical ratios it is important to choose the correct one. Follow these steps:

- Identify the sides of the triangle as 'opp', 'adj' or 'hyp' to the angle you are interested in.
- Write down:  $S\frac{\text{opp}}{\text{hyp}}$   $C\frac{\text{adj}}{\text{hyp}}$   $T\frac{\text{opp}}{\text{adj}}$

- Select the correct ratio.

---

## ■ EXAMPLE 3

Find length $y$ to 3 SF.

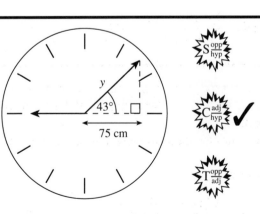

| [F] | See diagram. |
| --- | --- |
| [E] and [S] | $\cos 43° = \dfrac{75}{y}$ |
| [W] | $y \times \cos 43° = 75$ |
| | $y = \dfrac{75}{\cos 43°}$ |

$75 \boxed{\div} 43 \boxed{\text{cos}} \boxed{=} 102.549\,6$ to 7 SF

Therefore $y = 103$ cm to 3 SF.

## ___ **Exercise 28**

Give your answers to 3 SF.

**1** Find each side $x$.

**a**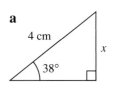

**b**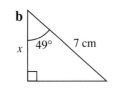

**c**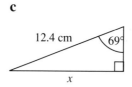

**d**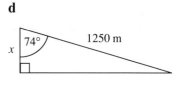

**2** Find each side $y$.

**a**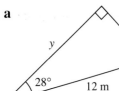

**b**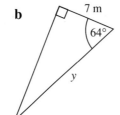

**c**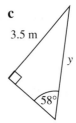

**d**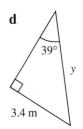

**3** A 3.8 m ladder rests against a vertical wall, making a 65° angle with the ground. How far away is the foot of the ladder from the base of the wall?

**4** A kite is at the end of a 70 m string, which makes an angle of 75° with the ground. How high is the kite above the ground?

**5** The triangles shown are isosceles.
  **a** Find BC.

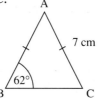

  **b** Find LM.

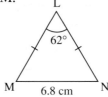

**6** This cable car climbs at 48° to the horizontal up the mountain-side. BC = 52 m, DE = 37 m. Calculate:
  **a** The total length of the cable AC.
  **b** The vertical height gained from E to A.

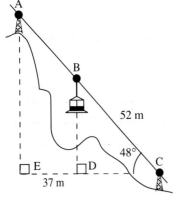

**7** A submarine dives for 150 m. The diving angle, measured from the vertical, is 75°. How deep is the front of the submarine at the end of its dive?

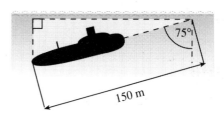

**8** In this triangle, calculate **a** AD  **b** BD  **c** area ABC  **d** angle C.

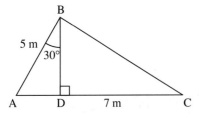

MASTERMINDERS

**9** A regular pentagon is inscribed inside a circle of radius 5 cm. What is the length of one side?

**10** In triangle EFG, EF = 6.3 cm, angle F = 62°, angle G = 46°. If ET is an altitude (height), find FT, ET and EG.

## —— Calculating angles

## —— *Activity 11*

**1** You want to find angle $\theta$ and you are given the **opposite** side and the **hypotenuse** in a right-angled triangle. First, find the sine ratio:

$$\sin \theta = \frac{\text{opp}}{\text{hyp}}$$

Then use your calculator to find the value of $\theta$ (check the calculator is in degree mode). To find $\theta$ in degrees, enter the value of $\sin \theta$ and press **INV** **sin** .

Copy and complete the table for $\theta°$ to the nearest degree.

| $\sin \theta°$ | 0 | 0.259 | 0.500 | 0.707 | 0.819 | 0.866 | 0.966 | 1 |
|---|---|---|---|---|---|---|---|---|
| $\theta°$ | | | 30° | | | | | 90° |

**2** This time you want to find angle $\theta$ and you are given the **adjacent** side and the **hypotenuse** in a right-angled triangle. First, find the cosine ratio:

$$\cos \theta = \frac{\text{adj}}{\text{hyp}}$$

Then use your calculator to find the value of $\theta$. This time, enter the value of $\cos \theta$ and press **INV** **cos** .

Copy and complete the table for $\theta°$ to the nearest degree.

| $\cos \theta°$ | 1 | 0.966 | 0.866 | 0.819 | 0.707 | 0.500 | 0.259 | 0 |
|---|---|---|---|---|---|---|---|---|
| $\theta°$ | 0 | | | | | 60° | | |

93

■ *EXAMPLE 4*

Find $\alpha$ to 2 SF.

| | |
|---|---|
| [F] | See diagram. |
| [E] and [S] | $\cos \alpha = \frac{1.5}{2}$ |
| [W] | Calculator operations: |

1.5 ÷ 2 = INV cos 41.409 62 to 7 SF

$\alpha = 41°$ to 2 SF.

■ *EXAMPLE 5*

Find $\beta$ to 2 SF.

| | |
|---|---|
| [F] | See diagram. |
| [E] and [S] | $\sin \beta = \frac{3.5}{4.3}$ |
| [W] | Calculator operations: |

3.5 ÷ 4.3 = INV sin

= 54.484 02 to 7 SF

$\beta = 54°$ to 2 SF.

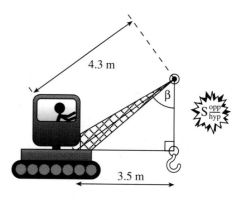

---

*REMEMBER*

When choosing a ratio:
- Identify the sides as 'opp', 'adj' or 'hyp'.
- Write down:

- Select the correct ratio.
- To calculate an angle from a ratio, use the

INV sin , INV cos OR INV tan buttons.

---

## — Exercise 29

Give your answers to 3 SF.

**1** Find the angles marked $\alpha$.

**a**

4 cm    3 cm

$\alpha$

**b**

75 mm    $\alpha$    67 mm

**c**

2 cm

$\alpha$    4.1 cm

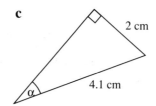

**d**

3 cm

$\alpha$

4.2 cm

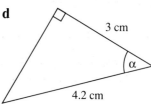

**2** Find the angles marked $\beta$.

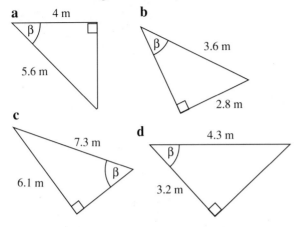

**a** 4 m $\beta$ 5.6 m

**b** $\beta$ 3.6 m 2.8 m

**c** 7.3 m 6.1 m $\beta$

**d** 4.3 m $\beta$ 3.2 m

**3** The World Trade Centre (see photograph) is 413 m high. If the distance from a point on the ground to the top of the building is 483 m, calculate the angle of elevation from this point to the top of the building.

**4** A train travels 4 km along a straight track and during this time has risen 500 m vertically. Calculate the angle of slope of the track.

**5** A 'control line' aircraft at the end of a 15 m wire is flying in a horizontal circle of radius 5 m. What angle does the wire make with the ground?

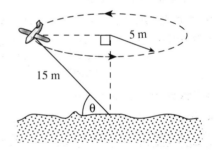

5 m

15 m

$\theta$

**6** A rectangle has a side of 10 m and diagonals of 25 m. Find the angle between the longer side and the diagonal.

**7** A woman cycles 15 km North and then 4 km East. Find:
**a** How far she is from her starting point.
**b** The bearing from her starting point.

## MASTERMINDERS

**8** Calculate the area of an equilateral triangle of side 10 cm.

**9** ABCD is a quadrilateral, BÂD and DĈB are right angles, AB = 8 cm, DB = 9 cm and DC = 4.5 cm. Calculate AB̂C.

# 5.4 Miscellaneous problems

## Exercise 30

Give your answers to 3 SF.

**1** Find the marked angle or side.

**a**

**b**

**c**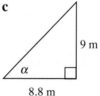

**d**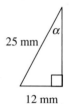

**2** Find the marked angle or side.

**a**

**b**

**c**

**d**

**3** Find the marked angles and sides.

**a**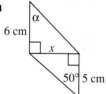

**b**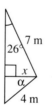

**c**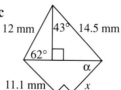

**d**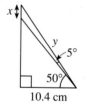

**4** A lighthouse is 60 m high. From its top, the angles of depression of two buoys due North of it are 33° and 29°. How far apart are the buoys?

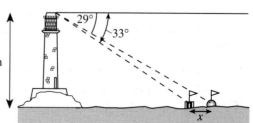

**5** A tripod, made of rods 1.75 m long, is put up so that its feet are equally spaced on a circle of radius 52 cm. What angle do the rods make with the vertical?

**6** A is due North of B and C is 215 km East of the line AB. An aeroplane flies from A to C on a bearing of 144° and from C to B on a bearing of 252°. Find the distance it travels.

**7** Calculate the height $H$ of these stairs.

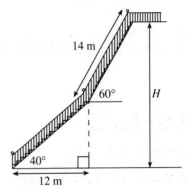

**8** **a** Calculate the car driver's 'blind' distance $D$.
**b** Why is this distance important in the car design?

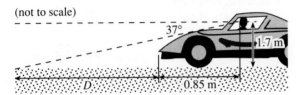

**9** Calculate **a** OB **b** the area of triangle AOB.

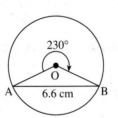

**10** The centre of the clock face rests in a tower 20 m above the ground. The hour hand is 1.1 m long. How far above the ground is the end of the hour hand at: **a** 02:00 **b** 07:00 **c** 10:30?

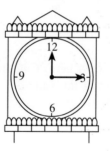

## MASTERMINDERS

**11** A motor-boat is 10 km South of a lighthouse and on a course of 053°. What is the closest distance that the motor-boat passes to the lighthouse?

**12** The diagram shows a rectangular packing case ABCD leaning against a vertical wall XY. AB is 2 m, AD is 3 m and the angle DCZ is 25°.
Find the height of A above the floor YZ.

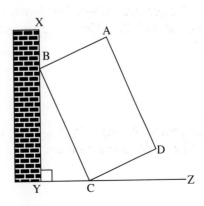

## ___ Revision Exercise 5

Give your answers to 3 SF unless otherwise stated.

**1** Find the marked angles and sides.

**a**    **b**    **c** 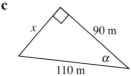   **d**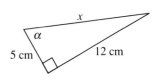

**2** In the following questions, the triangle ABC has a right angle at B.
  **a** In triangle ABC, $\hat{C} = 23°$, AC = 14 cm. Calculate AB.
  **b** In triangle ABC, $\hat{A} = 70°$, BC = 8 km. Calculate AB.
  **c** In triangle ABC, AB = 3 mm, BC = 7 mm. Calculate angle ACB.
  **d** In triangle ABC, AC = 9 m, AB = 4 m. Calculate angle BAC.

**3** Find the marked angles and sides.

**a** 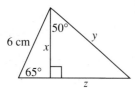   **b** 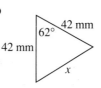   **c** 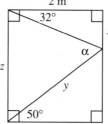   **d**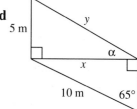

**4** A cross-section of a railway
   bridge is shown here. Calculate:
   **a** The depth of the valley.
   **b** The length of the bridge.

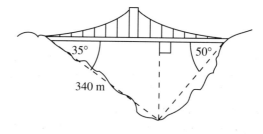

**5** A hot-air balloon drifts at a constant height on a bearing of 285° at a steady speed of 12 km/h.
   How far is it from its starting point after 90 minutes: **a** North or South? **b** West or East?

**6** A helicopter hovers in a fixed position 150 m
   above the ground. The angle of depression from
   the helicopter to church A (due West of the
   helicopter) is 32°.
   The angle of elevation from church B (due
   East of the helicopter) to the helicopter is 22°.
   Calculate the distance between the churches.

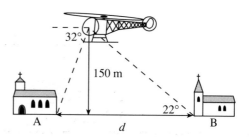

**7** A SCUBA diver's dive is shown below. He dives directly from A to B to C, then onto the seabed floor at D.
When the diver is at D he realises that he has only four minutes of air left in his tank. He can ascend vertically at 10 cm/s. (AB = 8 m, BC = 12 m, CD = 16 m.)
Can he reach the surface before his air supply is empty?

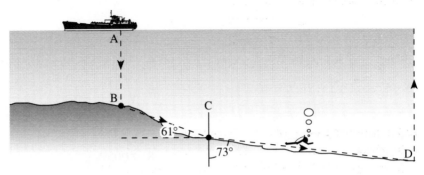

**8** Calculate the area of the triangles ABC below:

**a**
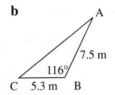
6 cm, 80°, C, 10 cm, B, A

**b**
7.5 m, 116°, C, 5.3 m, B, A

**c**
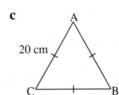
20 cm, A, C, B

**d**
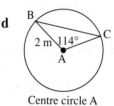
B, 2 m, 114°, C, A
Centre circle A

**9** A hiker walks from her camp for 10 km on a bearing of 050° and then walks for a further 14 km on a bearing of 140°. At this point she decides to return directly to the camp.
**a** Find the distance and bearing of the return journey.
**b** She hikes at a constant speed of 1.5 m/s. If her return journey starts at 15:00, at what time will she arrive at camp?

## MASTERMINDER

**10** A cunning rabbit wishes to cross a busy new road. He calculates that the angle of elevation from the edge of the road to a lamp-post on the other side is 25°. From a position 12 m back from the road the angle is 15°.
**a** Find the width of the new road.
**b** He can hop across the road at 1 m/s. Find the time taken to cross the road.
**c** Vehicles on this road travel at 60 mph. Find how far apart the vehicles must be in order for him to cross safely. (1600 m ≈ 1 mile)

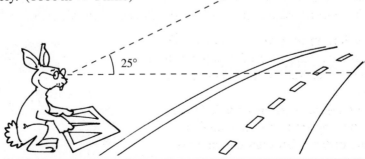

## ___ Basics Test 3

**A** Calculator
Give all your answers to 3 SF.

**1** Solve for $a$: $20.6 \div a = 24$

**2** Solve for $b$: $10^3 = 6.9 \times 10^5 + b$

**3** $10^3 - \sqrt{361 \times 10^{-1}}$

**4** $(4.5 \times 10^{-2}) + (6.7 \times 10^{-3})$

**5** $(4.5 \times 10^2) \times (6.7 \times 10^{-3})$

**6** $\sqrt{\frac{4.5 \times 10^2}{6.7 \times 10^3}}$

**B** Paper and pencil

**7** $1\frac{3}{5} \div \frac{4}{5}$

**8** $0.005 + \frac{3}{8}$

**9** Decrease 120 seconds by 15%.

**10** Convert $15.3\,\text{m}^3$ to $\text{cm}^3$.

**11** A rectangular lawn of area $32\,\text{m}^2$ has a length twice its width. What is the width?

**12** A map has a scale of 1 : 25 000. How long is a road which is shown on the map as 3.5 cm long?

**13** Find the largest integer $x$ which satisfies the inequality: $4 + 3x \leqslant 9$.

**14** A train takes 30 minutes to travel $9 \times 10^5$ cm. What is its average speed in km/h?

**15** Simplify: $\frac{a}{5} + \frac{b}{4}$

**C** Mental
Ten questions will be read out to you. You need the following information for Questions 16–20.

| Cinema tickets | | | |
|---|---|---|---|
| Adult £12.50 | Student £7.50 | Child £3.25 | O.A.P. £2.00 |

## ___ Puzzlers

**1** **Practical** Devise a suitable method, and use it, to measure the length of ribbon on an electric typewriter spool.

**2** Anil runs faster than Bertram, and David will always beat Charles in a race. Bertram is never beaten by Edward. One day all five race against each other. Which of the following results is possible?

    **a** ABCDE     **b** BEDAC     **c** ABCED     **d** ADBCE     **e** ADCEB

**3** The five tyres of a car (four road tyres and one spare) were used equally on a car that had travelled 20 000 km. Work out the number of kilometres of use of each tyre.

# Coursework: Aviation flight paths

The map shows all the main civil aviation corridors across the South West of England. Radio beacons are at Land's End, Berry Head and Southampton. The distance between each Northing and each Easting represents 50 km.

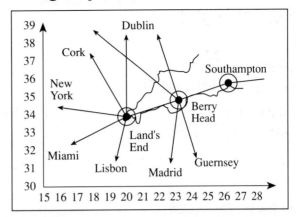

**1**  Use the information below to make a copy of the map. Use the largest possible scale.

Radio beacons are at 200340, 230350 and 260360.
Air corridors pass over 220380, 200360, 180390, 170390, 160345, 160320, 190310, 225320, 240320.

**2**  Show by calculation that:
**a** The bearing of Berry Head from Land's End is 072°, to the nearest degree.
**b** From Southampton the bearing of Berry Head is 252°, to the nearest degree.
**c** The distance between Southampton and Land's End is 316.2 km, correct to 4 SF.

**3**  An aeroplane passes over Southampton and sets a course to pass over Land's End. If, however, the plane flew 1° off course at Southampton, how near would it fly to Land's End?

**4**  A plane is at 15 000 feet over Southampton and climbs at a constant rate until it reaches a height of 32 000 feet over Land's End. Find the mean angle of ascent.

**5**  At 16:06 an aeroplane passed over Berry Head, flying at 450 km/h, and bound for Guernsey. 23.2 minutes later it crashed into the sea. Show that the disaster occurred at approx 241317.
**a** Show by measurement that the distance between the crash and Land's End and the crash and Southampton is approximately 235 km.
**b** Rescue helicopters leave for the crash as shown in the table. Copy and complete this table and find out which helicopter arrived at the scene of the crash first. (Remember to show all your working.)

| Place of departure | Time of departure | Time of arrival | Bearing of course | Speed of helicopter |
|---|---|---|---|---|
| Land's End | 16:34 | | | 100 km/h |
| Berry Head | 16:53 | 18:53 | | |
| Southampton | 17:00 | | | 125 km/h |

## EXTENSION

**6**  A plane takes half an hour to fly from Dublin to Cork. **Investigate** as much as possible about its flight.

# 6 PROPORTION

## 6.1 Basic principles

When two quantities are related together in a problem, we can use the 'Unitary Method' to solve it. Many different problems in Mathematics and Science can be solved in this way. Here is a summary of the Unitary Method.

*REMEMBER*

1 The Question quantity is always put on the lefthand side (LHS).

2 The Answer quantity is put on the righthand side (RHS).

3 If necessary, the Question quantity is changed to unity (one).

4 All quantities are clearly labelled with the correct units.

5 The two quantities are linked using words.

■ *EXAMPLE 1*

At maximum speed the QE2 uses 10 litres of fuel per second. Find, to the nearest second, the time it takes to use 1 cubic metre of fuel.

$$\begin{array}{ll} \textit{Question quantity} & \textit{Answer quantity} \\ 10 \text{ litres are used in} & 1 \text{ second} \\ 1 \text{ litre is used in} & \frac{1}{10} \text{ second} \\ 1000 \text{ litres } (1 \text{ m}^3) \text{ are used in} & \frac{1}{10} \times 1000 = 100 \text{ seconds} \end{array}$$

Time taken to use $1 \text{ m}^3$ of fuel is $100$ seconds.

■ *EXAMPLE 2*

£1 can be exchanged for 10.8 French francs. How many pounds could be exchanged for 24.3 francs?

$$\begin{array}{ll} \textit{Question quantity} & \textit{Answer quantity} \\ \text{Fr } 10.8 \text{ can be exchanged for} & £1 \\ \text{Fr } 1 \text{ can be exchanged for} & £\frac{1}{10.8} \\ \text{Fr } 24.3 \text{ can be exchanged for} & £\frac{1}{10.8} \times 24.3 \\ & = £2.25 \end{array}$$

£2.25 can be exchanged for 24.3 francs.

■*EXAMPLE 3*

The scale of a map is 1 : 50 000. Find the distance between two points on the map in mm if they are 5 km apart on the land.

*Question quantity*    *Answer quantity*

50 000 km is represented by    1 km

     1 km is represented by    $\dfrac{1}{50\,000}$ km

     5 km is represented by    $\dfrac{1}{50\,000} \times 5 \times 10^6$ mm

                        $= 100$ mm

The distance on a map between two points 5 km apart on the land is 100 mm.

■*EXAMPLE 4*

When 1.8 g of peanuts are burnt, 39 kJ (kilojoules) of energy are produced. How much energy is produced if 24 g of peanuts are burnt?

*Question quantity*    *Answer quantity*

   1.8 g produces    39 kJ

      1 g produces    $\dfrac{39}{1.8}$ kJ

   24 g produces    $\dfrac{39}{1.8} \times 24$ kJ

                 $= 520$ kJ

520 kJ of energy are produced when 24 g of peanuts are burnt.

■*EXAMPLE 5*

A Boeing 737 uses 15 400 litres of fuel when cruising for $5\frac{1}{2}$ hours. Find the time for which the aircraft could cruise on 1000 litres (1 m$^3$) of fuel.

*Question quantity*    *Answer quantity*

15 400 litres are used in    5.5 h

     1 litre is used in    $\dfrac{5.5}{15\,400}$ h

1000 litres are used in    $\dfrac{5.5}{15\,400} \times 1000$ h

            $= \dfrac{5.5}{15\,400} \times 1000 \times 60$ min

            $= 21.428\,57$ minutes to 7 SFs

A Boeing 737 could cruise for 21 minutes (to 2 SF) on 1000 litres (1 m$^3$) of fuel.

## —— Exercise 31

**1** A car travels 17.1 km and uses 1.5 litres of petrol. Find the distance it travelled on:
**a** 1 litre   **b** 25 litres.

**2** On Hawaii it rains an average of 50 mm every 47 hours. How long would you expect it to take for the following amounts to fall: **a** 1 cm   **b** 183 cm (6 feet)?

**3** A human kidney has a volume of 150 cm$^3$. It contains 1.35 million nephrons (small tubes). How many nephrons would you expect in: **a** 1 cm$^3$   **b** 0.001 cm$^3$ (1 mm$^3$)?

**4** Six identical tapes cost £47.70. What is the cost of **a** 1 tape   **b** 7 tapes?

**5** On average, 108 tonnes of Mars bars are produced every 24 hours. How many tonnes would you expect to be produced in **a** 1 hour   **b** 20 minutes?

**6** A carpet manufacturer produces, on average, 3240 m of carpet every 24 hours. What length of carpet would you expect to be produced in **a** 1 hour   **b** 365 days?

**7** In 8 hours, one million cans of Heinz baked beans are sold. How many cans, to the nearest whole number, are sold in **a** 1 minute   **b** 1 second?

**8** An average adult can read 44 100 words every 147 minutes. How many words would you expect an average adult to read in five minutes?

**9** Fifteen identical sheets of block board cost £216. How much do seven cost?

**10** £1 can be exchanged for 245 Spanish pesetas (Ptas). How many pounds can be exchanged for Ptas 833?

**11** On a map, a straight road is 3.5 cm long. If the scale of the map is 5 cm to 1 km, what is the actual length of the road?

**12** If this can costs £1.60, how much would you expect to pay for a can weighing 1.4 kg?

**13** A lump of aluminium has a mass of 140.4 g and a volume of 52 cm$^3$. Find the mass of 36 cm$^3$ of aluminium.

**14** The sub-continent of India moved at the rate of 10 cm per year for 50 million years before colliding with Asia. How far did it move?

**15** It takes 24 hours to fill 489 600 bottles of Cola at a bottling plant. How long does it take to fill 340 bottles?

# ___ 6.2 Change of units

The following table gives you the conversions needed when answering questions in this chapter. You may also find it useful in other parts of the course.

|  | Conversions (correct to 4 SF) | Equivalents |
|---|---|---|
| Length | 1 inch = 2.540 cm<br>1 yard = 0.9144 m<br>1 mile =1.609 km | 1 foot = 12 inches<br>1 yard = 3 feet<br>1 mile = 1760 yards |
| Mass | 1 ounce = 28.35 g<br>1 pound = 0.4535 kg | 1 pound = 16 ounces (oz)<br>1 stone = 14 pounds |
| Volume and capacity | 1 pint = 0.5682 litre<br>1 gallon = 4.546 litres | $1 \text{ cm}^3 = 1$ ml<br>$1 \text{ m}^3 = 1000$ litres<br>1 pint = 20 fluid oz<br>1 gallon = 8 pints |
| Area | 1 acre = 0.4047 hectare (ha) | $1 \text{ ha} = 10\ 000 \text{ m}^2$ |
| Temperature | $5 \times (°\text{Fahrenheit} - 32) = 9 \times °\text{Celsius}$ | |

# ___ *Activity 12*

Different cookery books use different units – Fahrenheit, ounces and pints in one book, gas regulos, grams and litres in another. The aim of this Activity is to make a 'Kitchen Units Converter' for temperature, mass and capacity.

**1** Copy onto graph paper all the information shown below.

KITCHENS UNITS CONVERTER

MASS
Ounces  0  4  8  12  16  20  24  28  32  36
Grams
Pounds

CAPACITY
Litres  0  0.1  0.2  0.3  0.4  0.5  0.6  0.7  0.8  0.9
Fluid oz
Pints

TEMPERATURE
°C  120  140  160  180  200  220  240  260  280  300
°F
Gas  1  12

2 Write on your converter, to 2 SF:
a The number of grams for each of the ounces shown.
b The number of fluid ounces for each of the litres shown.
c The temperature in degrees Fahrenheit for each of the temperatures shown.

3 In the correct place, write on your converter:
a The pounds from $\frac{1}{4}$, $\frac{1}{2}$, ... to 2, $2\frac{1}{4}$.
b The pints from $\frac{1}{4}$, $\frac{1}{2}$, ... to $1\frac{1}{4}$, $1\frac{1}{2}$.
c The gas settings from 2 to 11.

4 Cut out your converter, glue it onto a piece of card (and keep it in the kitchen).

## Exercise 32

For Questions 1 to 3, write down the letter which represents the correct answer.

1 Coal is sold in 56 pound sacks. This is approximately **a** 25 kg **b** 50 kg **c** 110 kg.

2 Clare walks four miles in one hour. Her average speed is approximately **a** 1.8 m/s **b** 9 m/s **c** 0.5 m/s.

3 A sprinter runs the 100 m in 10 s. This is approximately **a** 10 km/h **b** 20 km/h **c** 40 km/h.

4 Which is the greater distance, 5000 m or 3 miles?

5 Which is the smaller mass, half a pound of flour or 250 g of sugar?

6 Hamish is six feet tall and Bill is 183 cm tall. Who is the taller?

7 Maggie has a mass of 58 kg and Gill has a mass of 126 pounds. Who is the lighter?

8 A playing field has an area of 1 km² and a park has an area of 0.38 square miles. Which has the larger area?

9 Which has the greater capacity, a 16 pint barrel or a 9 litre can?

10 I need about five pints of milk, but the shop sells milk in litres and half litres. Should I buy **a** 3 litres **b** $2\frac{1}{2}$ litres **c** 2 litres?

11 As a percentage, how much faster is 50 mph than 80 km/h?

12 As a percentage, how much less is 3000 m than 2 miles?

13 Find the percentage error when assuming that 25 mm = 1 inch.

14 Given that 1 mm = 0.039 371 inches, which is the more accurate: 1 inch = 25.4 mm or 1 km = 0.6214 miles?

15 **Investigate** the size of 13 twist drills in a set which ranges from one sixteenth of an inch to a quarter of an inch.

MASTERMINDERS

16 Find the percentage error in the following statements:
   **a** 1 pint of water has a mass of $1\frac{1}{4}$ pounds.
   **b** 1 cubic foot of water has a mass of 1000 ounces.

17 Show that 1 gallon of water has a mass of 10.0 pounds, correct to 3 SF.

18 How many mm$^3$ are there in a cubic light year? (Light travels at $3 \times 10^8$ m/s.)

## ___ *Activity 13*

The aim of this Activity is to produce a table of **approximate** conversions, useful for quick mental work. You should learn these, as they will be needed for certain tests and examinations.

Copy the information shown below. Use the information on page 105 to help complete it.

| Length | [    ] is about 2.5 cm<br>12 inches is about [    ] cm<br>1 yard is just under [    ] m<br>1 mile is about 1600 [    ]<br>5 [    ] is about 8 km |
|---|---|
| Mass | 2.2 pounds is about [    ] |
| Volume and capacity | 1.75 pints is about [    ]<br>1 [    ] is about 4.5 litres |
| Area | 2.5 acres is about [    ] |
| Temperature | °F ≈ ([    ] × 2 + 30) °C |

## ___ **6.3** Exchange rates (mental)

In a foreign country, it is useful to work out mentally the approximate costs of things in pounds. To do this we use an **approximate** exchange rate. So that you can answer, mentally, the questions in Exercise 33, you should use the approximate rates below (copy these for use in Exercise 33):

*Approximate exchange rates*
   £1 = $1.5 (United States)
   £1 = Fr 11 (France)
   £1 = DM 3 (Germany)
   £1 = Ptas 225 (Spain)

## ___ Exercise 33

1   Change to DM:   **a** £40      **b** £1.20     **c** £2.50.
2   Change to Ptas:  **a** £2       **b** £4        **c** £3.
3   Change to $:     **a** £3       **b** £30       **c** £1.50.
4   Change to Fr:    **a** £12      **b** £0.70     **c** £30.
5   Change to £:     **a** Ptas 450 **b** Ptas 900  **c** Ptas 90.
6   Change to £:     **a** Fr 55    **b** Fr 99     **c** Fr 154.
7   Change to £:     **a** DM 69    **b** DM 195    **c** DM 12.75.
8   Change to £:     **a** $45      **b** $135      **c** $10.5.

MASTERMINDER

9   The price of a litre of petrol in four countries is shown below. In which country is it the most expensive?
United States $0.55   Spain Ptas 90   Germany DM 1.3   France Fr 4.4

## ___ 6.4 Comparative costs

We can use proportion and percentages to compare costs.
Look carefully at the following example.

■ *EXAMPLE 1*

**a**   Which of these cans is the better buy?
**b**   How much more, in percentage terms, would you get for your money if you bought a 415 g can rather than a 240 g can?

**a**   415 g can: 1p will buy $\dfrac{415}{67}$ g        240 g can: 1p will buy $\dfrac{240}{47}$ g

   $\quad\quad\quad\quad = 6.19$ g to 3 SF        $\quad\quad\quad\quad = 5.11$ g to 3 SF

Therefore the 415 g can is the better buy.

**b**   We are comparing the best value for money with the least, so we call the least value for money – the 240 g can – 100%. The ratio line looks this:

From the ratio line, $\dfrac{5.11}{100} = \dfrac{6.19}{x}$

$\quad\quad\quad 5.11x = 6.19 \times 100$

$\quad\quad\quad\quad\quad x = \dfrac{6.19 \times 100}{5.11} = 120\%$ to 2 SF

Therefore you get about 20% more for your money if you buy the 415 g can.

| | 240 g can | 415 g can |
|---|---|---|
| g/p 0 | 5.11 | 6.19 |
| % 0 | 100 | x |

108

## — *Activity 14*

**Investigate** the following information. (The number in brackets is the percentage of the joint which is **not** edible.)

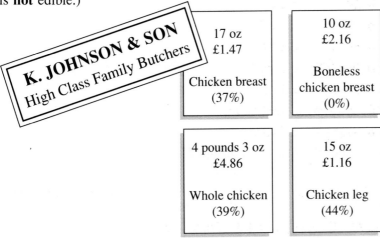

K. JOHNSON & SON
High Class Family Butchers

17 oz
£1.47

Chicken breast
(37%)

10 oz
£2.16

Boneless
chicken breast
(0%)

4 pounds 3 oz
£4.86

Whole chicken
(39%)

15 oz
£1.16

Chicken leg
(44%)

## — **Exercise 34**

1   The table below shows details of baked beans sold in 1977 and 1987.

|      |      | *Mass (g)* | *Cost (p)* |
|------|------|------------|------------|
| 1977 | i    | 794        | 28.5       |
|      | ii   | 142        | 7          |
|      | iii  | 447        | 15         |
|      | iv   | 567        | 20         |
| 1987 | v    | 840        | 51         |
|      | vi   | 150        | 15         |
|      | vii  | 450        | 21         |
|      | viii | 580        | 38         |

**a** Investigate these figures.
**b** Collect your own details of baked beans sold in different sized cans and analyse your figures.

2   A 330 ml bottle of lager costs 64p. How much should a $\frac{1}{2}$ pint bottle of the same type of lager cost?

3   A man goes to an Off Licence with an empty 2 litre bottle and asks for it to be filled with cider which costs £1.90 per pint. How much does he pay?
    If on another occasion he was charged £6 for 2 litres, how much was he paying per pint?

4   The gas in a Calor Gas cylinder has a mass of 4.5 kg. To replace the gas costs £7.50. The cost of replacing a Camping Gas cylinder, which contains 190 g of gas, is £1.70. How many times more expensive is it to use Camping Gas rather than Calor Gas? Comment on your answer.

MASTERMINDER

5  The table gives details of the cost of certain liquids sold in 1979 and 1985.

| Type of liquid | Cost (£) | | Volume |
| --- | --- | --- | --- |
| | 1979 | 1985 | |
| Brandy | 7.29 | 9.25 | 680 cm³ |
| Ink (cartridge) | 0.30 | 0.60 | 7.5 cm³ |
| Petrol | 1.30 | 1.90 | 1 gallon |
| Ink (bottle) | 0.45 | 0.90 | 57 cm³ |
| Beer | 0.45 | 0.70 | 1 pint |

a Work out the cost per litre of each of the five types of liquid in 1979 and 1985.
b Work out the percentage increase over the six years to 2 SF.
c Draw a bar chart to illustrate your results.
d Find the cost per litre of similar liquids which are on sale today. Compare and comment on your findings.

# — 6.5 Problem solving

REMEMBER

When using the Unitary Method:
- Reduce the Question quantity to unity (one).
- Label the quantities with the correct units.

■ EXAMPLE 1

There are 4800 km of motorway in the UK. The total area of land used is 60 000 acres. Find the number of acres per mile of motorway. (Take 1 mile ≈ 1.61 km.)

$$\text{Question quantity} \qquad \text{Answer quantity}$$

$$\text{4800 km of motorway uses} \qquad \text{60 000 acres}$$

$$\text{1 km of motorway uses} \qquad \frac{60\,000}{4800} \text{ acres}$$

$$\text{1 mile (1.61 km) of motorway uses} \qquad \frac{600}{48} \times 1.61 \text{ acres}$$

$$= 20 \text{ acres to 2 SF}$$

1 mile of motorway uses about 20 acres of land.

## Activity 15

Work out, to 2 SF, how far each of the following travels, in metres, during 0.2 seconds.

**1**  A man walks 4 km in 1 hour.

**2**  A greyhound runs 400 m in 19.5 s.

**3**  A rifle bullet takes 1.79 s to travel 1 mile.

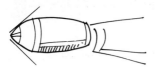

**4**  The equator turns at just over 1000 miles/h.

**5**  A thunderclap travels at $3.3 \times 10^4$ cm/s.

**6**  Lightning travels at $3 \times 10^{10}$ cm/s.

## Exercise 35

Give all answers correct to 3 SF.

**1**  It is estimated that by the age of eighteen the average American child has seen 350 000 commercials on TV. How many commercials is a child likely to have seen per day?

**2**  On average, a queen termite lays 950 eggs every 25 minutes. How long would you expect her to take to lay a million eggs?

**3**  In its twelve years of life, it is estimated that the Chimney Swift bird flies 1.25 million miles. How far would you expect it to fly in an hour?

**4**  In 25 minutes 900 million gallons of water cascade over the Niagara Falls. How much water cascades over these falls per second?

**5**  Red blood cells are replaced by the bone marrow at the rate of $2 \times 10^{11}$ per day. How many are replaced per second?

**6** A company claims to sell 114 062 500 packets of cornflakes a year. If each packet has a mass of 480 g, find the mean mass sold per day. Give your answer in tonnes.

**7** The total petrol used per year in the UK is 6000 million gallons. The total emission of lead through car exhaust is 3000 tonnes per year. Find the mean mass of lead in 1 gallon of petrol.

**8** On a map of Scotland the distance between Inverness and Aberdeen is 13.4 cm. If the actual distance between the two towns is 134 km, what is the scale of the map?

**9** There are $25 \times 10^{11}$ red blood cells in a human body. Suppose the total mass of red blood cells is 2.5 kg and the total volume is 2.75 litres. Find:
**a** The number of cells in 1 g.
**b** The density of red blood cells in g/cm$^3$.

**10** A camel can drink 45 litres of liquid in 5 minutes. How long would it take to drink a pint?

**11** One ounce of gold can be beaten out to cover 9.2 m$^2$. What mass of gold, in kg, could cover a hectare?

**12** In 4 m$^2$ of grassland there can be as many as 2500 worms. How many could there be in a hectare?

**13** The base area of a Monopoly house is 1 cm$^2$ (to 1 SF). The value of this area of land in the middle of Tokyo is £2500. What is the value of a football pitch, of area 1 ha, in the middle of Tokyo?

**14** In 365 days the average person in the UK uses 54 000 litres of water. How many gallons does the average person use in a fortnight? Compare your answer to the capacity of a large domestic oil tank (500 gallons).

**15** On a map of Africa the island of Madagascar is 4.1 cm long. If the scale of the map is 1 : 40 million, find the actual length of the island. What would be the length of the island on a map of scale: **a** 1 : 20 million **b** 1 : 1 million **c** 1 : 100 000 **d** 1 : 25 000?

## MASTERMINDERS

**16** The building plans of a house are drawn to a scale of 1 : 50.
**a** Find the length of the house, in metres, represented by a length of 30 cm on the plan.
**b** Find the length, in cm, which represents the height of the house on the plan, if the height of the house is 7 metres.
**c** Regulations require the cloakroom window to have an area of 3000 cm$^2$. Find the area, in cm$^2$, of this window on the plans.
**d** The area of the kitchen floor on the plan is 120 cm$^2$. Find the area, in m$^2$, of the kitchen floor of the house.

**17** Two cogged wheels, one of which has 16 cogs and the other 27, engage each other. If the latter turns 80 times in 45 seconds, how often does the former turn in 8 seconds?

# 6.6 Inverse proportion

## *Activity 16*

The following statement appeared in a national newspaper:

'The construction of the Channel Tunnel and associated activities will create about 100 000 man-years of employment in Britain'.

In theory, this is the same as saying that the tunnel can be built in:

    1 year by 100 000 men
    2 years by 50 000 men
    4 years by 25 000 men
    5 years by 20 000 men

We call this an 'inverse proportion' relationship.

1   How many men would be required to build the tunnel in 8 years?

2   How long would it take 40 000 men to build the tunnel?

3   How many men would be required to build the tunnel in $t$ years?

4   How many years would it take $n$ men to build the tunnel?

5   How long would you expect 100 000 men to build two similar tunnels?

6   Copy and complete the following:

    (i) 100 000 men could build 4 tunnels in ☐ years.

    (ii) 100 000 men could build ☐ tunnels in 2 years.

    (iii) 20 000 men could build 8 tunnels in ☐ years.

    (iv) ☐ men could build 2 tunnels in 6 months.

## Exercise 36

**1** It takes one man eight days to dig one trench.
  **a** Copy and complete this table:
  **b** Write down anything you notice about the numbers in each column.
  **c** How long would it take 16 men to dig two trenches?
  **d** How many men could dig four trenches in 16 days?
  **e** How many trenches could be dug by three men in 56 days?

| Number of men | Time in days to dig | | |
|---|---|---|---|
| | 1 trench | 2 trenches | 3 trenches |
| 1 | | | |
| 2 | | | |
| 4 | | | |
| 3 | | | |
| $n$ | | | |

**2** It has been estimated that it took 4000 men 30 years to build the largest pyramid in Egypt.
  **a** How long would it have taken to build with (i) 8000 men  (ii) 2000 men  (iii) 3000 men  (iv) 40 men (not necessarily the same men!)  (v) $x$ men?
  **b** How many men could have built it in (i) 6 years  (ii) 20 years  (iii) 1 year  (iv) 1000 years  (v) $y$ years?

**3** One mosquito can produce 9 million young in 500 hours. Copy and complete the following.
  **a** 1 mosquito can produce 18 000 young in ☐ hours.
  **b** 1 mosquito can produce ☐ young in 1 second.
  **c** ☐ mosquitoes can produce 9 million young in 1 hour.
  **d** 500 mosquitoes can produce ☐ young in 500 hours.

**4** During the University Boat Race, a commentator said: 'Every member of the crew does the equivalent amount of work as someone who lifts a 25 kg sack of potatoes, from the floor to shoulder height, 36 times a minute for 18 minutes'.

  **a** What total mass is 'lifted' by one crew member during the 18 minute race? Give your answer to 2 SF.
  **b** A lorry is to be loaded with sacks of coal each of mass 25 kg. Work out, to 1 SF, how long you would expect:
   (i) One crew member to load 4 tonnes.
   (ii) 8 crew members to load 4 tonnes.
   (iii) 4 crew members to load 4 tonnes.
   (iv) 8 crew members to load 1 tonne.

**5** One cow belches 200 g of methane in a day. Copy and complete the following.
  **a** 1 cow belches 1 kg of methane in ☐ days.
  **b** ☐ cows belch 1000 kg of methane in 5 days.
  **c** 3100 million cows belch ☐ tonnes of methane in 365 days.
  (It is estimated that there are about 3100 million cows in the world.)

MASTERMINDER

**6**  The average mass of a swarm of locusts is 80 000 tonnes.  Each locust eats its own mass in food per day.  There are about 40 billion locusts in a swarm.

**a** Estimate the total mass of food eaten by a swarm of locusts each day.

**b** What is the average mass of a locust?

**c** The amount of food eaten by a swarm of locusts in a day would be sufficient to keep half a million people alive for a year.

(i) How much food, to the nearest tonne, would be sufficient to keep half a million people alive for one day?

(ii) How much food, to the nearest 10 grams, would be sufficient to keep one person alive for one day?

# — **6.7** Science problems

## — *Activity 17*

The Earth was formed about 4600 million years ago.  If this time span is represented by a straight line 5 metres long, where should the following events be placed on this line?

| Appearance of | Approximate number of years ago |
|---|---|
| First living cells | $3200 \times 10^6$ |
| First land animals | $400 \times 10^6$ |
| First mammals | $225 \times 10^6$ |
| Giant dinosaurs | $135 \times 10^6$ |
| Man | $4 \times 10^6$ |

*REMEMBER*

- Density $(g/cm^3)$ = mass, in grams, of $1\,cm^3$ = $\dfrac{Mass(g)}{Volume(cm^3)}$

- Density of water = $1\,g/cm^3$ = $1\,kg/litre$ = $1\,tonne/m^3$

115

# 6 PROPORTION

■ *EXAMPLE 1*

Lead has a density of 11.4 g/cm³. Find the volume of a lump of lead which has a mass of 47.2 g.

$$\qquad \textit{Question quantity} \quad \textit{Answer quantity}$$

$$11.4\text{ g has a volume of} \quad 1\,\text{cm}^3$$

$$1\text{ g has a volume of} \quad \frac{1}{11.4}\,\text{cm}^3$$

$$47.2\text{ g has a volume of} \quad \frac{1}{11.4} \times 47.2\,\text{cm}^3$$

$$= 4.14\,\text{cm}^3, \text{ to 3 SF}$$

## ▬ Exercise 37

Give all answers correct to 3 SF.

1  The density of silver is 10.5 g/cm³. Find the volume of a silver necklace which has a mass of 7.8 g.

2  The density of iron is 7.85 g/cm³. Find the mass of an iron gate which has a volume of 1200 cm³.

3  The density of lead is 11.4 g/cm³. What mass of lead has a volume of one cubic metre?

4  The density of air is 1.2 kg/m³. What would be the mass of air in a classroom measuring 10 m by 8 m by 3 m?

5  The density of aluminium is 2.65 g/cm³. 3 cm³ of brass has a mass of 25.5 g. Which is heavier and by how much: 40 cm³ of aluminium or 12 cm³ of brass?

6  A piece of wire is 2.4 m long and has a resistance of 7 ohms.
   **a** What would be the resistance of a piece of wire 3.5 m long?
   **b** What length of wire would have a resistance of 23 ohms?

7  A virus is $5 \times 10^{-10}$ m in diameter. How many viruses would fit across a human hair of diameter 0.006 mm?

8  The amount of heat needed to raise the temperature of 1 gram of water by 1 °C is 4.2 joules.
   **a** How much heat would be needed to raise the temperature of 20 g of water by 1 °C?
   **b** How much heat would be needed to raise the temperature of 1 g of water by 30 °C?
   **c** How much heat would be needed to raise the temperature of 20 g of water by 30 °C?

9  Guy runs in an 800 m race and uses 520 kJ (kilojoules) of energy. 100 g of sugar is converted by the body into 1650 kJ of energy. How much sugar should Guy take to replace the energy he used in his 800 m race?

**10** The drawing represents a red blood cell. The
diameter of a red blood cell is $7 \times 10^{-6}$ m.
  **a** Approximately, by how many times has the red
  blood cell in the diagram been magnified?
  **b** How many could be placed in a straight line
  one centimetre long?

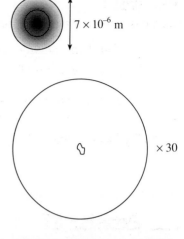

$7 \times 10^{-6}$ m

**11** The diagram shows the outline of an Amoeba as it
appears under the low power ($\times 30$) of a microscope.
Draw a circle of the same diameter. Inside your
circle draw the outline of the Amoeba as it would
appear under the medium power ($\times 100$) of the
microscope.

$\times 30$

**12** A four-day-old hamster has a mass of 67 g and a
skin area of 139 cm$^2$. An adult hamster has a mass
of 681 g and a skin area of 616 cm$^2$.
  **a** What area of skin is there for every gram of (i) a
  4 day-old hamster   (ii) an adult hamster?
  **b** Which has the greater area of skin per gram of
  body?

MASTERMINDER

**13** A molecule of water is a very small thing, so small that its volume is $10^{-27}$ m$^3$.
  **a** How many molecules are there in 1 m$^3$? If you wrote your answer in full, how many zero
  digits would there be?
  **b** If a molecule is assumed to be in the form of a cube, show that its side length is $10^{-9}$ m.
  **c** If a number of these molecules were placed touching each other in a straight line, how many
  would there be in a line one centimetre long?
  **d** Taking the volume of a cup of tea to be 200 cm$^3$, how
  many molecules of water would the cup hold? If all
  these were placed end to end in a straight line, how
  long would the line be? Taking the circumference of
  the Earth to be 40 000 km, how many times would the
  line of molecules go around the Earth?

## ___ Revision Exercise 6

Give all answers correct to 3 SF. You may consult the table of conversions on page 105.

1 William goes on a 13 mile cycle ride. How many kilometres is this?

2 Mrs Black buys $3\frac{1}{2}$ pounds of apples. How many kilograms is this?

3 Juliet buys three litres of vinegar. How many pints is this?

4 A field has an area of nine hectares. How many acres is this?

5 New potatoes are sold at £1.60 per pound. How much is this per kilogram?

6 What is the cost of peat per pound?

7 A painting measures five inches by eleven inches. What is its area in cm$^2$?

8 A man weighs 85 kg. Change this to stones and pounds.

9 The normal temperature for a human is 98.4 °F. Change this to degrees Celsius.

10 In percentage terms, how much larger is a square mile than a square kilometre?

11 At an airport shop the cost of a bottle of brandy is shown in two currencies:
Fr 125 (France)
DM 34 (Germany)
Copy and complete the following, to give the likely exchange rate.
'DM 10 can be exchanged for Fr....'

12 £1 can be exchanged for Fr 10.8. How many pounds can be exchanged for 59.4 francs?

13 In percentage terms, how much less is half a pint than a third of a litre?

14 A firm produces one type of cat meat and sells it in two different size cans.

    a Use the above facts to work out the likely cost of the 400 g can.
    b The volume of the 400 g can is 385 cm$^3$. Work out:
        (i) The density of the cat meat.
        (ii) The volume of the 415 g can.
    c If some of the meat were accidentally dropped into water, would it float?

**15** There are $6 \times 10^{23}$ atoms of silver in 127 g of silver. How many atoms of silver would weigh 1.905 kg?

**16** A piece of wire is 12.5 m long and has a resistance of 13.9 ohms. What length of wire would have a resistance of 20 ohms?

**17** In the blood of a human, there are $5 \times 10^{11}$ red cells per litre. Find the number of red blood cells per $mm^3$.

**18** It is estimated that by the age of eighteen the average American child has seen 15 000 murders on TV. How many murders is a child likely to have seen per day?

**19** A map has a scale of 1 : 25 000. How long is a road which is shown on the map as 3.5 cm long?

**20** There are a quarter of a million miles of roads in the UK and 18 million cars. How many cars for every 100 yards of road do these figures suggest?

**21** North Sea oil production reached a peak in 1985 when 665 million gallons of oil were pumped ashore every 7 days. How many gallons were likely to have been pumped ashore every 30 seconds?

**22** A soft drinks factory produces 2000 cans of drink per minute. Each can contains 0.33 litres. Assuming that this rate of production can be maintained, work out the total volume of drink produced per year. Approximately how many times would this volume fill your classroom?

**23** One honey bee has to travel 75 000 km to produce 500 g of honey.
Copy and complete the following:
**a** ☐ honey bees would each have to travel 3000 km to produce a total of 500 g of honey.
**b** 25 honey bees would each have to travel 60 km to produce a total of ☐ g of honey.
**c** 25 honey bees would each have to travel ☐ km to produce a total of 1 tonne of honey.

**24** It is estimated that 55 million people in France eat 500 million snails each year. On average, how often does one person in France eat one snail?

## MASTERMINDER

**25** **Investigate** whether the wellknown science fiction writer Charles Berlitz was right when he suggested that planet Earth was likely to be invaded by people from outer space to extract the gold from our oceans. Berlitz estimated that the value of gold in each cubic mile of ocean is $360 million. (Assume that gold is as valuable to people from outer space as it is to us.)

## Basic Algebra Test 2

**Section A**   (1 mark for each correct answer)

Simplify:

| | | | |
|---|---|---|---|
| **1** $2a + 6a$ | **2** $2a \times 6a$ | **3** $2a - 6a$ | **4** $2a \div 6a$ |
| **5** $\frac{x}{3} + \frac{x}{2}$ | **6** $\frac{x}{3} \times \frac{x}{2}$ | **7** $\frac{x}{3} \div \frac{x}{2}$ | **8** $\frac{x}{3} - \frac{x}{2}$ |
| **9** $a^2 \times 3ab$ | **10** $a^2 \div 3ab$ | **11** $4 - (3 - x)$ | **12** $2(3x)^2$ |

Find the value of each expression when $a = -2$.

| | | | |
|---|---|---|---|
| **13** $2a^2$ | **14** $2 + a^2$ | **15** $(2a)^2$ | **16** $(2 - a)^2$ |

Solve for $c$:

| | | | |
|---|---|---|---|
| **17** $3 - c = 9 + 2c$ | **18** $2(c + 5) = 15$ | **19** $\frac{4}{3} = \frac{2}{c}$ | **20** $\frac{1 + c}{3} = \frac{c}{5}$ |

Factorize completely:

| | |
|---|---|
| **21** $2b + 4b^2$ | **22** $a^2b - ab^2$ |

Solve the inequalities:

| | |
|---|---|
| **23** $4 - 3x \geqslant 6$ | **24** $3 + \frac{x}{2} < 11$ |

**Section B**   (2 marks for each correct answer)

Simplify if possible:

| | | | |
|---|---|---|---|
| **25** $\frac{3x}{5} + \frac{x}{4}$ | **26** $\frac{36ab^2c^3}{12bc^2}$ | **27** $\frac{2b^2 + b}{b}$ | **28** $\frac{x - 1}{3} - \frac{x + 2}{4}$ |

Solve for $x$:

| | | | |
|---|---|---|---|
| **29** $2 - x(x - 1) = -x^2$ | **30** $\frac{x - 3}{3} = \frac{x + 2}{2}$ | **31** $\frac{2}{3} = \frac{x + 2}{x - 3}$ | **32** $\frac{x + 1}{5} - \frac{x - 1}{2} = -2$ |

## Puzzlers

**1**   Only three circles need be moved in order to make the triangle point downwards. What is the sum of the numbers in the circles?

**2**   Evaluate:   $9 + \dfrac{\frac{26}{35}}{1 - \dfrac{2}{3 + \dfrac{1}{6 - \frac{1}{2}}}}$

**3**   747 is a palindromic number, reading the same from left to right as from right to left. How many palindromic numbers are there between 100 and 1000?

**4**   If two foxes kill two chickens in two minutes, how long would you expect 100 foxes to take to kill 100 chickens?

# Coursework: The solar system

Our solar system, with the Sun at its centre, is one small part of the Milky Way. As you work through this Coursework you may begin to realize how insignificant our planet is.

| Celestial body | Mean diameter (km) | Mean distance from the Sun (km) |
|---|---|---|
| Sun | 1 390 000 | – |
| Mercury | 4880 | $57.9 \times 10^6$ |
| Venus | 12 100 | $108 \times 10^6$ |
| Earth | 12 800 | $150 \times 10^6$ |
| Mars | 6790 | $228 \times 10^6$ |
| Jupiter | 143 000 | $778 \times 10^6$ |
| Saturn | 121 000 | $1430 \times 10^6$ |
| Uranus | 51 000 | $2870 \times 10^6$ |
| Neptune | 48 000 | $4500 \times 10^6$ |
| Pluto | 3000 | $5950 \times 10^6$ |
| Moon | 3480 | * |
| Nearest star | * | $3.97 \times 10^{13}$ |
| Largest star | $3.75 \times 10^7$ | * |

(Remember to use the memory function on your calculator.)

1  **a** Measure the height of your classroom and let this represent the diameter of the Sun.
(i) How large should each of the planets and the Moon be if they are to be drawn to this scale?
(ii) Write this scale as $1 : n$ where $n$ is correct to 1 SF.
  **b** Draw a circle of diameter 200 mm. If this represents the planet Jupiter, draw separate circles to the same scale to represent each of the other planets. Using this scale, calculate the diameter of (i) the Sun   (ii) the largest star.

2  The distance from the Sun to Pluto is represented by a line five metres long.
  **a** Where should the other planets be placed along this line?
  **b** Using this scale, where would you have to place the nearest star?
  **c** By what number do you have to multiply or divide your answers in part **a** and **b**, to make a model where Pluto is placed (i) 5 cm   (ii) 20 cm   (iii) 100 m from the Sun? Draw a diagram to one of these scales showing the relative distances of the planets from the Sun.

EXTENSION   (Assume the shortest distance)

3  We see the planets and the nearest star as they were how long ago?
Comment on your last answer. (Speed of light $\approx 300\,000$ km/s.)

4  A Mega-booster space craft travels at 40 000 km/h. What problems would it have if it set out to explore our corner of the Milky Way?

# 7 ALGEBRA II

## — 7.1 Equations

### — *Activity 18*

In order to solve equations, you need to know how they are 'assembled' and 'dismantled'.

1  The flow diagram below shows the input, the output and three 'function boxes'.

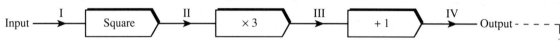

**Flow diagram**

If 2 is the input, the output is 13.

$$2 \rightarrow 4 \rightarrow 12 \rightarrow 13$$

Copy Table 1 below and use the flow diagram to help you complete it.

2  If you are given the output number from the flow diagram, and you want to find the input number, you use another flow diagram showing the **inverse operations**. (Note the direction of the arrows this time.)

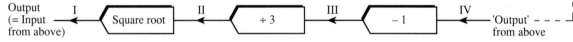

**Inverse flow diagram**

If 109 is the output from the original flow diagram, from the inverse flow diagram you will find that the input is 6.

$$6 \leftarrow 36 \leftarrow 108 \leftarrow 109$$

Copy Table 2 below and use the **inverse flow diagram** to help you complete it.

| input (I) | (II) | (III) | output (IV) | input (I) | (II) | (III) | output (IV) |
|-----------|------|-------|-------------|-----------|------|-------|-------------|
| 2 | 4 | 12 | 13 | 6 | 36 | 108 | 109 |
| 5 | | | | | | | 49 |
| 7 | | | | | | | 244 |
| $x$ | | | | | | | $p$ |
| | 49 | | | | | 363 | |
| | 1 | | | | | 27 | |
| | 9 | | | | | 745 | |
| | $y$ | | | | | | $q$ |

**Table 1**                    **Table 2**

122

## ___ *Activity 19*

Activity 18 showed how an equation ($y = 3x^2 + 1$) is formed ('assembled') and solved ('dismantled'). This principle helps us solve many types of equation.

Play this game with a partner. Ask her to think of an input number to enter into the flow diagram below and to tell you **only** the resulting output number.

Input → | Square | → | × 4 | → Output

You must now tell her the input number she thought of! (Explain why she must have started with 5 or $-5$ if she finished with 100.

Now play this game with a partner using a different flow diagram to the one above, and use three or more operations.

Study Examples 1 and 2 very carefully before starting Exercise 38.

### ■ EXAMPLE 1
Solve $3x^2 = 48$.

First sketch the flow and the inverse flow charts, like this:

$$3x^2 = 48 \quad \text{(Divide both sides by 3)}$$
$$x^2 = 16 \quad \text{(Square root both sides)}$$
$$x = \pm 4$$

**We have to include both plus and minus signs because the squares of both +4 and −4 give 16.** (Check: $3 \times 4 \times 4 = 48$ and $3 \times -4 \times -4 = 48$)

### ■ EXAMPLE 2
Solve $\frac{5x - 9}{7} = 3$.

First sketch the flow and the inverse flow charts, like this:

$$\frac{5x - 9}{7} = 3 \quad \text{(Multiply both sides by 7)}$$
$$5x - 9 = 21 \quad \text{(Add 9 to both sides)}$$
$$5x = 30 \quad \text{(Divide both sides by 5)}$$
$$x = 6$$

(Check: $\frac{30 - 9}{7} = \frac{21}{7} = 3$)

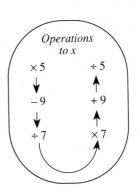

123

## ___ Exercise 38

Before solving each of Questions 1 to 38, sketch the appropriate flow charts, as in Examples 1 and 2 (page 123). After solving, check your answer by substitution.

**1** $2x + 1 = 5$  **2** $3x - 1 = 8$  **3** $1 + 5x = 46$  **4** $8 - 2x = 4$

**5** $1 + \frac{2x}{3} = 7$  **6** $\frac{4x}{19} - 1 = 7$  **7** $2(x + 3) - 4 = 7$  **8** $3(x - 19) + 7 = 40$

**9** $9 + 3(x + 5) = 18$  **10** $7 - 4(x - 2) = 5$  **11** $\frac{2x + 1}{3} = 11$  **12** $\frac{4x - 1}{19} = 5$

**13** $\frac{2x - 3}{11} = 5$  **14** $\frac{5x + 1}{3} = 12$  **15** $4x^2 = 100$  **16** $7x^2 = 63$

**17** $10x^2 = 490$  **18** $\frac{x^2}{4} = 25$  **19** $\frac{x^2}{9} = 9$  **20** $x^2 + 7 = 32$

**21** $x^2 - 17 = 64$  **22** $x^2 - 69 = 100$  **23** $5x^2 = 3.2$  **24** $x^2 + 0.56 = 2$

**25** $\frac{x^2}{0.5} = 50$  **26** $x^2 + 4 = 200$  **27** $2x^2 + 3 = 203$  **28** $3x^2 + 12 = 600$

**29** $5x^2 + 0.8 = 8$  **30** $\frac{x^2 + 0.19}{5} = 0.2$  **31** $\sqrt{x - 8} = 2$  **32** $8 = \sqrt{\frac{x}{9}}$

**33** $2 = \sqrt{x + 5}$  **34** $\sqrt{\frac{x}{2}} + 3 = 10$  **35** $\sqrt{\frac{x - 4}{8}} = 2$  **36** $10 = \sqrt{3 + \frac{x}{2}}$

**37** $\frac{\sqrt{x}}{2} + 3 = 10$  **38** $0 = 4\sqrt{x} - 4$

Solve for $x$ in each of the flow diagrams below.

**39**

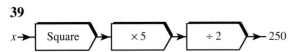

**40**

**41**

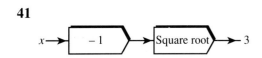

**42**

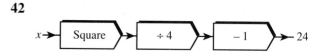

## MASTERMINDERS

Solve for $x$.

**43** $(3x)^2 = 225$  **44** $(x + 3)^2 = 169$

**45** $4(4 - x)^2 = 9$  **46** $2 = \sqrt{22 - 8x^2}$

**47** $x^5 = 80$ to 3 SF  **48** $\sqrt[5]{x} = 3$

**49** $\sqrt{\dfrac{(4 + \sqrt{x + 3})^2}{6}} + 3 = 3$

**50** $\sqrt{\dfrac{(1 + \sqrt{2x - 1})^2}{4}} + 1 = 2$

# — 7.2 'Trial and improvement' solution

This diagram shows a golfer's attempts to hole her ball.
The first stroke puts her quite close to the hole at $A_1$.
She improves on this position taking her to $A_2$.
A similar process then takes her to $A_3$ and then to $A_4$.
At $A_4$ she has solved the problem by holing the ball.

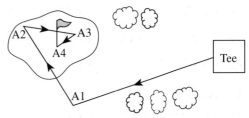

This demonstrates the process called **iteration**: first the answer to a problem is guessed or estimated; then this inaccurate answer is used to find a better one, and so on until a desired degree of accuracy is reached. (The accuracy could be 1 SF, 2 DP, etc.)

## — *Activity 20*

What can you say about the side length $x$ metres of a square lawn of area greater than $36\,\text{m}^2$ but less than $49\,\text{m}^2$?

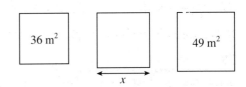

*(Usually a calculator is used to find the side length of a square of a given area, but in this activity you are NOT allowed to use the square root button!)*

Carefully study this example, noting the layout of the working.

I want to find the side length of a square lawn of area $42.25\,\text{m}^2$. 42.25 lies between 36 ($6^2$) and 49 ($7^2$). My first guess is 6.4 m as this is between 6 m and 7 m. Then I start to iterate, as shown in the table.

| Guess (m) | Area (m²) | Conclusion |
|-----------|-----------|------------|
| 6.4 | 40.96 | Too short |
| 6.6 | 43.56 | Too long |
| 6.5 | 42.25 | Correct |

The method is summarized in this partially completed flow diagram.

a   Copy and complete the flow diagram.
b   Use this method to find the side length of a square which has an area of: (i) $72.25\,\text{cm}^2$
(ii) $84.64\,\text{cm}^2$   (iii) $114.49\,\text{m}^2$   (iv) $127.69\,\text{m}^2$

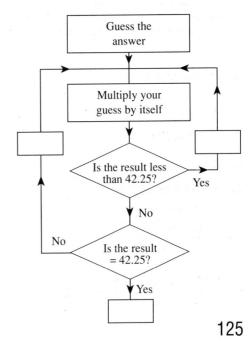

## Exercise 39

In this exercise you are **not** allowed to use the square root button on your calculator.
Use the flow diagram in Activity 20 to help you solve the questions by the 'trial and improvement' method. For each question write down the result of your guesses in a table (as in Activity 20).

**1** Find the side length of a square of area:
  **a** $30.25\,\text{cm}^2$      **b** $12.96\,\text{m}^2$      **c** $342.25\,\text{mm}^2$      **d** $0.1225\,\text{km}^2$

**2** Solve for $x$ to 3 SF:
  **a** $x^2 = 19$      **b** $3x^2 = 7$      **c** $2x^2 + 1 = 6$      **d** $1.2x^2 - 1.3 = 2$

**3** **a** The rectangle and the square have equal areas. Find the side length and the perimeter of the square.

**b** The triangle and the square have equal areas. Find the side length and the perimeter of the square.

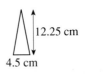 

**4** The rectangle ACDF consists of a large square BCDE and three small squares. The area of the rectangle is $6.75\,\text{cm}^2$. Find the side length of the large square.

**5** This diagram shows a square garden plot with a border path made from square paving stones. The area of the enclosed plot is $20.25\,\text{m}^2$. Find:
  **a** The side length of each paving stone.
  **b** The area of the border path.

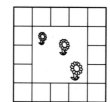

## MASTERMINDERS

**6** This rectangular window has an area of $1.125\,\text{m}^2$. Find its dimensions.

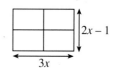

**7** This rectangular box has a volume of $0.648\,\text{m}^3$. Find its dimensions.

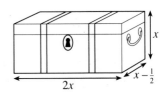

# ___ 7.3 Inequalities

Sentences involving 'greater than' ($>$), 'less than' ($<$) or 'at least' ($\geq$) are very common. Mathematically, they can be written as inequalities. (Look back to page 56 to remind yourself of the meaning of the symbols.)

■ *EXAMPLE 1*

Form an inequality from this advert:

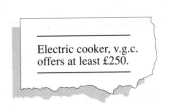

Electric cooker, v.g.c. offers at least £250.

Let $P$ be the price of the cooker. Then

$$P \geq £250$$

■ *EXAMPLE 2*

The width of a rugby pitch must be between 55 m and 69 m inclusive; the length of the pitch must be between 120 m and 144 m inclusive. Find the maximum and minimum area of the pitch.

Let $A$ be the area of the pitch.

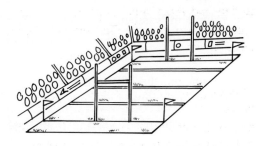

Minimum area = $55 \times 120 = 6600\,\mathrm{m}^2$
Therefore $A \geq 6600\,\mathrm{m}^2$

Maximum area = $69 \times 144 = 9936\,\mathrm{m}^2$
Therefore $A \leq 9936\,\mathrm{m}^2$

Combining the two inequalities:

$$6600\,\mathrm{m}^2 \leq A \leq 9936\,\mathrm{m}^2$$

■ *EXAMPLE 3*

A superstore's car park has an area of $1350\,\mathrm{m}^2$; $150\,\mathrm{m}^2$ is allowed for turning space.
Each car is given $20\,\mathrm{m}^2$ parking space.
Form an inequality and solve it to find the maximum number of cars that the car park can hold.

Let $N$ be the number of cars. Then:

$$150 + 20N \leq 1350 \quad \text{(Subtract 150 from both sides)}$$
$$20N \leq 1200 \quad \text{(Divide both sides by 20)}$$
$$N \leq 60$$

The maximum number of cars is 60.

## ___ *Activity 21*

Form as many inequalities as you can
from this job advertisement:

> "..8 G.C.S.E.'s and 3 A levels required. The
> applicant must be over 18 years old and have
> minimum shorthand of 120 w.p.m. and typing
> speed of 60 w.p.m. Hours of work are at least
> 35 per week. Salary $15 000 to $18 000
> depending on experience..."

## ___ **Exercise 40**

1   Form an inequality for each of the situations below. Use letters, stating clearly what each one
    represents.

a 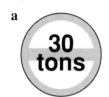   b    c 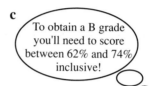   d
HOLIDAY CHALETS
to let
For between 2 and 8
people

2   A room is to be 6 m wide and $L$ m long. The area is planned to be between $36\,m^2$ to $48\,m^2$
    inclusive. Form an inequality for $L$.

3   The volume of water in a rectangular swimming pool of constant depth varies from $375\,m^3$ to
    $500\,m^3$ inclusive. The width and length of the pool are 10 m and 25 m respectively. Form an
    inequality for the depth of water $h$ m.

4   Dafydd can run the 400 m at a speed varying from 6.25 m/s to 6.4 m/s inclusive. Form an
    inequality for the time $t$ seconds in which he can complete the race.

5   A car travels at speeds varying from 20 m/s to 30 m/s inclusive. Form an inequality for the
    distance $d$ miles travelled by the car in 2 hours. (1 mile $\approx$ 1600 m)

6   The cabin of a new passenger aircraft is planned to have an area of $350\,m^2$. The gangway takes
    up $50\,m^2$. Each passenger seat is allowed $4\,m^2$. Form an inequality for the number of seats $N$
    and hence state the maximum number of passengers in the aircraft.

7   The safety limit of a service lift states that it can carry 'less than 830 kg'. Steven weighs 80 kg
    and enters the lift having loaded $N$ five-kilogram bricks into it. Form an inequality for $N$ and
    solve it to find the maximum number of bricks that the lift can safely transport with Steven on
    board.

8   A travelling salesman has daily expense allowances as follows:

    Travel by car: 25p per mile     Food and drink: £25

If his expenses for five days came to less than £312.50, form an inequality to help you find how
many miles $m$ he could have travelled over the five days. (Assume he spends his entire food
and drink allowance every day.)

# __ 7.4 Circumference of a circle

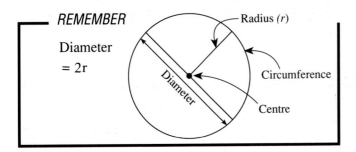

*REMEMBER*

Diameter
= 2r

Radius (*r*)

Diameter

Circumference

Centre

## __ *Activity 22*

1   Take a circular object such as a screw-on lid and measure its diameter $d$ and circumference $C$. Work out the ratio of circumference to diameter. Repeat this for three other circular objects. Use the headings below to tabulate your results.

| Object | Circumference (C) | Diameter (d) | $\dfrac{C}{d}$ |
|--------|-------------------|--------------|------|
|        |                   |              |      |

2   What do you notice about the numbers in the last column? If your measurements were accurate, you should have found that $C \div d$ was about 3.14 for all cases. This ratio is always denoted by the Greek letter $\pi$ (pi).

$$\frac{C}{d} = \pi$$

Therefore $C = \pi d$.

*REMEMBER*

- Circumference of a circle = $2\pi r$
- When using $\pi$ in a calculation, press the $\boxed{\pi}$ button on your calculator.

3   **a** Two thousand years ago Archimedes proved that the value of $\pi$ lay between $3\frac{1}{7}$ and $3\frac{10}{71}$. Which of these is nearest to 3.14?
    **b** Long before the time of Archimedes, the Chinese wondered if $\pi$ was equal to $\sqrt{10}$. Which is greater, $\sqrt{10}$ or $3\frac{1}{7}$?
    (In the last century, one American state, thinking it was being rather helpful, passed a law making $\pi = 3$!)

129

By means of a computer, $\pi$ has been calculated to thousands of decimal places. It is written here correct to 267 decimal places. You can see from this that $\pi$ is neither a terminating nor a recurring decimal and therefore cannot be written as a fraction.

Sir, what is $\pi$?

$\pi = 3.141\ 592\ 653\ 589\ 793\ 238\ 462\ 643$
$383\ 279\ 502\ 884\ 197\ 169\ 399\ 375\ 105$
$820\ 974\ 944\ 592\ 307\ 816\ 404\ 286\ 208$
$998\ 628\ 034\ 825\ 342\ 117\ 067\ 982\ 148$
$086\ 513\ 282\ 306\ 647\ 093\ 844\ 609\ 550$
$582\ 231\ 725\ 359\ 408\ 128\ 481\ 117\ 632$
$096\ 647\ 249\ 485\ 300\ 003\ 576\ 710\ 314$
$449\ 545\ 130\ 644\ 798\ 574\ 889\ 956\ 612$
$405\ 137\ 220\ 038\ 558\ 058\ 881\ 426\ 511$
$431\ 118\ 708\ 046\ 553\ 470\ 421\ 731\ 924...$

## Activity 23

A 'trundle wheel' is used to measure distances.

A group of pupils make a trundle wheel using the front fork and wheel of a BMX bicycle.

1   They measure the radius of the wheel to be 24.5 cm. Work out the circumference of the wheel (this is the distance through which it moves in one revolution). Copy and complete the table.

| Number of revolutions | Distance covered (m) |
|---|---|
| 10 | |
| 20 | |
| 30 | |
| 40 | |
| 50 | |
| 60 | |

Use your table to plot a graph. Comment.

2   The pupils then decide to check the accuracy of their trundle wheel by rolling it parallel to a long tape measure. They find that their trundle wheel is not very accurate. Suggest some possible reasons for this.

■EXAMPLE 1

Find to 3 SF the circumference of a wheel of diameter 53.4 cm.

[F]      $d$  = 53.4 cm, therefore $r = 26.7$ cm.

[E]      $C$  = $2\pi r$ cm

[S]      $C$  = $2\pi 26.7$ cm

[W]      $C$  = 168 cm to 3 SF

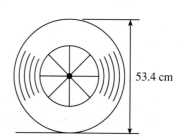

53.4 cm

■ *EXAMPLE 2*

Find the radius of a can of circumference 20 cm. Give your answer to 3 SF.

[F]     $C = 20\,cm$

[E]     $C = 2\pi r$

[S]     $20 = 2\pi r$   (Divide both sides by $2\pi$)

[W]     $\dfrac{20}{2\pi} = r$

        $r = 3.18\,cm$ to 3 SF.

Circumference 20 cm

r

BAKED
BEANS

## ___ Exercise 41

Give your answers to 3 SF.

**1** Find the circumference of a circle when its radius is:
   **a** 3 cm      **b** 8 m      **c** 16.7 cm   **d** 34 m      **e** 1.9 mm    **f** 214 cm

**2** Find the circumference of a circle when the diameter is:
   **a** 3 cm      **b** 7 m      **c** 19.8 m    **d** 56 m      **e** 18 mm     **f** 140 cm

**3** Find the radius of a circle when its circumference is:
   **a** 123 cm    **b** 45 m     **c** 98 cm     **d** 16 mm     **e** 12.4 m    **f** 420 mm

**4** Which has the longer perimeter, a square of side length 10 cm or a circle of radius 6.37 cm?

**5** The handle of a bucket is a semicircle of length 70 cm.
   Calculate the diameter of the bucket.

**6** The wheels of a railway carriage have a diameter of 105 cm. Find:
   **a** The circumference of each wheel.
   **b** The number of revolutions made by each wheel when the carriage travels from London to
   Leeds, a distance of 297 km.

**7** A car is travelling at 100 km/h. The diameter of its wheels is 60 cm.
   **a** Find the circumference of one of its wheels.
   **b** Find the number of revolutions each wheel makes when the car travels 100 km.
   **c** Find the number of revolutions each wheel makes in one hour.
   **d** Find the number of revolutions each wheel makes per second.

**8** The Earth moves in a circular orbit around the Sun
   once every $365\frac{1}{4}$ days. If the distance from the
   Earth to the Sun is 90 million miles, find the speed
   in mph of the Earth around the Sun.

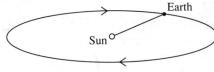
Earth

Sun

**9** The planet Uranus moves in a circular orbit around the Sun once every 84 years. If the distance
   from Uranus to the Sun is 1.8 billion miles, find the speed in mph of Uranus around the Sun.

**10** The Earth spins about its North to South axis once every 24 hours. London and Singapore are 3970 km and 6380 km respectively from this axis.

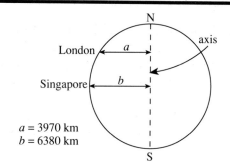

$a = 3970$ km
$b = 6380$ km

**a** Find the speed at which a pupil moves about the axis (i) in London (ii) in Singapore.

**b** How far will each pupil travel during a 45-minute Maths lesson?

**11** A bicycle wheel has a diameter of 70 cm. If the bicycle is ridden along a straight path of 700 m in 2 minutes, find:

**a** The number of revolutions made by the wheel.

**b** The mean number of revolutions made by the wheel per second.

**c** The number of revolutions made by the pedals if one revolution of the pedals makes four revolutions of the wheel.

**12** The end of the minute hand of 'Big Ben' has moved 33 333 km in 130 years. Find the length of the hand. (Take 365 days in a year.)

**13** How long would the minute hand of a clock have to be if its end were to move at 100 mph?

**14** A fly sits on the circumference of a 30 cm diameter long-playing record. If it remains there while one side of the record is played, and there are 1180 grooves across the diameter, find how far the fly travels.

**15** Find the perimeter of the figures.

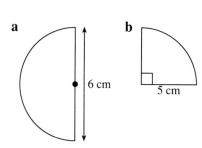

**a** 6 cm

**b** 5 cm

MASTERMINDERS

**16** A family goes on a cruise around the world. They have a pet hamster which remains in their cabin, which is at sea-level, throughout the voyage. The captain has a parrot on the bridge. If the bridge is 35 m above sea-level, calculate how much further the parrot travels than the hamster. (Assume that the world is a sphere and that the voyage is a circular orbit.)

**17** Eratosthenes in 250 BC noticed that at a particular time of the day, the Sun could be seen from the bottom of a deep well at Syene, and that at the same time a monument cast a shadow at Alexandria 500 miles due North.
**Investigate** how he deduced that the circumference of the Earth was about 24 000 miles.

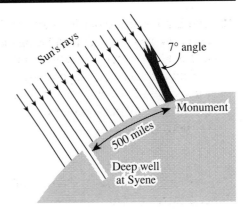

# __ 7.5 Area of a circle

## __ *Activity 24*

This Activity will show why the following is true:

> *NOTE*
>
> Area of a circle = $\pi r^2$

**1**  On a piece of card draw a circle of radius 3.5 cm. Draw 18 diameters such that the angle between any adjacent pair is 10°.
Carefully cut out the 36 areas (called sectors).

**2**  On a separate piece of paper, draw a rectangle whose length is equal to one half of the circumference of the circle and whose width is equal to the radius of the circle. Carefully stick all your sectors onto the rectangle as shown below. (You will need to cut one sector in half.)

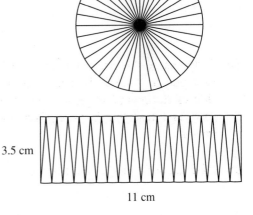

3.5 cm

11 cm

This shows that the area of the circle and rectangle are equal.

We can also show this by calculation.

Area of the circle (from equation above) = $\pi 3.5^2 = 38.48 \, \text{cm}^2$ to 4 SF

Area of rectangle (from part 2) = $\frac{1}{2} \times$ Circumference of the circle $\times$ Radius of the circle

(Circumference of circle = $2\pi 3.5 = 21.99 \, \text{cm}$ to 4 SF)

Therefore area of rectangle = $\frac{21.99}{2} \times 3.5 = 38.48 \, \text{cm}^2$ to 4 SF.

# 7 ALGEBRA II

## ■ EXAMPLE 1

Find the area of a circular window of radius 1.1 m.

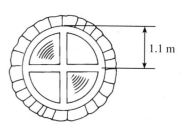

[F]           $r = 1.1$ m

[E]           $A = \pi r^2$

[S]           $A = \pi 1.1^2$

[W]          $A = 3.80\,\text{m}^2$ to 3 SF

## ■ EXAMPLE 2

Find the radius of a circular pond of area $20\,\text{m}^2$.

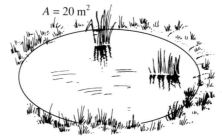
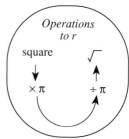

[F]           $A = 20\,\text{m}^2$

[E]           $A = \pi r^2$

[S]           $20 = \pi r^2$

[W]          $\dfrac{20}{\pi} = r^2$

$$\sqrt{\dfrac{20}{\pi}} = r$$

$$r = 2.52\,\text{m} \text{ to 3 SF}$$

## ■ EXAMPLE 3

The diagram shows a circle drawn inside a square. Find the shaded area. (Remember that a small dot inside a circle denotes its centre.)

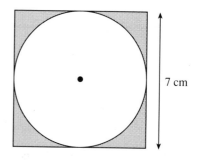

[F]      See diagram.

[E]      Shaded area = Area square − Area circle

[S]      Shaded area = $7^2 - \pi(3.5)^2$

[W]      Shaded area = $10.5\,\text{cm}^2$ to 3 SF

## ■ EXAMPLE 4

A goat is tethered to a peg fixed at the base of a stone wall by a rope of length 3.9 m. Calculate the area of field available for the goat to graze.

[F]      See diagram. Let $A$ = grazing area.

[E]      $A = \frac{1}{2} \times \pi r^2$

[S]      $A = \frac{1}{2}\pi 3.9^2$

[W]      $A = 23.9\,\text{m}^2$, to 3 SF

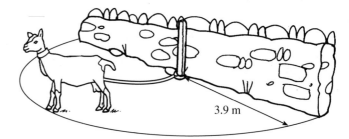

## ___ Exercise 42

Give your answers to 3 SF.

**1** Find the area of a circle when its radius is:
   **a** 4 cm     **b** 6.9 cm     **c** 12 mm     **d** 7.2 m     **e** 30 m     **f** 47.3 mm

**2** Find the radius of a circle when its area is:
   **a** 8.4 cm$^2$     **b** 3 cm$^2$     **c** 46 mm$^2$     **d** 8 m$^2$     **e** 46 m$^2$     **f** 31 km$^2$

**3** Find the diameter of a circle when its area is:
   **a** 5 cm$^2$     **b** 8 cm$^2$     **c** 5.9 mm$^2$     **d** 9 m$^2$     **e** 12.9 m$^2$     **f** 130 km$^2$

**4** A farmer irrigates part of a field with a high pressure hose which sprays water over a circular area of radius 75 m. Find the area irrigated in hectares. (1 hectare = 10 000 m$^2$)

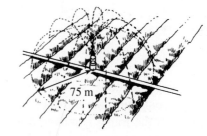

**5** Which has the greater area, a square of side length 10 cm or a circle of radius 5.8 cm?

**6** Find the area of the shapes.

**a**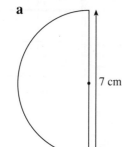
7 cm

**b**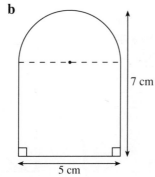
7 cm
5 cm

**c**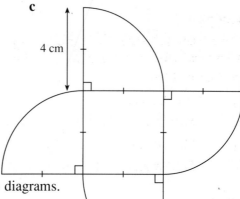
4 cm

**7** Find the area of the shaded region in each of the diagrams.

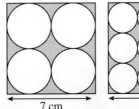
7 cm

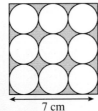
7 cm

Use your answers to work out the shaded region of a similar figure with 100 identical circles.

**8** The diagram shows the cross-section of a metal pipe. Find the area of the shaded part.

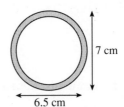
7 cm
6.5 cm

**9** Find the value of $x$ in each of the following:

**a**
Area = 20 cm²

**b**
$x$
Area = 45 cm²

**c**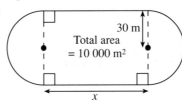
30 m
Total area = 10 000 m²
$x$

**d**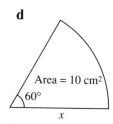
Area = 10 cm²
60°
$x$

**10** Find the area of each of the shaded regions.

**a**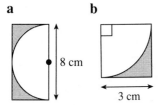
8 cm

**b**
3 cm

**c**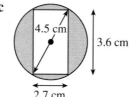
4.5 cm
3.6 cm
2.7 cm

**d**
4 cm
3 cm

**e**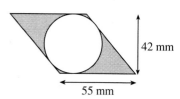
42 mm
55 mm

**11** The diagram shows a sash window in which the frame containing the top four panes slides up and down. If the frame is moved down 9 cm, what area of window is opened?

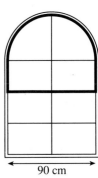
90 cm

**12 Investigate** how to measure as accurately as possible the radius of a £1 coin using only a ruler. Use your answer to find the area of one side of the coin.

## MASTERMINDERS

**13** Find the area of the shaded regions.

**a**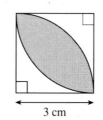
3 cm

**b**
3 cm

**14** A rescue helicopter has a searchlight switched on.
**a** Find the radius of the illuminated circle when the light is (i) 50 m (ii) 100 m above the ground.
**b** Find the area illuminated for **a** (i) and (ii).
**c Investigate** the relationship between the vertical height of the beam and the area illuminated.

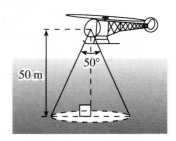
50°
50 m

**15** The area of the shaded region is 20 cm². Find the value of $x$.

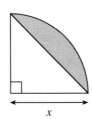
$x$

**16** A sector of a circle of radius $r$ has a perimeter of $4r$. Show that its area is $r^2$.

# ▬ 7.6 Pythagoras' theorem

## ▬ *Activity 25*

**1** Use your ruler to draw the grid shown in Figure 1. Onto your grid draw the numbered areas.

Use your drawing as a template to copy Figure 1 onto a piece of card. Cut out the six pieces and number them.

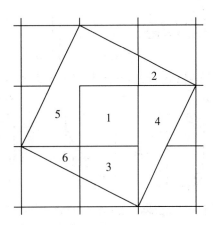

**Figure 1**

**2** Use your pieces to help make a copy of Figure 2.

Look at the three different-sized squares. What do you notice about the area of the two smaller squares relative to the area of the largest?

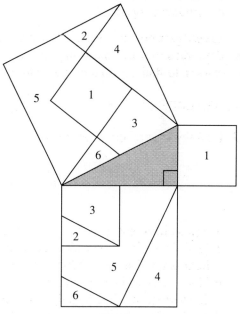

**3** If the width of your ruler is $x$ cm, write down in terms of $x$ the area of each of the six pieces. Use your answers to write down the area of the two largest squares in terms of $x$. What do you notice?

The result of your experiment shows that, in a right-angled triangle, the following is true:

**Figure 2**

┌─── *NOTE*

**Pythagoras' theorem:**
$$a^2 = b^2 + c^2$$

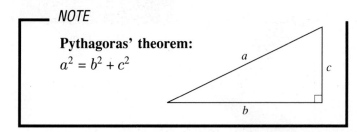

This formula works for all right-angled triangles. It was first discovered by the Egyptians over 3000 years ago, but it was not until 500 years later that the Greek mathematician Pythagoras actually proved this remarkable fact.

■ *EXAMPLE 1*

Find the value of $x$ to 3 SF:

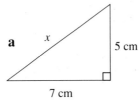

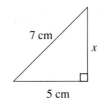

**a**    [F]           See diagram.

       [E] and [S]    $x^2 = 7^2 + 5^2$    (Square root both sides)

       [W]             $x = \sqrt{7^2 + 5^2}$

                       $x = 8.60$ cm to 3 SF

**b**    [F]           See diagram.

       [E] and [S]        $7^2 = x^2 + 5^2$    (Subtract $5^2$ from both sides)

       [W]          $7^2 - 5^2 = x^2$    (Square root both sides)

            $\sqrt{7^2 - 5^2} = x$

               $x = 4.90$ cm to 3 SF

■ *EXAMPLE 2*

Find the perpendicular height of A above BC in the isosceles triangle ABC.

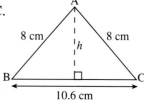

       [F]              See diagram. (The perpendicular from A bisects the base BC.)

       [E] and [S]        $8^2 = h^2 + 5.3^2$

       [W]      $\sqrt{8^2 - 5.3^2} = h$

               $h = 5.99$ cm to 3 SF

## ▬ Exercise 43

Give all your answers to 3 SF.

**1**    Find the value of $x$.

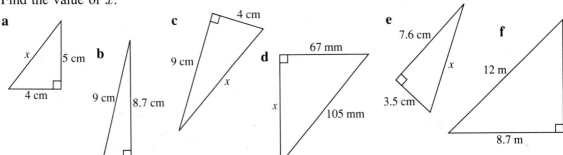

**2** Find the length of a diagonal of a rectangle with sides of 9.3 m and 17.3 m.

**3** The diagonals of a rhombus are 53 cm and 37 cm. Find its perimeter.

**4** Triangle ABC is isosceles. Copy and complete the table below. Show your working for each part. All lengths are in centimetres.

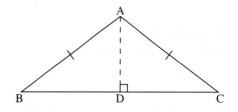

| | AD | BD | AB | BC | Area of triangle ABC |
|---|---|---|---|---|---|
| **a** | 3 | 4 | | | |
| **b** | 6 | | 10 | | |
| **c** | | 7 | 9 | | |
| **d** | 5 | | | 9.8 | |
| **e** | | | 8 | 15 | |
| **f** | | | | 20 | 45 cm² |
| **g** | 8 | | | | 18 cm² |

**5** The diagram shows the side of a 'lean-to' shed. Find:
**a** The height of the door AB.
**b** The area of the side of the shed.

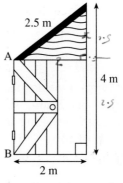

2.5 m

4 m

2 m

**6** Calculate the area of a square whose diagonals are each 10 cm long.

**7** A television tower stands on level ground and is supported by a wire from the top which is fixed to the ground 220 m from the base of the tower. If the wire is 500 m long, calculate the height of the tower.

**8** Calculate the distance between the points (7, 3) and (−5, −2) in the units used.

**9** Can a brick which measures 9 cm by 12 cm by 25 cm pass down a cylindrical pipe of internal diameter 14 cm?

**10** A ship travels four sea-miles North-East and then eight sea-miles North-West. How far is the ship from its starting point?

**11** A fierce dog is tethered by a rope 13 m long to a post 5 m from a straight path. For what distance along the path is one in danger?

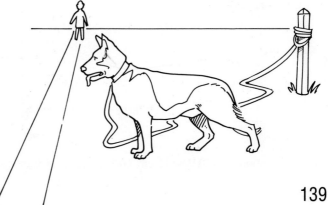

## MASTERMINDERS

**12** A triangle has sides of 5 cm, 3.3 cm, and 6 cm. Is the triangle obtuse, right-angled or acute?

**13** ABCD is a rectangle with sides of 4 cm and 3 cm. Find the area of triangle CDQ.

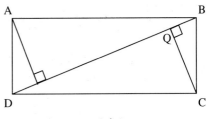

**14** A tunnel has a semicircular cross-section and a diameter of 10 m. If the roof of a bus just touches the roof of the tunnel when its wheels are 2 m from one side, how high is the bus?

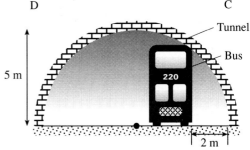

**15** ABCD represents a rectangular piece of paper with sides of 10 cm and 20 cm. If corner A is folded onto corner C, the resulting fold is shown as EF. Find the length of EF.

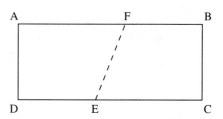

**16 a** A circle of radius $r$, has a circumference $C$ and area $A$. Express, in its simplest form, the area $A$ in terms of $C$ and $\pi$.
  **b** Calculate the height of an equilateral triangle which has the same area as a circle whose circumference is 10 cm.

**17 Investigate** the triangle ABC which is made from a rectangular piece of paper in the following way:

Fold the paper in half.

Fold corner A onto the first fold.

  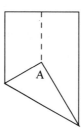 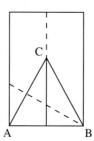

**18** In Question 4, if AB = 15 cm and the area of the triangle ABC is 60 cm², find AD, BD and BC.

# — 7.7 The cylinder

Any solid with parallel sides has a constant cross-section. The volume of such a solid is the product of the cross-sectional area and the length (or height). These solids are called **prisms**.

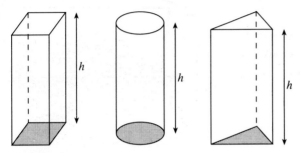

---

*NOTE*

Volume of prism = Cross-sectional area × Height

---

# — *Activity 26*

Take a rectangular piece of paper and make it into a hollow cylinder, like this:

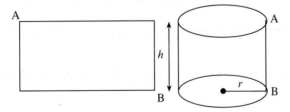

Draw a dotted line from A to B which is the shortest route around the curved surface.

Use your paper cylinder to explain why a cylinder has the following properties:

---

*REMEMBER*

- Volume $V = \pi r^2 \times h$
- Curved surface area $A = 2\pi r h$
- AB $= \sqrt{h^2 + (2\pi r)^2}$

---

## Exercise 44

Give your answers to 3 SF.

Questions 1 to 4 refer to the cylinder drawn in Activity 26.

**1**  The height $h$ of a cylinder is 12 cm. Find its volume if its radius ($r$) is:
    **a**  10 cm        **b**  25 cm        **c**  5.6 cm        **d**  35 cm

**2**  The diameter of a cylinder is 6 cm. Find the curved surface area if its height ($h$) is:
    **a**  4 cm        **b**  12 cm        **c**  7.9 cm        **d**  67 cm

**3**  The radius of a cylinder is 7 cm. Find the length of AB if its height ($h$) is:
    **a**  6 cm        **b**  19 cm        **c**  5.7 cm        **d**  28 cm

**4**  Copy the table below and complete it when the radius of a cylinder is 5 cm. (Show your working clearly.)

|   | Height (cm) | Volume (cm³) | Curved surface area (cm²) | AB (cm) |
|---|---|---|---|---|
| **a** |  | 11 |  |  |
| **b** |  | 22 |  |  |
| **c** |  |  | 45 |  |
| **d** |  |  | 90 |  |
| **e** |  |  |  | 160 |
| **f** |  |  |  | 320 |

**5**  Twelve cans of baked beans are tightly packed into a box as shown. If each tin has a volume of 508 cm³ and a height of 11.5 cm, find the internal dimensions of the box.

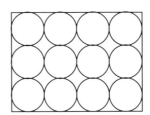

## MASTERMINDERS

**6**  **Investigate**, by calculation, the length of toothpaste which can be squeezed from a tube of toothpaste.

**7**  The largest salami ever made was 18.7 m long, had a circumference of 61 cm and a mass of 545.4 kg. Find the mass in grams of one cm³. What is this a measure of?

# ___ 7.8 Formulae

A formula is an equation which is used to help solve problems, especially when a calculation is repeated many times. You will have met several already in mathematics (for example, for the area of a triangle) and science (for example, for density).

## ___ Exercise 45

Give your answers to 3 SF.

1   The surface area $A$ of a sphere is given by $A = 4\pi r^2$.
    Calculate $A$ when:
    **a** $r = 2$   **b** $r = 8$   **c** $r = 16$.

2   The area $A$ of a triangle PQR is given by $A = \frac{1}{2}qr \sin \hat{P}$.
    Calculate $A$ when:
    **a** $q = 2$, $r = 5$, $\hat{P} = 30°$   **b** $q = 3$, $r = 7$, $\hat{P} = 60°$   **c** $q = 4$, $r = 9$, $\hat{P} = 25°$.

3   The volume $V$ of a sphere is given by $V = \frac{4}{3}\pi r^3$.
    Calculate $V$ when:
    **a** $r = 2$   **b** $r = 4$   **c** $r = 2.5$.

4   The volume $V$ of a pyramid is given by $V = \frac{Ah}{3}$.
    Calculate $V$ when:
    **a** $A = 5$, $h = 6$   **b** $A = 9$, $h = 12$   **c** $A = 7.5$, $h = 10.5$.

5   The distance $s$ fallen by a stone after time $t$ is given by $s = ut + \frac{1}{2}gt^2$.
    Calculate $s$ when:
    **a** $u = 2$, $t = 3$, $g = 9.8$   **b** $u = 4$, $t = 5$, $g = 9.8$   **c** $u = 0$, $t = 10$, $g = 9.8$

6   The time $T$ seconds for a simple pendulum, of length $\ell$ metres, to swing to and fro is given by

$$T = 2\pi \sqrt{\frac{\ell}{g}}$$

    Calculate $T$ when:
    **a** $\ell = 1.1$, $g = 9.8$   **b** $\ell = 1.5$, $g = 9.8$   **c** $\ell = 2.5$, $g = 9.8$.

7   'Tidal waves' (Tsunamis) are the result of earthquakes in the sea bed. The speed of a Tsunami, $V$ m/s, at an ocean depth of $d$ metres is given approximately by $V = \sqrt{9.8d}$.
    **a** Calculate $V$ when (i) $d = 25$ m   (ii) $d = 50$ m   (iii) $d = 1$ km.
    **b** The fastest ever Tsunami registered a speed of 790 km/h. Calculate the ocean depth in metres at this point.

**8** The speed $V$ m/s that a golf ball leaves the club face is given by $V = \frac{MU(1 + e)}{M + m}$.
  Calculate $V$ when:
  **a** $M = 300$, $m = 40$, $U = 50$, $e = 0.7$
  **b** $M = 250$, $m = 45$, $U = 45$, $e = 0.6$
  **c** $M = 275$, $m = 50$, $U = 47$, $e = 0.8$

**9 a** Find a formula for the shaded area in terms of $a$, $b$ and $c$.
  **b** Calculate the values of this area, $A \text{ cm}^2$, if:
   (i) $a = 10 \text{ cm}$, $b = 7 \text{ cm}$, $c = 5 \text{ cm}$
   (ii) $a = 12 \text{ cm}$, $b = 8 \text{ cm}$, $c = 8 \text{ cm}$
   (iii) $a = 10 \text{ cm}$, $b = 9 \text{ cm}$, $c = 11 \text{ cm}$

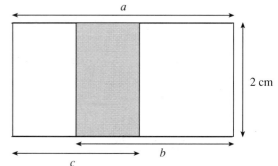

## MASTERMINDER

**10** Rows of flowered tiles are surrounded by plain tiles.

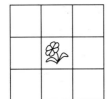 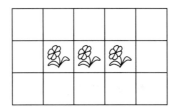

  **a** Find out how many plain tiles are required to surround:
   (i) five flowered tiles   (ii) six flowered tiles   (iii) $n$ flowered tiles.
  **b** How many flowered tiles are surrounded by 100 plain tiles?

# __ 7.9 Rearranging formulae

Sometimes an equation has to be rearranged to make one letter the 'subject', that is, on its own on one side. Look carefully at the following examples.

■ *EXAMPLE 1*
Make $x$ the subject in $ax + c = b$.

$ax + c = b$   (Subtract $c$ from both sides)
$\quad ax = b - c$   (Divide both sides by $a$)
$\quad\ x = \dfrac{b - c}{a}$

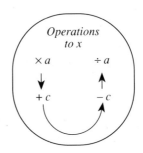

■ *EXAMPLE 2*

Make $v$ the subject in $s = \frac{(u+v)t}{2}$.

$$s = \frac{(u+v)t}{2} \quad \text{(Divide both sides by } t)$$

$$\frac{s}{t} = \frac{(u+v)}{2} \quad \text{(Multiply both sides by 2)}$$

$$\frac{2s}{t} = u + v \quad \text{(Subtract } u \text{ from both sides)}$$

$$\frac{2s}{t} - u = v$$

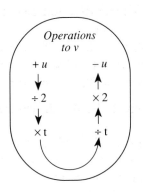

## ___ Exercise 46

Rearrange the following formulae to make $x$ the subject.

**1** $y = 4x$      **2** $y = px$      **3** $h = x + a$      **4** $g = 2x - h$

**5** $t = r + 2x$      **6** $a = 2 - 3x$      **7** $w = yx + z$      **8** $p = r + sx$

**9** $v = ut - tx$      **10** $c = gh - dx$      **11** $y = \frac{3}{x}$      **12** $y = \frac{ab}{x}$

**13** $s = \frac{t}{x} + v$      **14** $k = \frac{rt}{x} - 1$      **15** $y = a - \frac{b}{x}$      **16** $z = 1 - \frac{gh}{x}$

**17** $f = a(g + x)$      **18** $k = a(x - g)$      **19** $w = \frac{a}{x+b}$      **20** $f = \frac{a}{b-x}$

**21** $a^2 = v^2 + 2ax$      **22** $a = b^2 + cx$      **23** $r^2 = dc - hx$      **24** $f = \pi(3 - tx)$

**25** $A = \pi x^2$      **26** $A = \pi x(a + h)$      **27** $mn = b + \frac{d}{x}$      **28** $0 = \frac{A}{a+x} - B$

**29** $a = \frac{b}{cx} - b$      **30** $\frac{a^2}{x} = b - c$      **31** $f = \frac{g^2}{x} - h$      **32** $b = 2c^2 - \frac{d}{x}$

**33** $y = \frac{2z}{3(x-1)}$      **34** $y = \frac{3z}{2(1-x)}$      **35** $y = \sqrt{x}$      **36** $2y = \sqrt{2x}$

**37** $y$ is given by the formula $y = ut + \frac{1}{2}at^2$.
Rearrange the formula to make $a$ the subject and use it to find $a$ when:
**a** $y = 10$, $u = 4$, $t = 1$    **b** $y = 20$, $u = 2$, $t = 2$    **c** $y = 17.5$, $u = 2.5$, $t = 2$

**38** The total surface area $A$ of a cone is given by the formula $A = \pi r(r + \ell)$, where $r$ is the base radius and $\ell$ is the slant height. Rearrange the formula to make $\ell$ the subject and use it to find $\ell$ to 3 SF when:
**a** $A = 20$, $r = 2$    **b** $A = 750$, $r = 12$    **c** $A = 823.5$, $r = 9.3$.

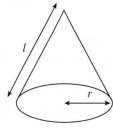

MASTERMINDER

**39** The volume $V$ of a sphere is given by the formula $V = \frac{4}{3}\pi r^3$, where $r$ is the radius of the sphere.
Rearrange the formula to make $r$ the subject and use it to find $r$ to 3 SF when: **a** $V = 10$    **b** $V = 125$    **c** $V = 812.7$.

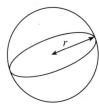

## ▬ Revision Exercise 7

**1** Solve the following equations:

   **a** $2x - 5 = 11$       **b** $1 - 5x = 76$       **c** $3 - 4(x + 1) = 7$   **d** $\frac{3x+2}{2} = 25$

**2** Solve the following equations:

   **a** $2x^2 = 72$       **b** $4x^2 + 11 = 75$      **c** $\frac{x^2}{2} = 162$        **d** $\frac{x^2}{2} - 9 = 329$

**3** Solve the following equations:

   **a** $\sqrt{x} - 2 = 6$      **b** $\frac{\sqrt{x}}{3} = -4$       **c** $\sqrt{\frac{x+3}{4}} = 5$     **d** $\frac{\sqrt{2x-1}}{3} = 6$

**4** Use 'trial and improvement' to solve the following equations: (Show all your attempts in a table.)

   **a** $x^2 = 90.25$      **b** $3x^2 + 1 = 22.87$   **c** $x(x + 1) = 3.75$   **d** $x^2 - 2x = 27.09$

**5** A new roundabout is planned for a busy section of road. Its diameter has to be at least 15 m and at most 22 m. Form inequalities for:

   **a** $C$, the roundabout's circumference.

   **b** $A$, the area of the roundabout.

   **c** Use these inequalities to state the roundabout's (i) maximum circumference   (ii) minimum area, to 3 SF.

**6** Charlotte has 75p to spend. However, she must leave 21p for her bus-fare home. Lemon-drops ($L$) cost 5p each and toffees ($T$) 6p each.

   **a** Form an inequality involving $L$ and $T$, to show how Charlotte could spend her money.

   **b** If she decides not to buy any toffees, what is the maximum number of lemon-drops she can buy?

**7** The equation relating a temperature in degrees Fahrenheit ($F$) to a temperature in degrees Centigrade ($C$) is $F = \frac{9C}{5} + 32$.

   **a** Find the value of $F$ when $C$ is (i) 15   (ii) 20   (iii) $-15$.

   **b** Rearrange the formula to give $C$ in terms of $F$ and use this to find the values of $C$ when $F$ is (i) 86   (ii) 68   (iii) $-40$.

   **c** At what temperature is $C$ equal to $F$?

**8** Find a formula for the area, $A$, of this shape in terms of $a$, $b$ and $c$, showing all your working.

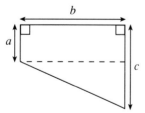

   **a** Use this formula to find the value of $A$ when $a = 10$ cm, $b = 18$ cm and $c = 20$ cm.

   **b** Rearrange the formula to give $c$ in terms of $A$, $a$ and $b$. Use it to find the values of $c$ when:

     (i) $A = 108$ m$^2$, $a = 3$ m, $b = 12$ m

     (ii) $A = 749$ mm$^2$, $a = 12.5$ mm, $b = 40$ mm.

**9** For each of the shapes below, calculate to 3 SF (i) the perimeter    (ii) the area.

**a**

7 cm

**b**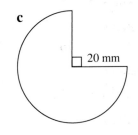

4 m

**c**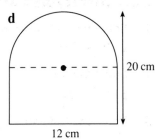

20 mm

**d**

20 cm

12 cm

**10** Find the lengths of the lettered sides to 3 SF.

**a**

7 cm    $x$

4 cm

**b**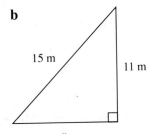

15 m    11 m

$x$

**c**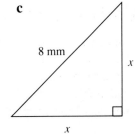

8 mm    $x$

$x$

**d**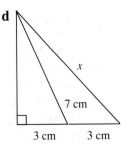

$x$

7 cm

3 cm    3 cm

**11** A solid cylinder of radius 8 cm and height 12 cm is melted down to be recast into a solid cube. Calculate the side length of the cube.

**12** Oil flows through a circular pipe of internal diameter 2 cm at a speed of 8 cm/s. Calculate the rate of flow in litres per second of the oil from the pipe to 3 SF. (Assume the pipe to be full.)

## MASTERMINDERS

**13** A 3 m ladder rests against a vertical wall with its foot 1 m from the base of the wall. Its foot slips a further 50 cm away from the wall. How far has the top of the ladder slipped down the wall?

**14** These circles are concentric and the 20 cm line is a tangent to the inner circle. Find the shaded area.

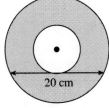

20 cm

**15** There is an interesting five-digit number. With a 1 after it, it is three times as large as with a 1 before it. What is the number?

## ___ Aural Test 2

Twenty questions will be read out to you. You may do any workings on a piece of paper. You will need the following information to answer Questions 11 to 20.

**11** and **12** The figure is a regular hexagon.

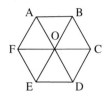

**13** Given $52 = \dfrac{2496}{48}$.

**14**

BMS
DRIVING SCHOOL
£15 : 1 HR
£25 : 2 HRS

**15** to **17** The chart shows the distance in miles between seven towns.

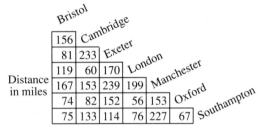

**18** and **19**

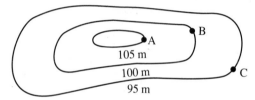

**20 a** 75 kg   **b** 750 g   **c** 750 kg   **d** 750 pounds   **e** 750 ounces

## ___ Puzzlers

**1** **Practical** Estimate how long it would take to count to a million. (Remember it takes longer to say 'six thousand and sixty-six' than 'six'!)

**2** In how many different ways can a careless postman deliver four letters (to four people) so that no one receives the right letter?

**3** Each letter in the diagram represents a number. The totals of three lines and three columns are shown. Find the total of the top line.

| P | E | A | T |      |
|---|---|---|---|------|
| T | T | A | E | 207  |
| P | P | P | E | 186  |
| E | A | T | T | 207  |

195      183  222

**4** Copy the triangular array of dots. Draw three straight lines to make a triangle so that 19 dots are inside the triangle and 19 dots remain outside.

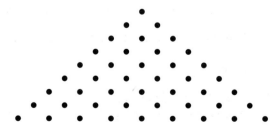

# Coursework: The Active Maths puzzle

All the constructions in this Coursework must be done only with a ruler and pencil. You are are not allowed to use the markings on a ruler, or graph paper.

1 Make a copy of the AM square shown in Figure 1. Mark all the lines which have the same length as the diagonal of the area marked IV.

2 **a** Construct a rhombus using the parallel sides of your ruler. Draw the two diagonals. Explain how you can construct a right angle using only a ruler.
**b** Construct a grid of 12 squares as shown in Figure 1. (Make sure that you construct the 90° angle accurately.) Use your grid to draw the AM square.
**c** Use your drawing as a template to make the six pieces out of card. Label each piece with its correct number.

3 Figure 2 shows piece III and half of piece IV.
**a** Explain, with the aid of a diagram, why BA is equal to the width of your ruler.
**b** If the width of your ruler is 4 cm, work out the area of each of the two triangles.

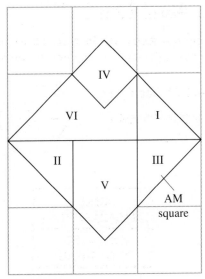

**Figure 1**

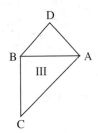

**Figure 2**

4 Copy this table. Use your answers to part 3 to help complete it.

| Piece number | Area (cm²) | Perimeter (cm) to 3 SF |
|---|---|---|
| I | | |
| IV | | |
| V | | |
| VI | | |

5 Taking the width of your ruler as 4 cm, calculate the side length of your AM square by
**a** using Pythagoras' theorem  **b** using the area of the whole square.

6 Use your six pieces to **demonstrate** Pythagoras' theorem.

## EXTENSION

7 If the width of your ruler is $x$ cm, find the area of each of the six pieces in terms of $x$ and hence **demonstrate** Pythagoras' theorem algebraically.

# Fact Finders: The Channel Tunnel

The building of the Channel Tunnel between Folkestone and Calais is the largest civil engineering project ever undertaken in Europe. The first proposal for such a connection was in 1802, but was ill-timed due to war resuming between Britain and France. The tunnel due for completion in 1994.

The tunnel itself is in fact three: two running and one service tunnel. The tunnels are 30.7 miles in length with 23.6 miles under the English Channel, 25–40 m below the sea bed reaching 100 m below sea level at the deepest point.

The internal diameters of the running and service tunnels are 7.6 m and 4.8 m respectively and their maximum gradient is about 1 : 90.

Conditions underground during construction were hot, damp, noisy and dangerous. The main engineering challenge was having to drill through fractured chalk saturated with water; this problem being particularly acute on the French side where tunnellers were expected to progress at half the speed of their English counterparts. Special boring machines were fitted with a seal behind the cutting head to prevent water gushing in as boring progressed; in fact water had to be pumped away at 9 gallons per second! The British workers advanced at 300 m per week (100 m more than planned) while the French also exceeded their target of 100 m per week.

The total cost of the construction is estimated at approximately £6 billion, and there were 15 000 workers on site at its busiest.

The crossing by ferry takes 90–100 minutes, but the train crossing takes 45–50 minutes. The high-speed trains (HSTs) are designed to travel at 100 mph in the tunnel and at 150 mph once outside, reducing the travel time between London and Paris from five hours twelve minutes to just three hours, not much longer than by air!

## — Questions on the Channel Tunnel

1 After how many years since its first proposal was the Channel Tunnel completed?

2 What percentage of the tunnels are actually under the English Channel?

3 Calculate the total volume of air in the tunnels in $m^3$ expressed in standard form to 3 SF. (Assume the tunnels are empty and 1 mile $\approx$ 1600 m.)

4 All tunnels are to be internally coated with sealant at a cost of £1.15 per square metre. Calculate the cost of this coating.

5 According to initial estimates, how long after tunnelling begins (to the nearest week) would the British tunnellers meet the French tunnellers?

6 How many litres of water were pumped away per 24 hours by one boring machine? (Answer in standard form to 3 SF and let 1 gallon $\approx$ 4.5 litres.) Compare this answer to the volume of water in a 10 m × 50 m × 1.5 m deep swimming pool.

7 The whole project started in 1987 and is due for completion in 1994. Calculate the mean cost of the scheme per second until completion.

8 Calculate the maximum and minimum percentage time saved by using the tunnel as opposed to taking a ferry crossing.

9 London is 75 miles from Folkestone and Calais is 150 miles from Paris. Estimate the total connection (waiting) time for this journey at the tunnel entrance/exit.

10 Use the photograph to show that the diameter of the drill-head is about 10 m.

# 8 GRAPHS II

## 8.1 Basic principles

### Co-ordinates and lines

A point can be plotted as a co-ordinate $(x, y)$ on a graph of $y$ against $x$. For example, the points A $(3, -2)$, B $(-1, 3)$ and C $(-2, -2)$ are shown alongside.

Several points can be plotted whose co-ordinates are determined by an equation. For example, the equation $y = x$ gives points $(1, 1)$, $(2, 2)$ ...... $(-1, -1)$, etc., which lie on a straight line. Every co-ordinate on this line has equal $x$ and $y$ values. This line and lines for other simple equations are shown alongside.

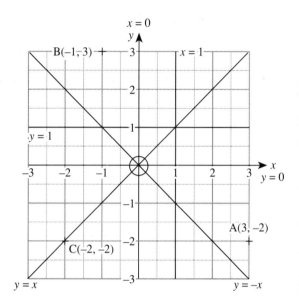

### Gradient of a line

The gradient of a line can be positive or negative. Look at the lines AB and CD.

$$\text{Gradient AB} = \frac{+1}{+3} = \frac{1}{3}$$

$$\text{Gradient CD} = \frac{+2}{-1} = -2$$

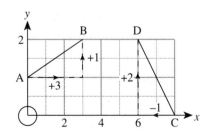

# 8.2 Graphs of $y = ax$

## Activity 27

In the equation $y = 4x$, when $x = 2$, $y = 8$.

We can write this pair of numbers as a co-ordinate (2, 8) and plot it on a graph of $y$ against $x$.

Then we can find other pairs of numbers from this equation and plot them on a graph. The straight line joining these points represents the equation $y = 4x$.

1   Copy and complete this 'table of values' for $y = 4x$.

| $x$ | −2 | 0 | 2 |
|---|---|---|---|
| $y$ | | | 8 |

2   Draw suitable $x$ and $y$ axes and plot the three points from the table of values. Hence draw the graph of $y = 4x$.

3   Find the gradient of this line. What do you notice?

## Activity 28

1   For each of the following equations, copy and complete a table of values:

| $x$ | −2 | 0 | 2 |
|---|---|---|---|
| $y$ | | | |

**a** $y = x$      **b** $y = 2x$      **c** $y = 3x$      **d** $y = 5x$
**e** $y = -2x$      **f** $y = -4x$      **g** $y = \frac{x}{2}$      **h** $y = -\frac{x}{2}$

2   Draw one set of suitable $x$ and $y$ axes and on it plot the graph of each of the eight equations in part 1. Label each graph with its equation. What do you notice?
(The scale on the $y$ axis need not be the same as the scale on the $x$ axis.)

3   Copy and complete the table for all the graphs drawn in part 2. What do you notice?

| Equation | Gradient | Equation | Gradient |
|---|---|---|---|
| $y = x$ | 1 | $y = 2x$ | |
| $y = 3x$ | | $y = 5x$ | |
| $y = -2x$ | | $y = -4x$ | |
| $y = \frac{x}{2}$ | | $y = -\frac{x}{2}$ | |

153

> **REMEMBER**
>
> The graph of $y = ax$ is a straight line through (0, 0) with a gradient of $a$.

## Exercise 47

**1** A stone is dropped from a cliff. Its speed is measured and shown in the table below.

| Time $t$ (s) | 0 | 1 | 2 | 3 | 4 |
|---|---|---|---|---|---|
| Speed $v$ (m/s) | 0 | 10 | 20 | 30 | 40 |

  **a** Draw the graph of $v$ against $t$, in the range $0 \leqslant t \leqslant 4$.
  **b** Use the graph to find:
    (i) The stone's speed after 2.5 s.
    (ii) When the stone's speed is 18 m/s.
  **c** What equation describes the relationship between the stone's speed $v$ and time $t$?

**2** The exchange rate for 3 German marks (DM) is £1.
  **a** Copy and complete the table below.

| $n$ (£) | 0 | 10 | 20 | 30 |
|---|---|---|---|---|
| $d$ (DM) | | | | |

  **b** Draw the graph of $d$ against $n$ in the range $0 \leqslant n \leqslant 30$.
  **c** Use the graph to find:
    (i) the number of DMs exchanged for £25.
    (ii) the number of £s exchanged for DM 50.
  **d** What equation describes the relationship between $d$ and $n$?

**MASTERMINDER**

**3** The area $A$ cm$^2$ of a sector of a circle is proportional
to the angle $\theta °$ of the sector. Look at this circle:

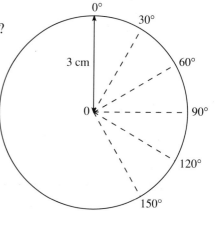

  **a** Copy and complete the table below to 3 SF.

| Angle $\theta °$ | 0 | 90 | 180 | 270 | 360 |
|---|---|---|---|---|---|
| Area $A$ (cm$^2$) | 0 | | | | 28.3 |

  **b** Draw a graph of $A$ against $\theta$ in the range $0° \leqslant \theta \leqslant 360°$.
  **c** Use this graph to estimate the value of $A$ when $\theta$ is (i) 120° (ii) 300°.
  **d** Use this graph to estimate the value of $\theta °$ when $A$ is (i) 10 cm$^2$ (ii) 25 cm$^2$.
  **e** What equation describes the relationship between $A$ and $\theta$?

# 8.3 Graphs of $y = ax + b$

## Activity 29

1 For each of the following equations, copy and complete the table of values:

| $x$ | $-2$ | 0 | 2 | |
|---|---|---|---|---|
| $y$ | | | | |

a $y = x - 1$      b $y = -x + 1$      c $y = 2x - 1$

d $y = -2x + 1$      e $y = 3x - 1$      f $y = -3x + 1$

2 Draw one set of suitable $x$ and $y$ axes and on it plot the graph of each of the six equations. Label each graph with its equation.

3 Copy and complete the table for all the equations you have just drawn. (The 'intercept with the $y$ axis' is the value of $y$ where the line crosses the $y$ axis.) What do you notice?

| Equation | Gradient | Intercept with y axis |
|---|---|---|
| $y = x - 1$ | 1 | $-1$ |
| $y = -x + 1$ | | |
| $y = 2x - 1$ | | |
| $y = -2x + 1$ | | |
| $y = 3x - 1$ | | |
| $y = -3x + 1$ | | |
| $y = ax + b$ | | |

**REMEMBER**

The graph of $y = ax + b$ is a straight line whose intercept with the $y$ axis is $b$ and whose gradient is $a$.

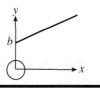

## Exercise 48

1 Find the gradient and the intercept on the $y$ axis of lines:

a $y = x + 2$      b $y = 2x + 3$      c $y = 3x + 1$

d $y = 4x - 2$      e $2y = 6x + 3$      f $y + 3x + 1 = 0$

**2** The cost £$C$ of glass for windows is related to the area $A$ m$^2$ of a window by the formula:

$C = 6A + 7$

**a** Copy and complete the table of values for $A$ and $C$.

| $A$ (m$^2$) | 2 | 4 | 6 | 8 | 10 |
|---|---|---|---|---|---|
| $C$ (£) | | | | | |

**b** Draw a graph of $C$ against $A$ using a suitable scale.

**c** Use your graph to find (i) the cost of glazing a 5 m$^2$ window   (ii) the area of window costing £49 to glaze.

**d** Suggest what the '+7' of the equation represents.

**3** The distance $D$ km travelled on one litre of petrol is approximately related to engine size $E$ litres, of various cars, by the formula:

$$D = 15 - \frac{7E}{2}$$

**a** Copy and complete the table of values for $E$ and $D$.

| $E$ (litres) | 1.0 | 1.2 | 1.6 | 1.8 |
|---|---|---|---|---|
| $D$ (km) | 11.5 | | | 4.5 |

**b** Draw a graph of $D$ against $E$ using a suitable scale.

**c** Use your graph to find (i) how far a 1.5 litre engine would travel on one litre of petrol
(ii) what size of engine would travel 8 km on one litre of petrol.

**4** The cost £$C$ of maths tutor Mr Smart is related to the teaching time $t$ hours by the equation:

$C = 16t + 3$

**a** Copy and complete the table for Mr Smart's charge:

| $t$ (hours) | 0 | 1 | 2 | 4 |
|---|---|---|---|---|
| $C$ (£) | | | | |

**b** Draw the graph of $C$ against $t$ for Mr Smart.

**c** The charge of Mrs Bright, another maths tutor, is given by the equation:

$C = 4t + 9$

Copy and complete the table for Mrs Bright's charge:

| $t$ (hours) | 0 | | | 4 |
|---|---|---|---|---|
| $C$ (£) | | 13 | 17 | |

**d** Draw the graph for Mrs Bright's charge **on the same axes**.

**e** Using both graphs, answer the following: (i) Who charges more per hour?
(ii) When is Mr Smart's charge equal to Mrs Bright's? What is this charge?
(iii) You need a maths tutor for three hours. Who would be cheaper and by how much?

**f** Another tutor, Mr Cubic, charges £14/hour with a £3 call-out charge. Express Mr Cubic's charge as an equation relating $t$ to $C$.

MASTERMINDER

5   Glenda decides to carpet a room in her home. She sees two types of carpet advertised in her local newspaper. Both costs £$C$ are related to the area to be carpeted $A\,\mathrm{m}^2$.

Carpet P: $C = 15A + 26$

Carpet Q: $C = 19A - 14$

a Copy and complete the tables:

| Carpet P | $A$ (m²) | 1 | 10 |
|---|---|---|---|
| | $C$ (£) | 41 | 326 |

| Carpet Q | $A$ (m²) | 1 | 10 |
|---|---|---|---|
| | $C$ (£) | 5 | 366 |

b **On the same axes**, draw both graphs of $C$ against $A$.

c Using both graphs, answer the following:

(i) What size of room will cost the same to carpet?

(ii) What is the difference in cost between carpet P and carpet Q, if a room of size $15\,\mathrm{m}^2$ is to be carpeted?

(ii) What is the difference in area that carpet P and carpet Q would cover for £250?

# 8.4 Graphs of $y = ax^2$

## Activity 30

1   Copy and complete the tables of values for the equations shown.

a $y = x^2$

| $x$ | −2 | −1 | 0 | 1 | 2 |
|---|---|---|---|---|---|
| $y$ | | | | | |

b $y = 2x^2$

| $x$ | −2 | −1 | 0 | 1 | 2 |
|---|---|---|---|---|---|
| $y$ | | | | | |

c $y = -x^2$

| $x$ | −2 | −1 | 0 | 1 | 2 |
|---|---|---|---|---|---|
| $y$ | | | | | |

d $y = -2x^2$

| $x$ | −2 | −1 | 0 | 1 | 2 |
|---|---|---|---|---|---|
| $y$ | | | | | |

2   Draw one set of suitable $x$ and $y$ axes and on it plot each of the four equations. Label each graph with its equation. Each of your four graphs should form a **smooth** curve.

# 8 GRAPHS II

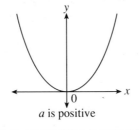

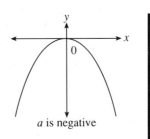

$a$ is positive          $a$ is negative

## Exercise 49

1   An engineer is designing a bridge, to cross a river, that
is to be supported by a parabolic arch. He chooses the
equation $y = -\frac{1}{2}x^2$ as the mathematical model.
a Copy and complete the table.

| $x$ | $-4$ | $-2$ | $-1$ | 0 | 1 | 2 | 4 |
|---|---|---|---|---|---|---|---|
| $y$ | | | | | | | |

b Use the same scale on both axes and draw the graph of the parabola.
c Draw the line $y = -6$ to represent the water level of the river. Use your completed graph to
estimate the width of the arch 10 m above the river, if the scale is one unit to 5 m.
d State three examples where you have come across a parabolic shape in everyday life.

2   The braking distance $d$ m of a car travelling at speed $v$ m/s is given by the equation:   $d = 0.08v^2$.
a Copy and complete the table.

| $v$ (m/s) | 0 | 10 | 20 | 30 | 40 |
|---|---|---|---|---|---|
| $d$ (m) | | | | | |

b Draw the graph of $d$ against $v$ in the range $0 \leqslant v \leqslant 40$.
c Use your graph to estimate: (i) the braking distance at 25 m/s   (ii) the speed for a braking
distance of 25 m. Check both your answers algebraically.
d What other factors should be considered to estimate overall stopping distance?

3   After $t$ seconds, the distance $s$ metres fallen by a pebble from a clifftop is given by the
equation:   $s = 4.9t^2$.
a Copy and complete the table to 3 SF.

| $t$ (s) | 0 | 1 | 2 | 3 |
|---|---|---|---|---|
| $s$ (m) | 0 | | | 44.1 |

b Draw the graph of $s$ against $t$ in the range $0 \leqslant t \leqslant 3$.
c Use your graph to estimate: (i) the distance fallen by the pebble after 2.5 seconds   (ii) the
time when the pebble has fallen 25 m. Check both your answers algebraically.
d If the pebble has fallen two thirds of its distance after 2.8 s, calculate the height of the cliff.

**4** A water tank has a square base, side length $x$ m, and height 2 m.

    **a** In terms of $x$, write down the formula for the volume of water $v$ m$^3$ in a full tank of water.

    **b** Copy and complete the table to 3 SF.

| $x$ (m) | 0 | 0.4 | 0.8 | 1.2 | 1.6 |
|---------|---|-----|-----|-----|------|
| $v$ (m$^3$) | 0 | | | | 5.12 |

    **c** Draw the graph of $v$ against $x$ in the range of $0 \leqslant x \leqslant 1.6$.

    **d** Use your graph to estimate: (i) the dimensions of the base to give a volume of 4 m$^3$   (ii) the volume of water held by the tank if its base is of area 0.36 m$^2$.

    **e** A hotel needs a water tank to hold at least 3 m$^3$. In order for the tank to fit into the roof space it cannot be more than 1.5 m wide. What range of $x$ values will meet these requirements?

MASTERMINDER

**5** The population $p$ of a rabbit warren after $t$ weeks is given (approx.) by the equation:   $p = kt^2$ where $k$ is a constant and the equation is valid for $2 \leqslant t \leqslant 10$.

    **a** Study the table carefully and use it to find $k$.

| $t$ (s) | 2 | 4 | 6 | 8 | 10 |
|---------|---|---|---|---|-----|
| $p$ | 10 | | | | 225 |

    **b** Copy and complete the table.

    **c** Draw the graph of $p$ against $t$ in the range $2 \leqslant t \leqslant 10$.

    **d** Use your graph to estimate: (i) the population after five weeks   (ii) the number of weeks after which the population exceeds 100.

## —— *Activity 31*

Graphs can be sketched very quickly and accurately using a computer and short programs. Use the program below to plot the graph of $y = \frac{1}{2}x^2$.

| Program | Explanation | |
|---------|-------------|--|
| `10  MODE 1` | | |
| `20  MOVE 0,500: DRAW 1279,500` | $x$-axis drawn across screen | |
| `30  MOVE 600,0: DRAW 600,1023` | $y$-axis drawn up screen | |
| `40  FOR H = -600 TO 600 STEP 2` | $x$ values in given range | |
| `50  LET Y = 0.5*H^2` | placed in $y = 0.5x^2$ | |
| `60  PLOT 69, H+600, Y/400+500` | to find $y$ values | |
| `70  NEHT H` | Curve scaled to fit screen | |

When you are happy that you understand the commands, modify the program and use it to plot the graphs below **after** you have made brief sketches of them.

**1** $y = 2x^2$   **2** $y = 3x^2$   **3** $y = 4x^2$   **4** $y = 10x^2$

Did they appear as you expected them to?

159

# 8.5 Graphs of $y = \dfrac{a}{x}$

## Activity 32

1 Copy and complete the tables of values for the equations shown.

**a** $y = \dfrac{3}{x}$

| $x$ | −3 | −2 | −1 | 0 | 1 | 2 | 3 |
|---|---|---|---|---|---|---|---|
| $y$ | | | | | | | |

**b** $y = -\dfrac{3}{x}$

| $x$ | −3 | −2 | −1 | 0 | 1 | 2 | 3 |
|---|---|---|---|---|---|---|---|
| $y$ | | | | | | | |

Why are there no $y$ values for $x = 0$?

2 Draw one set of suitable $x$ and $y$ axes and on it plot both equations. Label each graph with its equation.

> **REMEMBER**
>
> The graph of $y = \dfrac{a}{x}$
> is a **hyperbola**.
> Note that the curve
> approaches, but never
> touches, the axes.
>
>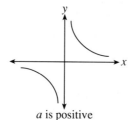
> $a$ is positive
>
>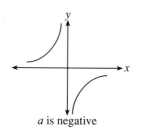
> $a$ is negative

## Exercise 50

1 The population $Y$ of an insect colony at time $t$ months is given approximately by the equation:

$Y = \dfrac{2000}{t}$  valid for $1 \leqslant t \leqslant 6$

**a** Copy and complete the table.

| $t$ (months) | 0 | 1 | 2 | 3 | 4 | 5 | 6 |
|---|---|---|---|---|---|---|---|
| $Y$ | | | | | | | |

**b** Draw the graph of $Y$ against $t$ in the range $1 \leqslant t \leqslant 6$.

**c** Use your graph to estimate: (i) when the population decreases by 75% from its size at $t = 1$
(ii) how long it takes for the population to decrease from 1500 to 500.

**2** A water tank springs a leak. The volume of water $V$ m$^3$ at time $t$ hours after the leak occurs is given by the equation:

$$V = \frac{1000}{t} \quad \text{valid for } 1 \leq t \leq 20$$

**a** Copy and complete the table.

| $t$ (hours) | 1 | 5 | | 15 | |
|---|---|---|---|---|---|
| $V$ (m$^3$) | | | 100 | | 50 |

**b** Draw the graph of $V$ against $t$ in the range $1 \leq t \leq 20$.

**c** Use your graph to estimate (i) when the volume of water is reduced by 750 m$^3$ from its value at $t = 1$ (ii) the volume decrease between eight hours and sixteen hours.

**3** Ron calculates that the temperature of a cup of tea, $T\,^\circ$C, $m$ minutes after it has been made, is given by the equation:

$$T = \frac{400}{m} \quad \text{valid for } 5 \leq m \leq 10$$

**a** Copy and complete the table.

| $m$ (minutes) | 5 | 6 | 7 | 8 | 9 | 10 |
|---|---|---|---|---|---|---|
| $T$ ($^\circ$C) | | | | | | 40 |

**b** Draw the graph of $T$ against $m$ in the range $5 \leq m \leq 10$.

**c** Use your graph to estimate (i) the temperature of a cup of tea after 450 seconds (ii) the time after which the temperature of a cup of tea is 60 °C.

**d** Ron is very fussy and will only drink tea of temperature at least 50 °C but no more than 75 °C. Use your graph to find the range of values of $m$ between which Ron will drink his beverage.

**4** Bill decides to go on a strict diet that claims his weight, $W$ kg, after $t$ days on the diet will be given by the equation:

$$W = \frac{2400}{t} \quad \text{valid for } 30 \leq t \leq 35$$

**a** Copy and complete the table.

| $t$ (days) | 30 | 31 | 32 | 33 | 34 | 35 |
|---|---|---|---|---|---|---|
| $W$ (kg) | 80 | | | | | |

**b** Draw the graph of $W$ against $t$ in the range $30 \leq t \leq 35$.

**c** Use your graph to estimate the number of days after the start of the diet that Bill's weight should be 74 kg.

**d** Why do you think there is only a limited range of values of $t$ for which this equation works?

MASTERMINDER

**5** Draw the graph of $xy = -10$ in the range $-5 \leq x \leq 5$ and use it to estimate the value of $y$ when $x$ is 2.5. Briefly explain why the curve approaches both the $x$ and $y$ axes but never touches either.

## Revision Exercise 8

1 Suggest everyday situations to match the following graphs. Find suitable equations for each (for example, $y = 2x$).

a y↑

b y↑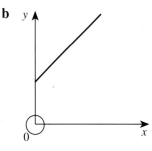

c y↑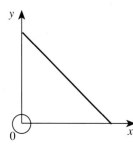

d y↑

e y↑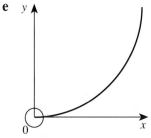

f y↑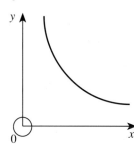

2 **Sketch** the following graphs (you are not expected to plot co-ordinates):

a $y = 3x$   b $y = -2x$   c $y = 2x^2$   d $y = -3x^2$   e $y = \frac{10}{x}$   f $y = -\frac{10}{x}$

3 **Sketch** the following graphs (you are not expected to plot co-ordinates) and state for each:
(i) The gradient.
(ii) The intercept on the $y$ axis.
(iii) The intercept on the $x$ axis.

a $y = 3x + 1$   b $y = -3x - 1$   c $2y = 5x + 6$   d $y + 3x - 4 = 0$

4 Square yards $Y$ are related to square metres $M$ by the equation:
$$Y \approx 0.836M$$

a Copy and complete the table to 3 SF.

| $M$ (m$^2$) | 0 | 5 | 10 | 15 | 20 | 25 |
|---|---|---|---|---|---|---|
| $Y$ (yd$^2$) | 0 | | | | | 20.9 |

b Draw the graph of $Y$ against $M$ in the range $0 \leqslant M \leqslant 25$.
c David decides to tile his kitchen floor with terracotta tiles. He likes two types: 'Country' at £30 a square metre, and 'Earth' at £25 a square yard. His kitchen has a plan area of 20 m$^2$. Use your graph to estimate which tile would be cheaper and by how much. Show your method clearly.

**5** The world high jump record, $h$ metres, $x$ years after 1900 is given approximately by the equation:

$$h \approx 0.005x + 1.89$$

**a** Copy and complete the table to 3 SF.

| $x$ (years) | 0 | 30 | 60 | 90 | 120 |
|---|---|---|---|---|---|
| $h$ (m) | 1.89 | | | | |

**b** Draw the graph of $h$ against $x$ for years 1900 to 2020.
**c** Use your graph to estimate:
   (i) The world records in 1950 and 2000; comment.
   (ii) The year when the world record is likely to be 2.40 m; comment.
**d** Why will this graph eventually go wrong?

**6** The speed, $v$ m/s, of a duck $t$ seconds after the start of its descent onto a pond is given by the equation:

$$v = \frac{10}{t} \quad \text{valid for } 1 \leqslant t \leqslant 20$$

**a** Copy and complete the table to 3 SF.

| $t$ (s) | 1 | 2 | 5 | 10 | 15 | 20 |
|---|---|---|---|---|---|---|
| $v$ (m/s) | 10 | | | | | 0.5 |

**b** Draw the graph of $v$ against $t$ in the range $1 \leqslant t \leqslant 20$.
**c** If the duck's speed of descent exceeds 0.9 m/s, after 12 seconds it will tumble on landing.
   Use your graph to estimate whether or not the duck has a smooth landing.

## MASTERMINDER

**7** The shaded area $A$ cm$^2$ in a square of side $L$ cm containing $n$ circles arranged as shown is given by the equation:

$$A = (1 - \frac{\pi}{4})L^2$$

**a** Copy and complete the table to 3 SF.

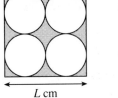
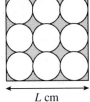

$L$ cm          $L$ cm

| $L$ (cm) | 0 | 5 | 10 | 15 | 20 |
|---|---|---|---|---|---|
| $A$ (cm$^2$) | 0 | | | | 85.8 |

**b** Draw the graph of $A$ against $L$ in the range $0 \leqslant L \leqslant 20$.
**c** Use this graph to estimate:
   (i) The value of $A$ when $L = 12$ cm.
   (ii) The value of $L$ when $A = 50$ cm$^2$.
**d** Show that $A = (1 - \frac{\pi}{4})L^2$.
   What can you conclude from this equation?

## ___ Basics Test 4

**A** Calculator
Give all your answers to 3 SF.

**1** Convert $\frac{1}{7}$ to a decimal.

**2** $\dfrac{3.1 \times 10^{-3}}{4.1 \times 10^{-4}}$

**3** Solve for $b$: $3b^2 = 19$.

**4** $(1.04)^5 \times (1.04)^3$

**5** $(3.1 \times 10^{-3}) - (4.1 \times 10^{-4})$

**6** $(1.04)^5 - (1.04)^3$

**B** Paper and pencil

**7** $\dfrac{5.6}{0.7}$

**8** $\dfrac{1}{2} + \dfrac{1}{3} + \dfrac{1}{4}$

**9** $2\frac{2}{3} \div 1\frac{2}{3}$

**10** Twelve pens cost £14.40. How much do 13 pens cost?

**11** What percentage of 170 is 34?

**12** Subtract 975 g from 12.12 kg.

**13** Solve for $c$: $3c + 1.4 = 5$

**14** Solve for $d$: $\dfrac{3}{2-d} = 4$

**15** A square field has an area of 22 500 m². What is its perimeter?

**C** Mental

Ten questions will be read out to you. Use the following information for Questions 16 to 20.

The diagram shows the distances, in miles, between some junctions on a motorway. The junctions are numbered [16], [17], ...

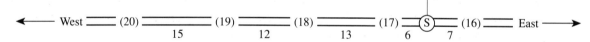

## ___ Puzzlers

**1** **Practical** Estimate how many revolutions a wheel of your family's car makes in an average year's motoring.

**2** In the cube, what is the angle ABC?

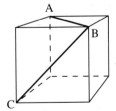

**3** Continue the sequence: 1, 4, 3, 11, 15, 13, 17, ...

**4** In the division sum, each of the nine digits 1 to 9 is used once. Find the two solutions.

# Coursework: Bicycle gears

The diagram shows the rear wheel of a bicycle connected to the pedal wheel by a chain from the sprocket wheel.

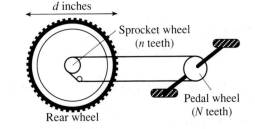

1  The pedal wheel rotates only once. If there are 30 teeth on the pedal wheel and 15 teeth on the sprocket wheel explain, with the aid of diagrams, why:

a The rear wheel will rotate exactly twice.

b The bicycle will move forward by exactly twice the circumference of the rear wheel.

c If the diameter of the rear wheel is $d$ inches, the bicycle will move forward $2\pi d$ inches.

These results are shown on the table below. Copy and complete this table.

| Number of teeth in | | Number of rotations of rear wheel | Distance in inches moved by bicycle |
|---|---|---|---|
| Pedal wheel | Sprocket wheel | | |
| 30 | 15 | 2 | $2\pi d$ |
| 20 | 10 | | |
| 10 | 10 | | |
| 60 | 15 | | |
| $N$ | $n$ | | |

From this table you should be able to see why, with one complete revolution of the pedal wheel, the distance moved by the bicycle is given by:

$$\frac{N}{n} \times \pi d \text{ inches}$$

2  Measure the diameter of the rear wheel of your bicycle and count the number of teeth on each sprocket wheel and the pedal wheel. Use this information to work out how far your bicycle will travel for one complete revolution of the pedal wheel, in each gear. Then verify your results by experiment. Work out the percentage error for each gear.

3  Suppose you have a bicycle with 52 teeth on its pedal wheel and sprocket wheels with 14, 17, 20, 24 and 28 teeth. If $R$ is the rate of pedalling in revolutions per minute (rpm), and $S$ is the speed of the bicycle in miles per hour (mph), then:

$$S = 0.08 \times \frac{N}{n} \times R$$

On one set of axes, draw the graphs of $S$ against $R$ for each of the sprocket wheels for speeds up to 40 mph and for revolutions up to 120 per minute.

a You pedal at 120 rpm. How much faster are you travelling in top gear than in bottom gear?

b The most efficient pedalling speed is 90 rpm. Which gear should you use when going up a hill at 20 mph?

c You are travelling at 15 mph. What are your possible pedalling speeds?

## EXTENSION

4  **Investigate** how a bicycle, with a 26 inch rear wheel, could travel at 100 miles per hour.

# 9 ARITHMETIC II

## 9.1 Tolerance

If a machine is constructed to make nails 3.2 cm long, it is unlikely that every nail will be exactly 3.2 cm. It may be sufficient for the nail lengths to be in the interval 3.1 cm to 3.3 cm. Then:

   Maximum nail length is 3.3 cm

   Minimum nail length is 3.1 cm

   Therefore **tolerance** = 3.3 cm − 3.1 cm = 0.2 cm

This interval, from 3.1 cm to 3.3 cm, can be written:

   $3.2 \pm 0.1$ cm

This method of describing intervals is often used for measurement in science experiments or in industry when we need to know the degree of inaccuracy.

## Exercise 51

1  Write each of the intervals as 'between ... and ...':
   **a** $3.5 \pm 0.1$   **b** $12.6 \pm 0.5$   **c** $5.6 \pm 0.01$   **d** $10.2 \pm 0.05$

2  Write each of the intervals in the form $a \pm b$:
   **a** 2.5 to 2.7   **b** 12.2 to 12.3   **c** 21.3 to 21.4   **d** 8.15 to 8.25

3  Two metal strips are made with the tolerances shown.

   Strip A: ($12.5 \pm 0.1$ cm)        Strip B: ($5.6 \pm 0.1$ cm)

   **a** If the two strips are placed end to end, find the maximum and minimum lengths.
   **b** If the strips are placed side by side as shown,
      find the minimum difference in length.

4  If $w = \dfrac{a+b}{c}$, and   $a = 1.2 \pm 0.05$ cm
   $$b = 3.7 \pm 0.03 \text{ cm}$$
   $$c = 1.1 \pm 0.1 \text{ cm},$$
   calculate the maximum and minimum value of $w$.

5  If $y = \dfrac{a+b}{c+d}$, and   $a = 4.2 \pm 0.1$ cm
   $$b = 3.2 \pm 0.1 \text{ cm}$$
   $$c = 2.2 \pm 0.1 \text{ cm}$$
   $$d = 1.2 \pm 0.1 \text{ cm},$$
   calculate the maximum and minimum value of $y$, and hence state the tolerance of $y$.

**6** If $h = \dfrac{a+b}{2(c-d)}$, and $\quad a = 32° \pm 1°$

$$b = 120° \pm 0.5°$$
$$c = 30° \pm 1°$$
$$d = 15° \pm 0.5°,$$

calculate the maximum and minimum value of $h$, and hence state the tolerance of $h$.

**7** If $p = \dfrac{x}{yz}$, and $\quad x = 23.1 \pm 0.5\,\text{kg}$

$$y = 12.1 \pm 0.3\,\text{kg}$$
$$z = 1.2 \pm 0.1\,\text{kg}$$

calculate the maximum and minimum value of $p$, and hence state the tolerance of $p$.

**8** The distance $x$ metres a boat is out to sea, when it is observed at an angle of depression $A$ from the top of a cliff $h$ metres high, is given by the formula:

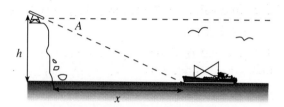

$$x = \frac{h}{\tan A}$$

You are given that $h = 80 \pm 5\,\text{m}$, and $A = 5°$ to the nearest degree.
Calculate the maximum and minimum values of $x$, and hence state the tolerance of $x$.
Comment on your answer.

# ▬ 9.2 Percentages

Previously (Chapter 1) we have calculated percentage increases and decreases using 'ratio lines' like this:

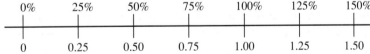

Another method is to use a 'multiplying factor', as shown in this table:

| Percentage | Fraction | Multiplying factor |
|---|---|---|
| 1% | 1/100 | 0.01 |
| 50% | 50/100 | 0.50 |
| 75% | 75/100 | 0.75 |
| 100% | 100/100 | 1.00 |
| 125% | 125/100 | 1.25 |

Can you think of a quick way of working out the multiplying factor, given a percentage?

## ___ Percentage increase

■ *EXAMPLE 1*

A car's price is increased by 25% from £6500. What is the car's new price?

The new price is 125% (100% + 25%) of the old price, so the multiplying factor is 1.25. Therefore

New price = 1.25 × £6500 = £8125

## ___ Percentage decrease

■ *EXAMPLE 2*

A radio's price is decreased by 25% from £120. What is the radio's new price?

The new price is 75% (100% − 25%) of the old price, so the multiplying factor is 0.75. Therefore

New price = 0.75 × £120 = £90

## ___ Exercise 52

1 Write down the multiplying factor to **increase** a number by the following percentages:

  **a** 15%     **b** 34%     **c** 65%     **d** 5%
  **e** 110%    **f** 176%    **g** 200%    **h** 0.1%

2 Write down the multiplying factor to **decrease** a number by the following percentages:

  **a** 10%     **b** 15%     **c** 45%     **d** 5%
  **e** 72%     **f** 95%     **g** $2\frac{1}{2}$%    **h** 0.1%

3 Copy and complete the following tables:

| Old price (£) | % increase | New price (£) |
|---|---|---|
| 1250 | 20 | |
| 750 | 58 | |
| 25 | 5 | |
| 180 | 115 | |
| | 16 | 52.20 |
| 32 | | 43.20 |

| Old price (£) | % decrease | New price (£) |
|---|---|---|
| 1600 | 5 | |
| 18 | 24 | |
| 940 | 62 | |
| | 18 | 77.90 |
| | 65 | 9.80 |
| 35 | | 30.10 |

4 Martin's salary of £12 140 is increased by 8%.
  Rajind's salary of £11 800 is increased by 12%.
  Who earns more afterwards, and by how much?

5 A car depreciates (loses) in value at the rate of 15% per year. If a car is bought for £8000, how much will it be worth in: **a** 1 year  **b** 2 years  **c** 3 years?

**6** An antique vase appreciates (gains) in value
at a rate of 15% per year. If the vase is bought
for £5000, how much will it be worth in:
**a** 1 year
**b** 2 years
**c** 3 years?

**7** By what percentage must: **a** the price of a £25 book be reduced to bring it down to £21
**b** the price of a £21 book be increased to bring it up to £25?

**8** Mrs Much has a salary of £34 000. She has a rise of 20%. Later she has another rise of 10%.
What is her salary now?

**9** The normal profit made by a shop on a bottle of wine is 25%. To clear the end of a line, the
shop offers a 10% discount. What profit is made by the shop on a bottle sold in this way?

## MASTERMINDERS

**10** A shopkeeper sells CDs at a 30% profit.
**a** How much does she charge for a CD for which she paid £6.30?
**b** What is her profit on a CD that she sells for £10.40?

**11** $p$ is the result of decreasing $q$ by 20%. $r$ is the result of increasing $p$ by 40%. $q$ and $r$ differ
by 30. What was $p$?

**12** A motorcycle depreciates in value at a rate of 10% per year. If the cost of a new motorcycle is
£3200, after how many years will it be worth half its original value?

**13** Mr Scrooge inherits £20 000 and decides to put it under his mattress for a 'rainy day'.
If inflation is running at 14% each year, calculate the value of this money after:
**a** 5 years      **b** 10 years      **c** 15 years      **d** 20 years.

**14** If the average inflation rate is 20% per annum (per year), estimate the cost of a £1.70 pint of
beer in 50 years time.

**15** If Julius Caesar had invested 1p at 1% per annum
compound interest, what would it be worth after 2000
years?

# 9.3 Wages and salaries

## Wages

A wage is money paid weekly and calculated at a certain rate for a set number of hours per week. Overtime is usually paid at a higher rate.

**■ EXAMPLE 1**

A shoe shop pays:

Normal time at £4.20 per hour
Overtime at $1.5 \times$ £4.20 per hour ('time and a half').

Hannah works the following hours in a week. Calculate her total wage.

| Time | Mon | Tues | Wed | Thurs | Fri | Sat |
|------|-----|------|-----|-------|-----|-----|
| Normal | 8 | 8 | 4 | 8 | 8 | |
| Overtime | | | 1 | | | 8 |

Hannah's wage = Normal time + Overtime
= 36 × £4.20 + 9 × 1.5× £4.20
= £207.90

## Salaries

A salary is a fixed annual (yearly) sum of money, usually paid each month.
(*Note*: 'per annum' means 'per year', and is often shortened to 'p.a.'.)

**■ EXAMPLE 2**

Paul was offered two jobs as a hair-dresser.

'Cutters' pay £11 700 per annum (p.a.)
'Clippers' pay £12 324 p.a.

How much more do Clippers pay per week?

Clippers pay per week $= £\dfrac{12\,324}{52} = £237$

Cutters pay per week $= £\dfrac{11\,700}{52} = £225$

Therefore Clippers pay £12 more per week.

## Exercise 53

**1** A restaurant pays normal time at £$x$ per hour, and overtime at £$2x$ per hour. Chris works the hours shown in the table, and earns £216. What is his normal pay per hour?

| Time | Mon | Tues | Wed | Thurs | Fri | Sat |
|---|---|---|---|---|---|---|
| Normal | 7 | 7 | | 7 | 3 | |
| Overtime | | | 4 | | 3 | 5 |

**2** A typist is paid a basic rate of £6.10 per hour. If she works more than 36 hours in a week, she earns overtime paid at 1.5 times the basic rate.
**a** One week she worked 42 hours. What was her wage that week?
**b** Another week her wage was £292.80. How many hours overtime did she work?

**3** A job is advertised at a starting salary of £9240 p.a., rising by annual increments (increases) of £340 to a maximum of £11 960 p.a.
**a** What is the difference between the starting and maximum salaries?
**b** How many increments are there?
**c** What is the salary for the third year?

MASTERMINDER

**4** Which salary would you prefer:
**a** £14 000 p.a. with annual increments of £500, or
**b** £12 000 p.a. with annual increments of 10% of the previous year's salary?

# 9.4 Taxation

The Government needs money to pay for health, education, defence, etc. It raises this money by **taxation**.

## Income tax

The calculation of income tax goes like this. Part of a person's income is 'tax free'. It is called the 'Personal Tax Allowance' and it depends on the status of the individual (single, married, etc.). Income tax is paid on the **remainder** of the income (called the taxable income).

In 1991 the basic rate of income tax was 25% in the pound for taxable incomes less than £23 700 and 40% in the pound for taxable incomes of more than £23 700.

In 1991 the Personal Tax Allowance was:

| Status | £ |
|---|---|
| Single person | 3295 |
| Married man | 5015 |
| Married woman | 3295 |

### ◼ EXAMPLE 1

Mr Williams is married and earns a salary of £30 000 p.a. Find the income tax he pays per month.

Annual income $= £30\,000$
Married man's allowance $= £5015$   (from table on page 171)
Taxable income $= £30\,000 - £5015 = £24\,985$

Tax to pay p.a.
(i) £23 700 @ at 25%
   $= £5925$
(ii) $£24\,985 - £23\,700$
   $= £1285$ at 40%
   $= £514$

TOTAL tax p.a. $= £5925 + £514$
   $= £6439$

Tax payable per month $= £6439 \div 12$
   $= £536.58$

## ▬ Value added tax (VAT)

This tax is added to the selling price of an article. In 1992 the rate of VAT was $17\frac{1}{2}\%$.

### ◼ EXAMPLE 2

A shopkeeper sells a bicycle for £98.80 plus VAT. Find the total cost.

Total cost $= 17\frac{1}{2}\%$ more than selling price
   $= £98.80 \times 1.175$
   $= £116.09$

## ▬ Exercise 54

1  Calculate the amount of income tax paid **monthly** by:
  **a** Mr Alpha, single, salary £16 685 p.a.
  **b** Mr Beta, married, salary £35 175 p.a.
  **c** Ms Gamma, single, weekly gross wage of £316.25.
  **d** Mrs Omega, married, monthly gross wage of £1800.

2  Gerry and Lisa are a married couple. Gerry's salary is £32 000 p.a. and Lisa's salary is £15 200 p.a. How much tax does the couple pay annually?

3  Calculate the VAT (at $17\frac{1}{2}\%$) on the following items:
  **a** A kettle costing £15 **before** tax.
  **b** A set of golf clubs costing £225 **before** tax.
  **c** A shirt costing £25 **after** tax.
  **d** A car costing £7500 **after** tax.

**4** A small survey is made at two DIY Stores.

| Store | 1 tin of paint | Wallpaper | Tiles |
|---|---|---|---|
| 'Paint It' | £9.20 | £16.60 | £7.80 |
| 'Brush It' | £7.50 | £14.00 | £6.60 |

The prices quoted at 'Paint It' include VAT, those quoted at 'Brush It' do not include VAT.
**a** Which store's prices are cheaper?
**b** If all the items listed above were purchased at the 'cheaper' store, how much less would the total bill be than at the 'expensive' store?
**c** What is the price of one tin of paint at the 'Paint It' store before VAT?

## MASTERMINDER

**5** **Investigate** why, to find the VAT (at $17\frac{1}{2}\%$) which is included in a given price, we can multiply the given price by the fraction $\frac{7}{47}$.

# __ 9.5 Interest and loans

If you place money in a Savings Account, Bank or Building Society, it will earn you extra money (interest) because they are borrowing your money. Similarly, if you borrow money you will have to pay interest on the loan. The amount of interest depends on the amount saved or borrowed and on the rate of interest.

## ■ EXAMPLE 1

Bob places £100 in the 'Saveright' Building Society who pay an interest rate of 8% p.a. If the interest earned stays in the account, how much will Bob have in his account at the end of the fifth year?

| Year | Amount saved |
|---|---|
| 1 | £100 × 1.08 |
| 2 | £100 × 1.08 × 1.08 = £100 × $(1.08)^2$ |
| 3 | ... |
| 4 | ... |
| 5 | £100 × $(1.08)^5$ = £146.93 |

## ■ EXAMPLE 2

A credit card enables Linda to buy goods and pay for them at the end of the month. Failure to do this results in an interest charge of 2% per month on the amount owing.
What interest would Linda pay on £500 for **a** 1 month's interest  **b** 12 month's interest?

**a** Interest to pay after 1 month = (£500 × 1.02) − £500 = £10

**b** Interest to pay after 12 months = (£500 × $1.02^{12}$) − £500 = £134.12

## — Exercise 55

**1** Calculate the interest earned on the following amounts:
    **a** £250 saved for 1 year at 8% p.a.     **b** £1250 saved for 1 year at 12% p.a.
    **c** £700 saved for 4 years at $12\frac{1}{2}$% p.a.     **d** £10 500 saved for 6 years at 14% p.a.

**2** £50 is invested in a Bank Account paying an interest rate of 10% p.a. After how many years will there be £100 in the account if all interest is kept in the account?

**3** Calculate the interest owed to 'Loan Shark Ltd' on the following amounts at an interest rate of 30% p.a.:
    **a** £5800 borrowed for 1 year.     **b** £1750 borrowed for 3 years.
    **c** £5000 borrowed for 1 month.     **d** £10 000 borrowed for 6 months.

**4** A sports car costs £15 000. Mark borrows the money to buy the car from a Bank and pays back the loan after a year at 16% p.a. interest. The car's value depreciates at 15% p.a.
    **a** How much more does Mark actually pay in interest?
    **b** How much does the car lose in depreciation?
    **c** At the end of the year, how much has the car really cost Mark?

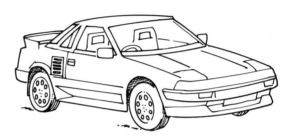

# — 9.6 Discount and hire purchase (HP)

## — Discount

To encourage customers to spend, goods may be sold at a price reduced (discounted) by a certain percentage.

■ *EXAMPLE 1*
How much would you pay for this racquet?

The selling price is 100% − 12% = 88% of the normal price.
Therefore the new price is £80 × 0.88 = £70.40.

> **FOR SALE**
> *DUNLUP TENNIS RACQUET*
> NORMALLY £80
> DISCOUNTED BY **12%**

## — Hire purchase (HP)

To enable expensive articles to be purchased, the payment can be spread over a certain time period. Usually an initial deposit is paid, followed by monthly payments. Hire purchase usually results in a much larger total cost than the 'cash down' payment.

■ *EXAMPLE 2*

A computer is advertised for £499.99 cash or a deposit of £100 followed by twelve monthly payments of £46. How much more does the hire purchase method of payment cost?

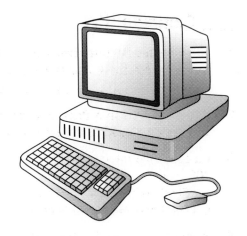

Hire purchase cost  = £100 + 12 × £46
                    = £652

Cost difference  = £652 − £499.99
                 = £152.01

## ___ Exercise 56

1   Copy and complete the table, to show the selling price of a number of items at varying discounts.

| Item | Cost | Selling price at discount of | | | |
|------|------|------|------|------|------|
|      |      | 5% | 8% | $12\frac{1}{2}\%$ | 15% |
| Tent | £60 | | | | |
| Video | £450 | | | | |
| Book | £3.50 | | | | |
| Car | £6350 | | | | |

2   A woman buys a set of golf clubs in a sale at 12% discount.

| Club | Selling price |
|------|------|
| Woods | £144 |
| Irons | £166 |
| Putter | £18.80 |

How much would the set of clubs have cost before the sale?

3   The cash price of a bicycle is £188. Jake pays an initial 10% deposit followed by twelve equal monthly payments. How much should each monthly payment be if he pays **a** no interest **b** 12% interest, on the monthly payments?

4   The cash price of a camera is £120. Ally pays an initial 12% deposit followed by equal monthly payments.

| Scheme A | Deposit + 12 monthly payments of £9 |
|------|------|
| Scheme B | Deposit + 18 monthly payments of £6.50 |

**a** Which scheme is cheaper, and by how much?
**b** By what percentage is Scheme B more expensive than the cash price?

## ___ Revision Exercise 9

**1** Find the maximum and minimum values, and the tolerance, for the following expressions when:
$$x = 9.05 \pm 0.05$$
$$y = 1.05 \pm 0.05$$

**a** $x + y$ **b** $x - y$ **c** $x - 2y$ **d** $xy$ **e** $\frac{x}{x+y}$ **f** $\frac{x}{x-y}$

**2** Ian cycles at $v$ m/s round a corner that is part of a circle of radius $r$ metres. He must lean at an angle of $A°$ to the vertical to negotiate the corner, where:
$$\tan A° = \frac{v^2}{rg}$$
Calculate the maximum and minimum values of angle $A$ if:
$v = 12 \pm 0.5$ m/s
$r = 48 \pm 0.1$ m
$g = 9.8$ m/s$^2$.

**3** A £70 000 house appreciates for three consecutive years at 8% p.a., then depreciates for two consecutive years at 4% p.a. Find the cost of the property after this five-year period.

**4** 'Saksuni Cars' pays its workers: *Normal time* at £$x$ per hour.
*Overtime* at £$1.5x$ per hour.

Graham's time sheet for a week in which he earns £262.50 is:

| Time | Mon | Tues | Wed | Thurs | Fri | Sat |
|---|---|---|---|---|---|---|
| Normal | 8 | 8 | 4 | 8 | 8 | |
| Overtime | | | 2 | | 4 | 5 |

What is his normal rate of pay per hour?

**5** Which salary would you prefer:
**a** £20 000 p.a. with annual increments of £500.
**b** £16 000 p.a. with annual increments of 10% of the previous year's salary?
Explain your answer.

For Questions 6 and 7 refer to the basic rates of tax and allowances on page 171.

**6** Calculate the amount of income tax paid **monthly** by:
**a** Mr Smith, single, salary £18 000 p.a.
**b** Mr Hurd, married, salary £18 000 p.a.
**c** Ms Tams, single, salary £28 200 p.a.
**d** Mrs Hill, married, salary £32 500 p.a.

**7** Bill and Alice decide to get married.
Bill's salary is £29 000 p.a.
Alice's salary is £19 000 p.a.
How much less tax per month do they jointly pay once they are married?

**8** Copy and complete the following table for VAT at $17\frac{1}{2}\%$.

| Item | Cost before VAT | Cost after VAT |
|---|---|---|
| Tie | £12 | |
| Blouse | £32 | |
| Computer | | £680 |
| CD player | | £350 |

**Homemaker Estate Agents**
Our unbeatable charges on house sales are:
*2% on sales up to £40000*
*$1^1/_2$% on sales over £40000*
All charges subject to VAT

**9** Calculate the charges owed to 'Homemaker Estate Agents' on houses sold for:
**a** £38 000
**b** £123 000
**c** £40 000

**10** Calculate the interest earned on the following amounts:
**a** £125 saved for 1 year at 9% p.a.
**b** £420 saved for 1 year at 14% p.a.
**c** £5420 saved for 5 years at 12% p.a.
**d** £14 600 saved for 10 years at $11\frac{1}{2}\%$ p.a.

**11** On the following items, calculate: **a** the hire purchase price **b** how much more is paid by HP than cash.

(i) Cash: £18 000
HP: Deposit £1000
24 monthly instalments of £800

(ii) Cash: £740
HP: Deposit £50
12 monthly instalments of £60

(iii) Cash: £420
HP: Deposit £10
12 monthly instalments of £35

(iv) Cash: £535
HP: No deposit
24 monthly instalments of £25

MASTERMINDER

**12 Investigate** how much tax a married man would pay per month if he earned £1 000 000 in a year!

## Basics Test 5

**A** Calculator
Give all your answers to 3 SF.

**1** $(\frac{3}{7} + 0.37)^3$

**2** $\frac{2.6}{11.4 \div 7.3}$

**3** Solve for $e$: $7\sqrt{e} = 27$.

**4** Solve for $x$: $4 = 9(x^2 - 2)$.

**5** $(10^5 \times 1.25 \times 10^{-6})^2$

**6** $\sqrt{4.1^3 - 3.1^3 - 2.1^3}$

**B** Paper and pencil

**7** $3\frac{1}{7} + 7\frac{1}{3}$

**8** Decrease $1.20\,\text{kg}$ by 35%.

**9** Divide £56 in the ratio 4 : 3.

**10** Solve for $d$: $0.5 = \frac{d}{0.03}$

**11** Winston runs the 200 m in 24 seconds. Find his average speed in km/h.

**12** Which produces the larger result: to increase £20 by 20% or to decrease £30 by 30%?

**13** What is the total surface area of a block of wood measuring 3 cm by 4 cm by 5 cm?

**14** How many 19p stamps can you buy for £10?

**15** If 65 m of platinum wire costs £1365, what is the cost per metre?

**C** Mental
Ten questions will be read out to you. Use the following information for Questions 16 to 20.

$x = -3$, $y = -4$, $z = 5$

## Puzzlers

**1** **Practical** Find the probability of a motorist having to wait at a certain set of traffic lights near to your home or school.

**2** The equation below gives the monthly repayments $S$ for a mortgage on a home over $n$ months on £$P$ borrowed at $R\%$.

$$S = \frac{PR\left(1 + \frac{R}{1200}\right)^n}{1200\left[\left(1 + \frac{R}{1200}\right)^{n-1} - 1\right]}$$

Calculate to 2 DP the monthly repayments on £50 000 over 25 years at **a** 8%  **b** 12%  **c** 17%.

**3** There is a unique solution to this multiplication, where each letter represents a single digit number. Find it!

$$
\begin{array}{r}
Y\ D \\
\times\ C\ D\ X\ Y \\
\hline
X\ B\ Y\ D\ B \\
\hline
X\ C\ S\ Y\ C\ Y \\
\end{array}
$$

# Coursework: World population

The population of the world is increasing by about 2% each year. This may not sound much, but if it continues at this rate the human race will face a large problem!

For this Coursework you will need the following facts:

Mass of the Earth = $6.6 \times 10^{21}$ tonnes
Diameter of the Earth = $12\,700$ km
Present world population = $4.5 \times 10^9$
70% of the Earth's surface is under water
Surface area of the Earth = $4\pi \times (\text{radius})^2$

1 Assuming that the population increases at 2% each year, the population of the world, after a given number of years, can be worked out as shown below.

| Number of years | Population to 2 SF |
|---|---|
| 0 | $4.5 \times 10^9 = 4.5 \times 10^9$ |
| 1 | $4.5 \times 10^9 \times (1.02) =$ |
| 2 | $4.5 \times 10^9 \times (1.02) \times (1.02) =$ |
| 3 | $4.5 \times 10^9 \times (1.02)^3 =$ |

a Copy and complete the above table.
b Explain why the population of the world, after $T$ years, is given by:

$$4.5 \times 10^9 \times (1.02)^T$$

Use this relationship to work out the world population after the following number of years: 10, 20, 30, 40, 50. Draw a graph of population against time for the first 50 years. Use your graph to estimate in how many years time the population will have doubled.
c Work out to 2 SF the world population after (i) 100 years   (ii) 224 years   (iii) 375 years (iv) 1600 years. How many times larger than the present population is each of your answers?

2 Assuming that the average mass of a human is 50 kg, work out to 2 SF the mass of the population in 1600 years' time. Compare your answer to the mass of the Earth.

3 a Show that the total land surface of the world is approximately $1.5 \times 10^8$ km².
   b Work out to 1 SF the number of humans per km² of land (i) at present   (ii) in 100 years (iii) in 224 years.
   c What would be the population of the world if there was an average of:
   (i) One human for every $20\,\text{m}^2$.
   (ii) One human for every 20 metres square.
   In how many years time would these two densities occur?

EXTENSION

4 **Investigate** why the world population will not continue to increase by 2% each year.

# 10 STATISTICS AND PROBABILITY

## 10.1 Basic principles

### Collection of data

Statistics is the science of collecting facts (data) and analysing them. The data can cover a wide range of subjects – from nuclear power to hair shampoo!

Suppose we want to find out about pupils and school dinners (and have only a limited time). Rather than asking **every** pupil about school dinners, we choose a **sample**, and ask them. The more carefully we choose our sample, the more accurate our results.

Statisticians talk about 'avoiding bias'. In the case of school dinners, a fair sample would **not** consist only of vegetarians, or sixth-formers, or the school basketball team.

We may wish to collect different types of data:

> 'Measurable' quantities, eg length, mass, number of school dinners, etc.

> People's opinions and preferences, eg political polls, market research questionnaires, etc.

Whichever sort of data we collect, we need to present it in a clear concise way that is easy to understand at a glance.

### Activity 33

The results of a large survey on TV and radio are shown below. This is a good example of how data can be displayed. **Briefly** explain the main features of each diagram.

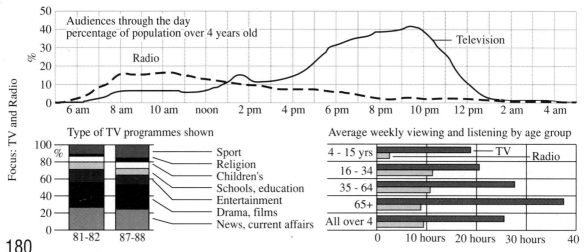

180

## ___ Representation of data

The following examples all refer to this table of information, which summarizes a survey of types of housing in Cityville.

| Type of house | | Number of people |
|---|---|---|
| Detached | (D) | 5000 |
| Semi | (S) | 8000 |
| Terraced | (T) | 4500 |
| Flats | (F) | 2500 |

**■EXAMPLE 1**

Represent these facts on a **pictogram**.

Key:

1000 people

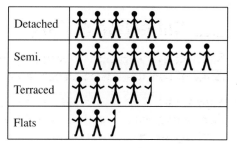

*Types of housing of people in Cityville*

(Pictograms are easy to understand, but they take time to draw and are difficult to read when 'bits' of pictures are shown.)

**■EXAMPLE 2**

Represent these facts on a **bar chart**.

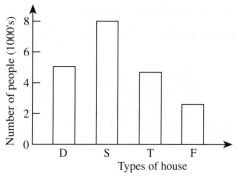

*Types of housing of people in Cityville*

(Bar charts are simpler to draw than pictograms, but perhaps not so easy to understand.)

**■EXAMPLE 3**

Represent these facts on a **pie chart**.

First we have to work out the angle of sector per person. The total number of people is 5000 + 8000 + 4500 + 2500 = 20 000. Therefore:

20 000 people are represented by 360°

1000 people are represented by $\frac{360°}{20} = 18°$

(Check: 90° + 144° + 81° + 45° = 360°)

| Type of house | Number of people | Angle of sector |
|---|---|---|
| Detached | 5000 | 5 × 18° = 90° |
| Semi | 8000 | 8 × 18° = 144° |
| Terraced | 4500 | 4.5 × 18° = 81° |
| Flats | 2500 | 2.5 × 18° = 45° |

(Pie charts can involve a number of calculations, and careful drawing.)

How 'user friendly' do you think these Examples are?

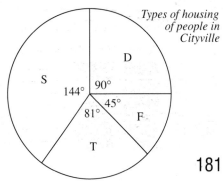

*Types of housing of people in Cityville*

## ___ *Activity 34*

Carry out a survey of all pupils in your class to investigate what sort of pet their family keeps, and represent this data on:

**a** A pictogram.

**b** A bar chart.

**c** A pie chart.

Comment on your results.

## ___ Sampling

We take **samples** of data because it is too time-consuming and expensive to collect information using every member of the 'parent population' (the population from which the sample is drawn).

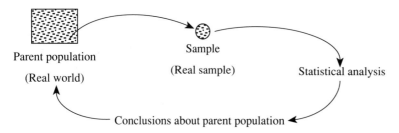

Parent population

(Real world)

Sample

(Real sample)

Statistical analysis

Conclusions about parent population

We want to 'avoid bias' when choosing our sample, or our conclusions will be misleading. And we need to have a large enough sample to be sure of the results – for example, just asking your two neighbours at table their opinions of school dinners would not be adequate.

## ___ *Activity 35*

Look carefully at the following data collections. State for each where there could be sources of bias. Briefly, how would you improve the sampling method?

**a** **Radio 1 opinion survey on the Top 20**: data was collected from people in a shopping centre at 10 am on a Thursday morning.

**b** **A US opinion poll in the 1940s on a Presidential Election**: people from the telephone directory were telephoned to ask who they would vote for.

**c** **A TV production line**: every twenty-fifth TV off a production line in a factory is checked for faults.

**d** **A football match**: Nottingham Forest FC have reached the FA Cup Final and outside a Nottingham pub a local newspaper has collected data on who people think will win.

# 10.2 Misuse of statistics

Data can be presented so as to give false impressions. Closer inspection shows that someone has been 'economical with the truth'.

For example, sales of pens from Penwrite plc are shown on Graph 1. This portrays a steady drop in sales over three years, followed by a small upswing.

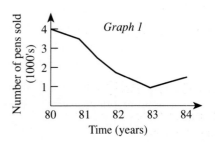

However, the company statistician in the PR (public relations) department presents the data to portray a dramatic upsurge in sales, by looking only at one year and by altering the vertical scale – see Graph 2.

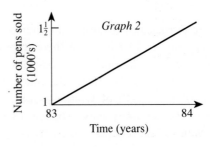

Crammer College publishes its apparently excellent A-level results (see the first two columns of the table below). The third column gives some interesting information not disclosed in the official results.

| Subject | Pass rate | Truth! |
|---------|-----------|--------|
| Italian | 100% | 1 candidate who was Italian |
| Maths | 100% | 4 pupils entered out of 30 |

# Activity 36

Can you see what is wrong in this diagram?

From newspapers and magazines, find three examples of misleading statistics and point out their defects.

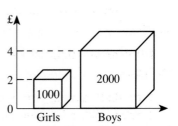

*Average weekly pocket money received by boys and girls under 15 (1992)*

# 10.3 Scatter graphs

A scatter graph is a graph that is plotted to discover if two sets of data are related. For example, this is a scatter graph of the heights of 20 pupils against the heights of their mothers.

The crosses on the graph cluster along a line, showing a definite relationship or **correlation** between the height of a child and the height of its mother. The line, called the **line of best fit**, allows us to estimate the height of a pupil in the class given the mother's height (or vice versa).

It is important not to jump to conclusions from scatter graphs. Just because there appears to be a straight-line relationship, it may not mean that one variable directly affects the other. (A scatter graph of the length of women's skirts and the state of the economy may produce a straight line but there is little connecting the two!)

Conversely, if there is **not** a straight line on a scatter graph, it does not necessarily mean that there is no relationship.

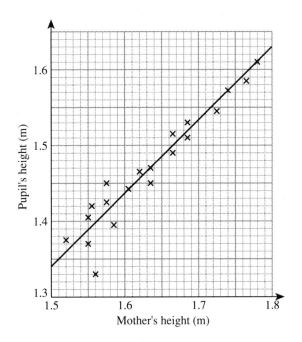

## Exercise 57

1   The marks of ten pupils in a French exam and a German exam were:

| French | 4 | 4 | 5 | 6 | 6 | 8 | 9 | 9 | 10 | 10 |
|--------|---|---|---|---|---|----|---|---|----|----|
| German | 3 | 5 | 5 | 5 | 7 | 10 | 8 | 7 | 9  | 8  |

a Draw a scatter graph for German marks against French marks and insert a 'line of best fit'.
b Use this line to estimate what mark you would expect a pupil to score in the German exam if he or she scored 7.5 in French.

2   The lengths and widths of eight leaves are given below:

| Length (mm) | 50 | 58 | 63 | 71 | 75 | 62 | 80 | 70 |
|-------------|----|----|----|----|----|----|----|----|
| Width (mm)  | 41 | 46 | 55 | 65 | 61 | 50 | 72 | 58 |

a Draw a scatter graph for leaf widths against leaf lengths, and insert a 'line of best fit'.
b What length would you expect a leaf 50 mm wide to be?

3   Sketch what sort of scatter graph you would expect for:
   **a** Daily rainfall against daily sunshine.
   **b** Weights of 10p coins against their ages.
   **c** Hand-spans against shoe sizes.
   **d** Heights of pupils against their weights.

4   Collect your own data for any survey from Question 3. Were your expectations correct?

## ___ Activity 37

Draw lines 9, 12, 15, 18, 21, 24, 27 and 30 cm long on separate blank sheets of paper. Give these sheets in random order to your partner, asking him or her to estimate and mark one third of the way along the line.

For each trisection, measure the error $y$ cm (ignoring whether the error is positive or negative). Plot $y$ against the accurate trisection length $x$ cm. State your conclusions.

# ___ 10.4 Calculating averages

There are three 'averages' used in statistics. The first one – the arithmetic mean, often just called the mean – you will have met before in Books 1 and 2. The median and the mode are defined below. We will use them all to look at the goals scored in a number of matches.

> ___ REMEMBER
>
> • The arithmetic mean $= \dfrac{\text{TOTAL sum of scores}}{\text{TOTAL number of scores}}$
> • The median: when scores are arranged in ascending or descending order, the median is the 'middle' score; it has equal numbers of scores above and below it.
> • The mode is the score that occurs most frequently.

■ *EXAMPLE 1*

The team scored 3, 5, 7, 9, and 11 goals in five matches this season. What was their mean goal score per match?

$$\text{Mean number of goals scored per match} = \frac{3+5+7+9+11}{5} = 7$$

■ *EXAMPLE 2*

Another team scored 3, 11, 9, 6, and 7 goals in their five matches. What is their median goal score per match?

First arrange the scores in order like this: 3, 6, 7, 9, 11. The middle score is 7. Therefore:

Median goal score per match = 7.

■ *EXAMPLE 3*

Find the median goal score per match of a team with the following scores: 3, 11, 9, 6, 8, 7.

First arrange the scores in order: 3, 6, 7, 8, 9, 11. The 'middle score' occurs between 7 and 8. Therefore:

$$\text{Median goal score per match} = \frac{7+8}{2} = 7.5.$$

■ *EXAMPLE 4*

Find the modal goal score if a team scores 3, 11, 6, 5, 4, 3, 3 goals.

The score which occurs most often is 3. Therefore:

Modal goal score per match = 3.

## ▬ Summary

Knowing which of these 'averages' to use for any particular situation is a matter of judgement.

| Advantages | |
| --- | --- |
| *Mean* | Uses all data and can be calculated exactly. |
| *Median* | Easy to understand and not affected by 'freak' scores. |
| *Mode* | Easy to understand and not affected by 'freak' scores. Useful to manufacturers of hats, gloves, etc. (Why?) |

| Disadvantages | |
| --- | --- |
| *Mean* | Can be 'skewed' if there are 'freak' scores. For example, if masses of 5 girls are 7, 8, 7, 9, 15 stones, then mean = 9.2 stone!  This is NOT representative of the group. |
| *Median* | Odd score distribution can give strange results. For example, given scores of 2, 2, 2, 7, 31, then median = 2.  This is NOT representative of the group. |
| *Mode* | Cannot be found exactly in 'grouped' data. |

## ___ Exercise 58

**1** For each set of numbers, calculate (i) the mean   (ii) the median   (iii) the mode:
   **a** 7, 12, 14, 14, 3.
   **b** 21, 31, 11, 16, 18, 4, 4.
   **c** 1.2, 0.9, 1.1, 3.1, 0.7, 0.5.

**2** Five pupils score the following marks (%) for a German test: 44, 56, 64, 35, 50.
   **a** Calculate the mean mark.
   **b** The teacher adds ten marks to each pupil's score. How does this affect the mean?

**3** A keen golfer plays four rounds of golf. If his scores were 88, 98, 91 and 91, which type of average (mean, median or mode) would he prefer to call his 'average'?

**4** A survey of 20 pupils was taken to find how many children there were in their families, with these results:

| Children | 1 | 2 | 3 | 4 | 5 |
|----------|---|---|---|---|---|
| Families | 3 | 6 | 5 | 4 | 2 |

   Calculate **a** the mean,   **b** the median   **c** the mode.
   State which is the most appropriate 'average' to use.

## MASTERMINDERS

**5** What is the mean of 1, 2, 4, 8, 16, 32? Use your answer to work out the mean of
   **a** 99, 100, 102, 106, 114, 130.
   **b** 49.5, 50, 51, 53, 57, 65.

**6** A certain group of 12 boys has a mean age of 10.75; one of them, aged 13.5, leaves the group. What is the mean age of the remaining boys?

**7** Which of the following:
   £12.50, £13, £13.50, £13.90, £14.30
   could not possibly be the mean cost of five books of which one (or more) cost £12, one (or more) cost £15 and the others cost between £12 and £15?

**8** The following five measurements are made of an angle:
   $232°, 233°, 235°, 237°, 238°$
   Two more measurements are made which are 1° apart, and the mean of **all** the measurements is now 234°. What were the extra two measurements?

**9** The mean of $N$ numbers is 7.3. Half the numbers have 1.2 added to them. What is the new mean?

**10** The mean of three numbers, $a$, $b$ and $c$, is 10. What is the mean of
   **a** $6a$, $6b$, $6c$.
   **b** $6a + 1$, $6b + 2$, $6c + 3$?

# 10.5 Frequency distributions

When collecting data, we often sort it into groups (or classes). For example, a school team might record its match goals in the groups 0–1, 2–3, 4–5, and 6 and over. Then a 'frequency table' can be constructed to show how often these scores are obtained.

**Frequency table**

| Number of goals | Frequency |
|---|---|
| 0–1 | 4 |
| 2–3 | 2 |
| 4–5 | 3 |
| 6 and over | 1 |

There are two types of data:

**Discrete**  Goals, typing errors on a page, road accidents, etc.
**Continuous**  Time, length, mass, etc.

## Discrete data

## *Activity 38*

In this Activity you will be testing a paper clip to destruction, recording your results in a frequency table, and combining the results of the whole class to produce a 'frequency distribution'.

Each member of the class will be given five paper clips. Each clip should be bent backwards and forwards through about 90° until it breaks. The number of times this has to be done, before breaking, for all the paper clips in the class should be noted on a table like the one below. (A bend backwards and forwards should count as two bends.)

| Number of bends | Tally | Frequency total |
|---|---|---|
| 1–2 | // | 2 |
| 3–4 | ++++ | 5 |

1   Draw a bar chart showing the results from the whole class. This bar chart is called a 'frequency distribution'. Find the modal class (the number of bends with the highest frequency).

2   Explain why some clips take longer to break than others.

3   Comment on the shape of your frequency distribution. Is it what you expected?

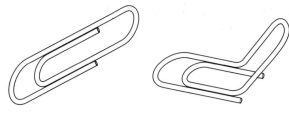

## Activity 39

Working in pairs, roll two dice sixty times, and keep a tally of the combined scores obtained.

1   Copy and complete this table, and enter the results of the whole class.

2   Draw a bar chart showing the frequency of each score, that is, a frequency distribution.

3   Comment on the shape of your frequency distribution. Is it what you expected?

| Score | Tally | Frequency total |
|-------|-------|-----------------|
| 2     |       |                 |
| 3     |       |                 |
| 4     |       |                 |
| 5     |       |                 |
| .     |       |                 |
| .     |       |                 |
| .     |       |                 |
| 12    |       |                 |

## Exercise 59

1   A golf club's annual tournament yields the following results:

| Score     | 76 | 77 | 78 | 79 | 80 | 81 | 82 |
|-----------|----|----|----|----|----|----|----|
| Frequency | 1  | 2  | 4  | 5  | 4  | 3  | 1  |

a Draw the frequency distribution as a bar chart.
b Is the general shape of the bar chart what you would expect? Why?
c What is the modal score?

2   'Fizz' matches claim to have a mean of 50 matches per box. A sample of ten boxes was taken and the number of matches noted:

   50, 51, 49, 52, 52, 47, 47, 51, 49, 50

a Make a frequency table and from it draw the frequency distribution as a bar chart.
b Is the manufacturer's claim justified?

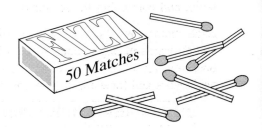

3   Sketch the shape for each of the expected frequency distributions below.
a One die is thrown many times.
b Two dice are thrown many times and the difference in score is noted.
b Three dice are thrown many times and their score combined.

4   Select a page from a book and construct a frequency table for the number of letters contained in each of the first 100 words.
a Draw the frequency distribution as a bar chart.
b Repeat this using the first 100 words from the start of a strip in a comic.
c Compare both frequency distributions, and comment.

189

## ___ Histograms

A histogram is similar to a bar chart because it also represents a frequency distribution. But its 'bars' have areas that represent the given frequencies. At this stage we shall look only at histograms for equal class widths.

■ *EXAMPLE 1*

In a survey of children's heights, the results were:

| Height (h cm) | Frequency |
|---------------|-----------|
| 120–125 | 2 |
| 125–130 | 3 |
| 130–135 | 5 |
| 135–140 | 6 |
| 140–145 | 5 |
| 145–150 | 3 |

Plot these data on a histogram.

The histogram should look like this:

( Note that:
(i) Class intervals for $h$ are:
$$120 \leqslant h < 125$$
$$125 \leqslant h < 130$$
$$130 \leqslant h < 135, \ldots$$
(ii) There are no gaps between the bars.)

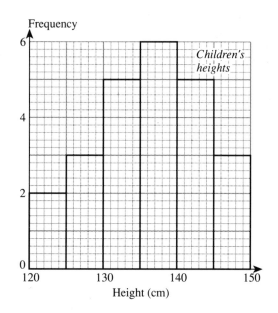

## ___ Frequency polygons

A 'frequency polygon' can be drawn by joining the mid-points of the tops of the rectangles of a histogram. (It is not always necessary to draw the histogram.)

| Time (s) | Frequency |
|----------|-----------|
| 100–120 | 2 |
| 120–140 | 8 |
| 140–160 | 9 |
| 160–180 | 7 |
| 180–200 | 4 |

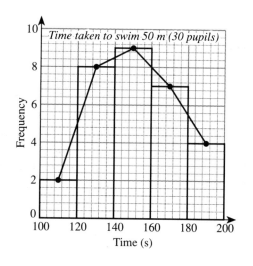

## ■ EXAMPLE 2

The masses at birth of 18 babies in a certain hospital had the following distribution:

| Mass (M kg) | Frequency |
|---|---|
| 2.0–2.5 | 1 |
| 2.5–3.0 | 6 |
| 3.0–3.5 | 9 |
| 3.5–4.0 | 2 |

Display these data on a histogram and then construct a frequency polygon.

The histogram and the frequency polygon for these data are plotted on the right.

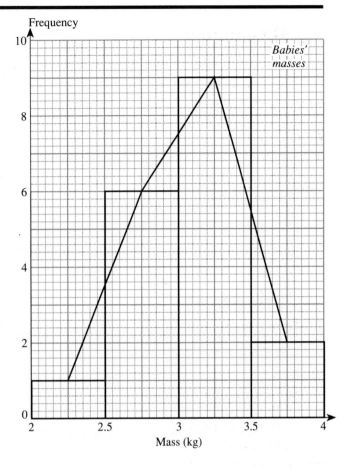

# ▬ Continuous data

# ▬ *Activity 40*

In this Activity your reaction time will be tested.

Pupil A holds a 30 cm ruler vertically between two fingers. Pupil B positions his or her fingers over 0 cm but not touching the ruler. Pupil A releases the ruler without warning and Pupil B aims to catch it as soon as possible. The distance ($y$) the ruler falls is called the 'reaction length'.

*(Continued)*

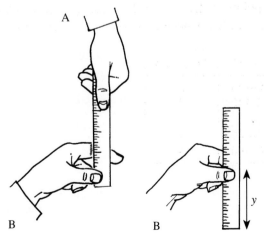

191

# 10 STATISTICS AND PROBABILITY

1   Each pupil in the class should be tested ten times. Enter the results from the class on a table like this:

In Activities 38 and 39 it is obvious in which group any result belongs. In this Activity, the data are continuous. Hence, if a result lies on the group boundary, it is placed in the 'above' group, for example 2–4 means '2 to less than 4', 4–6 means '4 to less than 6', ...

| Reaction length (cm) | Tally | Frequency Total |
|---|---|---|
| 2–4 | II | 2 |
| 4–6 | III | 3 |
| 6–8 | ЖІ | 6 |
| . | | |
| . | | |
| . | | |

2   Draw a histogram and a frequency polygon for these results.

3   Comment on the shape of your frequency distribution. Is it what you expected?

## ____ Exercise 60

1   The times of cross-country runners in a race were distributed as follows:

| Time (min) | 11.5–14.5 | 14.5–17.5 | 17.5–20.5 | 20.5–23.5 |
|---|---|---|---|---|
| Frequency | 3 | 7 | 11 | 4 |

Draw a histogram and a frequency polygon to illustrate the data. Comment on these results.

2   The ages (in completed years) of women who gave birth to a child in a local hospital during April 1990 were:

| Age (years) | 16–22 | 22–28 | 28–34 | 34–40 |
|---|---|---|---|---|
| Frequency | 19 | 64 | 51 | 26 |

Draw a histogram and a frequency polygon to illustrate the data. Comment on these results.

3   The heights of 32 men (in cm) were as follows:

165 174 171 166   181 175 180 173   171 165 168 179   175 172 181 169
165 178 179 181   189 169 188 176   166 177 190 183   179 178 176 166

a Group the data into a frequency table with classes 165–170, 170–175, 175–180, etc.
b Draw a histogram to illustrate the data, and comment on its shape.
c State the modal height class.

4   The sales of a mini-computer over two years were:

| Number sold/week | 1–11 | 12–22 | 23–33 | 34–44 |
|---|---|---|---|---|
| Number of weeks (1990) | 23 | 17 | 10 | 2 |
| Number of weeks (1991) | 3 | 11 | 17 | 21 |

Draw a frequency polygon to show sales in both years on the same grid, without drawing a histogram. Comment on the sales in 1990 and 1991.

# __ 10.6 Probability: single events

Probability theory enables us to calculate the chance of an event occurring if we know the circumstances surrounding it.

Consider the following statements:

'Liverpool will probably win the FA Cup'.
'It probably won't snow this summer'.
'I'll probably pass my maths exam'.

All of these have a degree of uncertainty that could be estimated.

## __ Experimental probability

If we carry out an experiment (often called a 'trial') many times, and count how often event A occurs, we can find the 'experimental probability' of A occurring. The experimental probability $p(A)$ is given by:

> **REMEMBER**
>
> $$p(A) = \frac{\text{Number of times A occurred}}{\text{Total number of trials}}$$

In probability theory we use the following notation:

> **NOTE**
>
> $p(A)$ means the probability of event A happening.
> $p(\overline{A})$ means the probability of event A **not** happening.

■ **EXAMPLE 1**

Event A is that a particular drawing pin lands on its back. It does this 30 times in 120 throws. Find the probability that, on the next throw, it will land on its back, and the probability that it will **not** land on its back.

$$p(A) = \frac{30}{120} = \frac{1}{4} \qquad p(\overline{A}) = \frac{90}{120} = \frac{3}{4}$$

What do you notice?

## *Activity 41*

What is the probability that a person chosen at random from your class was born on an even date? (For example, 2nd, 6th etc.)

1 Copy and complete this table for your class.

| Day | Tally | Total |
|-----|-------|-------|
| Even Odd | | |

2 If A is the event that a person is chosen at random from your class with an even birthday date, calculate **a** $p(A)$ **b** $p(\overline{A})$ **c** $p(A) + p(\overline{A})$.

What do you notice about your answer to part **c**?

## Theoretical probability

If all the possible outcomes are equally likely, we can deduce how many of them ought to be event A – that is, the 'theoretical probability' $p(A)$ – which is:

*REMEMBER*

$$p(A) = \frac{\text{Number of desired outcomes}}{\text{Total number of possible outcomes}}$$

■ *EXAMPLE 2*

A fair die is rolled. Calculate the probability of a prime number being thrown.

The prime numbers are 2, 3 and 5.

Therefore $p(\text{Prime}) = \dfrac{\text{Number of desired outcomes}}{\text{Total number of possible outcomes}} = \dfrac{3}{6} = \dfrac{1}{2}$

■ *EXAMPLE 3*

A two-tailed coin is tossed. If A is the event of a tail being thrown, calculate **a** $p(A)$ **b** $p(\overline{A})$.

**a** $p(A) = \dfrac{2}{2} = 1$   A certainty!

**b** $p(\overline{A}) = p(\text{Head})$

$= \dfrac{0}{2} = 0$   An impossibility!

All probabilities can be measured on a scale from 0 to 1 inclusive.

> ⌐ *REMEMBER*
>
> If A is any event, $0 \leqslant p(A) \leqslant 1$

## ⎯ *Activity 42*

Copy the scale below across your page.

On the scale, judge carefully where you would place the probability that:

**a**   A netball captain wins the toss.
**b**   A club is drawn from a pack of cards.
**c**   A club is not drawn from a pack of cards.
**d**   You will win the Wimbledon Singles title.
**e**   This book has been printed.

If A is any event, it either occurs (A) or it does not (not A or ($\overline{A}$)). Nothing else can happen! Hence:

$$p(A) + p(\overline{A}) = 1 \quad \text{or, more usefully:}$$

> ⌐ *REMEMBER*
>
> $p(\overline{A}) = 1 - p(A)$

## ■ *EXAMPLE 3*

A card is selected at random from a pack of 52 playing cards. Calculate the probability that a King is **not** chosen.

We call A the event that a King **is** selected. Then:

$$p(\overline{A}) = 1 - p(A)$$
$$= 1 - \frac{4}{52}$$
$$= \frac{12}{13}$$

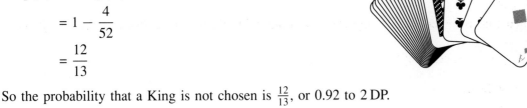

So the probability that a King is not chosen is $\frac{12}{13}$, or 0.92 to 2 DP.

## Exercise 61

1 A fair die is thrown. Calculate the probability of obtaining:
 a A one.
 b An odd number.
 c A number less than four.
 d A one or a six.

2 A 50p and a 20p coin are tossed. Write down all the possible outcomes and calculate the probability of obtaining: **a** two tails **b** a head and a tail.

3 A card is randomly selected from a pack of 52 playing cards. Calculate the probability of obtaining:
 a A black card.
 b A Queen.
 c A number card that is a multiple of 3.
 d A Jack, Queen or King.

4 A bag contains one red, two blue and three green marbles. A marble is selected at random. Calculate the probability that it is: **a** blue **b** green **c** yellow.

5 The bar chart below shows the number of pupils wearing different sock colours in a class.

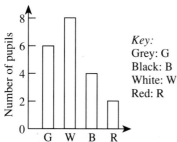

Key:
Grey: G
Black: B
White: W
Red: R

 If a pupil is chosen at random, calculate the probability that he or she will be wearing:
 a Grey socks.
 b White socks.
 c Black or red socks.

6 A pupil chooses a letter randomly from the word TRIGONOMETRY. Calculate the probability that it is:
 a 'T'.
 b A vowel.
 c An 'R' or an 'O'.

7 A coin is tossed and a die is rolled. List all the possible outcomes in a table and calculate the probability of obtaining:
 a A tail and a six.
 b A head and a prime number.
 c A tail and a seven.

**8** David and Melissa play battleships on two $10 \times 10$ grids of squares. Both have in their fleet:

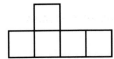

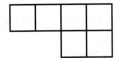

*A battleship*                  *A submarine*                  *An aircraft carrier*

David shoots first, choosing a square randomly. Calculate the probability that he hits:
**a** The aircraft carrier.
**b** The battleship or the submarine.

**9** Comment on the statement that, if a person reaches the age of 105, the probability of him or her living to 106 is 0.5.

## MASTERMINDERS

**10** A black die and a red die are thrown together and their scores added. Copy and complete the table showing all 36 possible outcomes.

|  | Red | | | | | |
|---|---|---|---|---|---|---|
|  | 1 | 2 | 3 | 4 | 5 | 6 |
| 1 | 2 | 3 | 4 | | | |
| 2 | 3 | 4 | | | | |
| Black 3 | 4 | | | | | |
| 4 | | | | | | |
| 5 | | | | | | |
| 6 | | | | | | |

**a** Use your table (called a 'probability space') to calculate the probability of obtaining:
(i) A total of six.
(ii) A total of twelve.
(iii) A total more than ten.
(iv) A total less than four.
**b** What is the most likely total?

**11** The black die and red die in Question 10 are again thrown together.
This time the scores are multiplied.
**a** Draw a probability space similar to that in Question 10. Use it to calculate the probability of obtaining:
(i) A four.
(ii) An even number.
(iii) An eight or a ten.
(iv) A number less than sixteen.
**b** What is the most likely score?

# — 10.7 Probability: combined events

## — Activity 43

In this Activity you will investigate the probability of combined events by throwing two dice.

1   Working in pairs, roll a pair of dice 36 times. Note the outcome of the lefthand (LH) and the righthand (RH) for each throw. Copy and complete the table below showing your scores and the scores for the whole class. (Your teacher will help you gather the latter data.)

Event X: A one is thrown.     Event $\overline{X}$: A one is not thrown.

| LH die | RH die | Scores (frequency) | |
|--------|--------|------|-------|
| | | Yours | Class |
| X | X | | |
| X | $\overline{X}$ | | |
| $\overline{X}$ | X | | |
| $\overline{X}$ | $\overline{X}$ | | |

2   Find, from your completed table of class results, the experimental probability of obtaining:
   **a** XX  **b** $X\overline{X}$  **c** $\overline{X}X$  **d** $\overline{X}\overline{X}$  **e** XX or $\overline{X}\overline{X}$  **f** $X\overline{X}$ or $\overline{X}X$

3   Copy and complete the table below showing all the 36 different outcomes of this Activity. This is its 'probability space'.

| | | RH die | | | | | |
|---|---|---|---|---|---|---|---|
| | | 1 | 2 | 3 | 4 | 5 | 6 |
| | 1 | X X | $\overline{X}$ X | | | | |
| | 2 | X $\overline{X}$ | $\overline{X}$ $\overline{X}$ | | | | |
| LH | 3 | | | | | | |
| die | 4 | | | | | | |
| | 5 | | | | | | |
| | 6 | | | | | | |

Using the table, calculate the theoretical probabilities of **a** to **f** in part 2, above.

4   Compare the experimental and theoretical probabilities, and comment.

This is a long-winded and impractical method to use all the time. Fortunately some simple rules exist that reduce the calculations necessary.

## Multiplication ('and') rule

If two events A and B can occur without being affected by the other (for example, a die is thrown and a coin tossed), then the probability of both A and B is:

### NOTE

$$p(A \ and \ B) = p(A) \times p(B)$$

### ■ EXAMPLE 1

A die is thrown and a coin tossed. Find the probability of the result being a multiple of 3 and a tail.

$p(\text{Tail}) = \dfrac{1}{2}$

$p(\text{Multiple of 3}) = \dfrac{2}{6}$

$p(\text{Tail } and \text{ Multiple of 3}) = \dfrac{1}{2} \times \dfrac{2}{6} = \dfrac{1}{6}$

## Addition ('or') rule

If two events A and B cannot occur at the same time (for example, selecting a King **or** a Queen from a pack of cards), then the probability of either A or B is:

### NOTE

$$p(A \ or \ B) = p(A) + p(B)$$

### ■ EXAMPLE 2

A card is randomly selected from a pack of cards. Find the probability that either a Queen *or* a King is selected.

$p(\text{Queen}) = \dfrac{4}{52}$

$p(\text{King}) = \dfrac{4}{52}$

$p(\text{Queen } or \text{ King}) = \dfrac{4}{52} + \dfrac{4}{52} = \dfrac{2}{13}$

## ▬ Tree diagrams

These are diagrams showing all the possible outcomes. Together with the 'and' and 'or' rules, they make problems easier to solve. Look carefully at the following example which shows how a tree diagram is used.

■ *EXAMPLE 3*

Two dice are thrown. Use a suitable tree diagram to help calculate each of the probabilities listed in part 2 of Activity 43 (page 198).

Event X: A one is thrown.
Event $\overline{X}$: A one is not thrown.

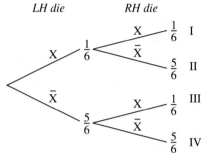

I  $p(XX) = \dfrac{1}{6} \times \dfrac{1}{6} = \dfrac{1}{36}$

II  $p(X\overline{X}) = \dfrac{1}{6} \times \dfrac{5}{6} = \dfrac{5}{36}$

III  $p(\overline{X}X) = \dfrac{5}{6} \times \dfrac{1}{6} = \dfrac{5}{36}$

IV  $p(\overline{X}\,\overline{X}) = \dfrac{5}{6} \times \dfrac{5}{6} = \dfrac{25}{36}$

Note that all the outcomes add up to $\frac{36}{36} = 1$.

Then, using the 'or' (addition) rule,

$$p(XX \text{ or } \overline{X}\,\overline{X}) = p(XX) + p(\overline{X}\,\overline{X})$$
$$= \frac{1}{36} + \frac{25}{36}$$
$$= \frac{26}{36} = \frac{13}{18}$$

$$p(X\overline{X} \text{ or } \overline{X}X) = p(X\overline{X}) + p(\overline{X}X)$$
$$= \frac{5}{36} + \frac{5}{36}$$
$$= \frac{10}{36} = \frac{5}{18}$$

## ___ Exercise 62

Use tree diagrams to help solve the following problems.

1   A fair six-sided die is thrown twice. Calculate the probability of obtaining:
    **a** Two sixes.
    **b** No sixes.
    **c** A six and not a six in that order.
    **d** A six and not a six in any order.

2   A bag contains two red beads and three green beads. One is randomly selected and replaced before another is chosen. Calculate the probability of obtaining:
    **a** Two red beads.
    **b** Two green beads.
    **c** A red and a green bead in that order.
    **d** A red and a green bead in any order.

3   A chest of drawers contains four yellow ties and six blue ties. One is randomly selected and replaced before another is chosen. Calculate the probability of obtaining:
    **a** Two yellow ties.
    **b** Two blue ties.
    **c** A yellow and a blue tie in that order.
    **d** A yellow and a blue tie in any order.

4   A hockey player's probability of scoring from a penalty is 2/3. If she attempts two penalties, calculate the probability that she scores:
    **a** Two goals.
    **b** One goal.
    **c** No goals.

5   About 10% of men are colour blind, and about 20% are lefthanded. If a man is selected randomly, calculate the probability that he is:
    **a** Colour blind and lefthanded.
    **b** Colour blind and righthanded.
    **c** Neither colour blind nor lefthanded.

6   Charlotte oversleeps one day in five, and on such occasions breaks a shoelace two out of three times. If both catastrophes happen together, she is late for school. What is the probability of her being late for school?

# 10 STATISTICS AND PROBABILITY

## ■ EXAMPLE 4

A fruit basket contains two oranges (O) and three apples (A). A fruit is selected at random and not replaced before another is randomly selected. Calculate the probability of choosing:

**a** An orange and apple in that order.
**b** An orange and apple in any order.
**c** At least one orange.

First draw a tree diagram. Note that when the second fruit is picked out, there are only **four** fruits left. Therefore the denominator for each probability is four.

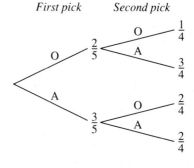

*First pick*   *Second pick*

**a** $p(OA) = \dfrac{2}{5} \times \dfrac{3}{4} = \dfrac{6}{20} = \dfrac{3}{10}$

**b** $p(OA \text{ or } AO) = p(OA) + p(AO)$

$$= \dfrac{6}{20} + \dfrac{6}{20} = \dfrac{12}{20} = \dfrac{3}{5}$$

**c** If at least one orange is selected, then two apples must **not** be selected. Therefore:

$p(\text{At least 1 orange}) = 1 - p(AA)$

$$= 1 - \dfrac{3}{10} = \dfrac{7}{10}$$

## ▬ Exercise 63

Use tree diagrams to solve the following problems.

1 A box contains two red marbles and five green marbles. One is randomly selected and not replaced before another is chosen. Calculate the probability of obtaining:
 a Two red marbles.
 b A red and a green marble in any order.
 c At least one green marble.

2 An archer fires his arrows at a target. The probability that he scores a bullseye in any one attempt is 1/3. If he fires twice, calculate the probability that he scores:
 a Two bullseyes.
 b No bullseyes.
 c At least one bullseye.

3 A chocolate box contains four milk chocolates and five plain chocolates. Helen loves milk chocolates and hates plain chocolates. She is told by her mother to select one randomly before a second is chosen, without replacing her first choice. Calculate the probability that:
 a Helen is very happy.
 b Helen is very unhappy.
 c Helen has at least one milk chocolate.

202

**4** A biased coin has $p(\text{Head}) = \frac{1}{3}$. It is tossed three times. Calculate the probabilities of obtaining:
**a** Three heads.
**b** Two heads and a tail in any order.
**c** At least two heads.

**5** Mr and Mrs Brood plan to have a family of three children. The probability of their producing a boy is equal to that of producing a girl. Calculate the probability that their family will contain:
**a** Three girls.
**b** Only one boy.
**c** More girls than boys.
**d** At least one boy.

**6** The probability that Mr Glum remembers his wife's birthday and buys her a present is $\frac{1}{3}$.

The probability that he does not lose it on the way home is $\frac{2}{3}$.

The probability that Mrs Glum likes the present is $\frac{1}{5}$.
Calculate the probability that Mrs Glum:
**a** Receives her birthday present.
**b** Receives her birthday present and doesn't like it.
**c** Is happy on her birthday.
**d** Is not happy on her birthday.

## MASTERMINDERS

**7** A box contains two red sweets and three green sweets. A sweet is selected at random. If a red sweet is picked on the first attempt, then two extra reds are placed in the box. If a green sweet is picked on the first attempt, then three extra greens are placed in the box. (Note that the first selected sweet is not replaced.) Calculate the probability of selecting from two attempts:
**a** Two red sweets.
**b** Two green sweets.
**c** No green sweets.
**d** At least one green sweet.

**8** A card is randomly selected from a pack of cards. Why is the following calculation, to find the probability that the card is either a Heart or a King, incorrect?

$p(\text{Heart } or \text{ King}) = p(\text{Heart}) + p(\text{King})$

$$= \frac{13}{52} + \frac{4}{52} = \frac{17}{52}$$

**9** Three dice are thrown. What is the probability of obtaining:
**a** Two sixes.
**b** Two of a kind.
**c** At least one six.

## _Activity 44_

Here are computer programs to solve two problems.

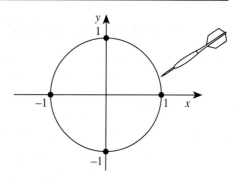

**1   How to estimate $\pi$ using the 'Monte Carlo method'**
If $N$ random shots are fired at a circular target
(equation $x^2 + y^2 = r^2$, where $r$ is the radius of
the circle), $\pi$ can be estimated by the formula:

$$\pi \approx 4 \times \frac{\text{Number of hits}}{\text{Number of throws}}$$

| Program | Explanation |
|---|---|
| 10 REM "MONTE CARLO APPROX FOR PI" | |
| 20 INPUT "NO. OF SHOTS    ", N | How many throws? |
| 30 LET H = 0 | Number of hits is zero |
| 40 FOR SH = 1 TO N | $N$ shots fired at target |
| 50 LET X = RND(1) | Random value of $x$ chosen |
| 60 LET Y = RND(1) | Random value of $y$ chosen |
| 70 LET R = X^2 + Y^2 | Equation of circle |
| 80 IF R<= 1 THEN LET H=H+1 | If point is in the circle this is a 'hit' |
| 90 NEXT SH | |
| 100 LET A = 4*H/N | |
| 110 PRINT "MONTE CARLO APPROX FOR PI IS "; A | |
| 120 END | |

What happens to your approximation to $\pi$ as $N$ is increased?

**2   Using a computer to 'simulate' throwing two dice** A faster method for gathering data in
Activity 43 is to use a computer program to simulate a large number of throws.

| Program | Explanation |
|---|---|
| 10 DIM F(12) | Sets up array F(0) to F(12) |
| 20 INPUT N | How many throws? |
| 30 FOR T = 1 TO N | For all $N$ throws |
| 40 LET X = RND(6) | $x$ is a random number 1 to 6 |
| 50 LET Y = RND(6) | $y$ is a random number 1 to 6 |
| 60 LET Z = X+Y | $z$ is a random number 2 to 12 |
| 70 PRINT Z | |
| 80 LET F(Z) = F(Z)+1 | |
| 90 NEXT T | |
| 100 PRINT TAB(6); "TOTAL FREQUENCY" | |
| 110 FOR Z = 2 TO 12 | |
| 120 PRINT Z, F(Z) | |
| 130 NEXT Z | |
| 140 END | |

Illustrate your results on a suitable bar chart. Comment.

## ▬ Revision Exercise 10

**1** A survey of musical tastes in a class of pupils gave the following results:

| Music | Classical | 'Pop' | Jazz | 'Rock' |
|---|---|---|---|---|
| Number of pupils | 6 | 8 | 3 | 7 |

Show this data in **a** a pie chart  **b** a bar chart.

**2** The pie chart shows the sales from a sports shop on a certain day. If the total sales were £8000, find the sales value of: **a** football boots (F)  **b** running shoes (R)  **c** tennis rackets (T)  **d** tracksuits (S).

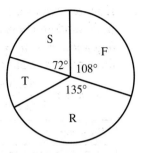

**3** Eight woman and four men attended a typing class. After two weeks the number of words that they could type per minute were:

| Women | 21 | 16 | 17 | 13 | 21 | 24 | 19 | 21 |
|---|---|---|---|---|---|---|---|---|
| Men | 15 | 19 | 23 | 23 | | | | |

Calculate the mean, median and mode words per minute for:
**a** the women  **b** the men  **c** the whole class.

**4** Anna's average score for her exams was 74%. Her individual scores were 75%, 62%, 85%, 59% and 70%, with only her History mark missing. What percentage did she obtain in History?

**5** Applicants for the Fire Brigade are asked to hold their breath for as long as possible. These results, together with their chest measurements, are shown below:

| Chest (cm) | 85 | 89 | 90 | 93 | 95 | 99 | 102 |
|---|---|---|---|---|---|---|---|
| Time (s) | 41 | 43 | 42 | 51 | 52 | 61 | 61 |

**a** Draw a scatter graph of chest measurement (cm) against breath holding time (s).
**b** Use this graph to estimate the breath-holding time of an applicant with a chest measurement of 92 cm.

**6** A batch of 150 apples had a mass distribution as follows:

| Mass (g) | 60–80 | 80-100 | 100–120 | 120–140 |
|---|---|---|---|---|
| Frequency | 12 | 41 | 52 | 45 |

Draw a histogram and a frequency polygon to illustrate the data. What do they tell you about this batch of apples?

**7** A survey of children's mean weekly pocket money in pence produced the following results:

```
20  25  20  30  45  50  40  80
85  75  70  30  60  65  70  90
45  40  80  65  75  75  70  80
```

**a** Group the data into a frequency table of classes 20p–30p, 30p–40p, 40p–50p, etc.
**b** Draw a histogram and a frequency polygon to illustrate this data. Comment on their shapes.

**8** A letter is randomly selected from the sentence, 'All the world's a stage and all the men and women merely players.' Calculate the probability that it is: **a** a   **b** t   **c** a vowel   **d** x.

**9** This pentagonal spinner is spun twice and the scores are added together. Copy and complete the probability space table showing the possible sums of the two scores.

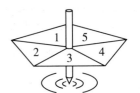

*1st spin*

|     | 1 | 2 | 3 | 4 | 5 |
|-----|---|---|---|---|---|
| 1   | 2 | 3 | 4 |   |   |
| 2   | 3 | 4 |   |   |   |
| 3   | 4 |   |   |   |   |
| 4   |   |   |   |   |   |
| 5   |   |   |   |   |   |

*2nd spin*

Use this table to calculate:
**a** $p$(The sum is 4).
**b** $p$(The sum is 6).
**c** $p$(The sum is 11).
**d** $p$(The sum is at least 7).
**e** $p$(The sum is less than 5).
What have you assumed about the spinner?

**10** A soccer player rates his chances of scoring a goal in a match as 2/7. Find the probability that in his next two matches he scores: **a** no goals **b** one goal in each **c** one goal.

**11** A box of chocolates contains two caramels, four turkish delights and three toffees. One is randomly selected and **not** replaced before another is chosen. Use a tree diagram to calculate the probability of obtaining:
**a** Two caramels.
**b** A turkish delight and a toffee in that order.
**c** A turkish delight and a toffee in any order.
**e** At least one caramel.

## MASTERMINDER

**12** Box X contains two black beads and three white beads.
Box Y contains three black beads and two white beads.
A bead is randomly taken from box X and is then placed in box Y. A bead is then randomly selected from box Y.
Find the probability that this bead is:
**a** black   **b** white.

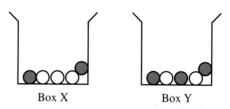

Box X          Box Y

## Aural Test 3

Twenty questions will be read out to you. You may do any workings on a piece of paper. You will need the following information to answer Questions 11 to 20.

**11 to 14** The table below shows the number of goals scored in 20 hockey matches by Miss Hitter's team.

| Goals | Frequency total |
|-------|-----------------|
| 0 | 2 |
| 1 | 4 |
| 2 | 6 |
| 3 | 5 |
| 4 | 2 |
| 5 | 1 |

**15 to 18** A telephone call is charged at the rate of 5p per unit. The table below shows the time allowed for one unit in seconds.

| Cheap rate 6 pm to 8 am | Standard rate 8 am to 9 am 1 pm to 6 pm | Peak rate 9 am to 1 pm |
|--------------------------|------------------------------------------|-------------------------|
| 360 | 90 | 60 |

Cheap Rate is charged all day Saturday and Sunday.

**19 a** 20 m/s   **b** 10 cm/s   **c** 0.1 km/s   **d** 10 m/s   **e** 5 m/s
**20 a** 1440   **b** 3600   **c** 2400   **d** 2000   **e** 6000

## Puzzlers

1 **Practical** Devise a suitable method, and use it, to divide a ball of string, or the ribbon on an electric typewriter spool, into ten equal lengths without using a tape measure or ruler.

2 The diagram shows a sailing boat with two masts of height 12 m and 8 m. If the supporting wires cross at a height of 4.8 m above the deck, **investigate** the distance between the masts.

3 Draw any triangle ABC. Find the position of a point T such that the three triangles ABT, BCT, ACT have equal areas.

4 Copy the six-pointed star and place the integers 1 to 12 in the circles so that the sum of the numbers along each of the six straight lines is 26.

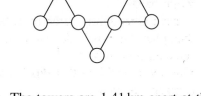

5 Archimedes (287–212 BC) developed a method to trisect an angle using only a pair of compasses and an unmarked ruler. How did he do it? (Note that he violated Plato's rules in that he made two marks on his ruler.)

6 The height of each tower of the Humber Bridge is 162.5 m. The towers are 1.41 km apart at the base but 36 mm further apart at the top. Estimate the radius of the Earth.

# Coursework: Traffic flow problem

A oneway road system is represented by the network shown in
Figure 1. The probability of a vehicle turning into a road at a junction
of two accessible roads is 1/2; at a junction of three accessible roads
is 1/3, etc. An arrow shows the direction of traffic flow.

In this Coursework  $p(A)$  means the probability of reaching A from X.
$p(B)$  means the probability of reaching B from X.

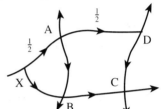

**Figure 1**

1  A car is at junction X. Copy the network in Figure 1 and write down the probability of going
   from X to B and from A to B.
   **a** Work out $p(A)$ and $p(B)$.
   **b** Sixty vehicles pass through X. How many vehicles would you expect to pass
      (i) junction A   (ii) junction B   (iii) junction B not via A?

2  The road system is extended as shown in Figure 2. A car is at
   junction X.
   **a** Copy the network and write down the probability of turning
      into each of the roads.
   **b** Find (i) $p(A)$   (ii) $p(B)$   (iii) $p(C)$   (iv) $p(D)$.
   **c** Sixty vehicles pass through X. How many would you expect
      to pass through the junction at (i) A   (ii) B   (iii) C   (iv) D?

**Figure 2**

3  You are now going to simulate traffic flow through the road network using a die. After a vehicle
   arrives at a junction, the die is thrown and the number dictates the vehicle direction as shown
   in Table 1.

| Die score | Junction |
|---|---|
| Odd | X → A |
| Even | X → B |
| 1, 2 | A → B |
| 3, 4 | A → D |
| Odd | B → C |
| Even | D → C |

**Table 1**

| Vehicle number | Die score | A | B | C | D |
|---|---|---|---|---|---|
| 1 | 3, 1, 4 | ✓ | ✓ | | |
| 2 | 6, 2 | | ✓ | | |
| 3 | 5, 5 | ✓ | | | |
| ⋮ | | | | | |
| 60 | | | | | |

**Table 2**

   **a** Copy and complete Table 2 for 60 vehicles starting at junction X, noting your final tally of
      vehicles through each junction. Write down the number of vehicles which pass through A, B,
      C and D.
   **b** Draw a frequency distribution for sixty vehicles entering the network at X using (i) the
      theoretical results from 2c and (ii) the experimental results from 3a. Compare and comment.

## EXTENSION

4  The planners want to reduce the traffic flow through C. 3600 vehicles per hour is the maximum
   flow through X. C is designed to cope with a maximum traffic flow of 1250 vehicles per hour.
   Two proposals are made: **a** a direct one-way road from B to D   **b** reversing the direction of
   traffic between C and D. Which would fulfil the design requirements?

# 11 GEOMETRY II

## ___ 11.1 Basic principles

Reflection, rotation and translation are three basic transformations. They change the position of an object but not its size or shape. Look carefully at these examples.

## ___ Reflections

**■ EXAMPLE 1**
Reflect point A (5, 1) in the line $y = x$ and label its image B.

The line joining point A to its image B is at right angles to the mirror line $y = x$.

A and B are the same distances from the mirror line.

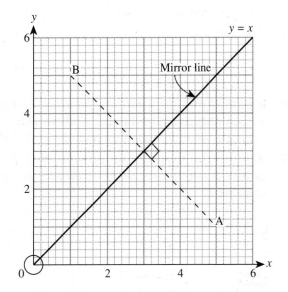

**■ EXAMPLE 2**
A is a pentagon with vertices (0, 0), (2, 4), (2, 2), (4, 0), (4, −2). Reflect A in the $y$-axis and label its image B.

(The construction lines joining points to their images have not been drawn. This is only necessary when the reflection is not straightforward.)

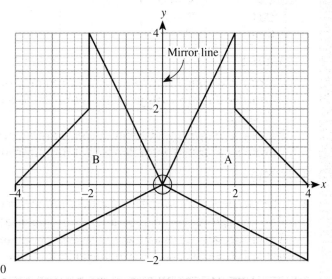

## __ Rotations

■ *EXAMPLE 3*

Rotate point A (4, 1) 90° anticlockwise about
centre (1, 1) and label its image B.

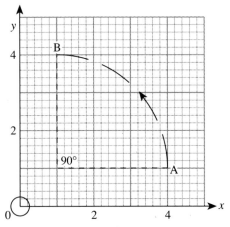

■ *EXAMPLE 4*

Flag A has vertices (4, 0), (4, 2), (4, 4), (6, 3).
Rotate flag A +90° about centre (0, −2) and label its image B.

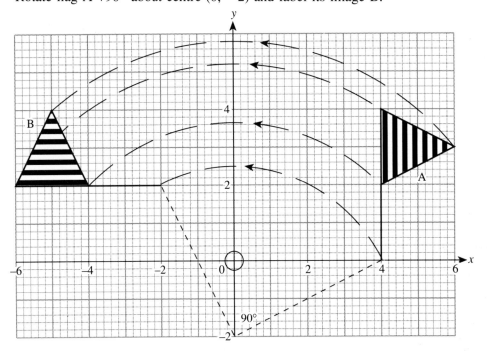

It is usually possible to simply draw the image of rotations by inspection. If you do find difficulty in
doing this, either use tracing paper or rotate the figure point by point and join up the rotated points
for the image.

210

# ▬ Translations

## ■ *EXAMPLE 5*

Translate point A (1, 2) along vector $\begin{pmatrix} 5 \\ -6 \end{pmatrix}$
and label its image B.

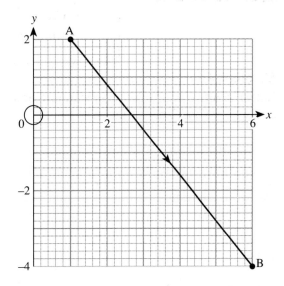

It is more usual to translate whole figures than single points.

## ■ *EXAMPLE 6*

A is an arrow head with vertices (2, 1), (4, 4), (6, 1), (4, 2). Translate A along vector $\begin{pmatrix} -6 \\ -4 \end{pmatrix}$
and label its image B.

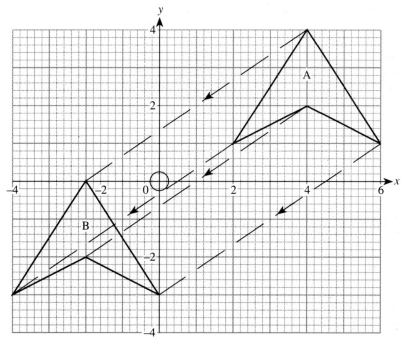

## — Notation

It is convenient to express transformations by a symbol, as in the following example.

If:     A is the translation along $\begin{pmatrix} 3 \\ -4 \end{pmatrix}$.

        B is the reflection in the line $x = 3$.

        C is the rotation of $+90°$ about the origin.

Then:   A(F) means 'Perform transformation A on F'.

        B(F) means 'Perform transformation B on F'.

        C(F) means 'Perform transformation C on F'.

We write the result of a transformation like this:

       A(F) → G, that is, F is 'mapped onto' G by transformation A.

Similarly B(F) → H, and C(F) → I. Check that these transformations are correct on the diagram below.

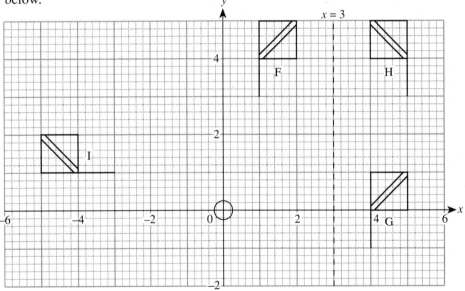

## — Exercise 64

1   Draw $x$ and $y$ axes from 6 to $-6$. Plot the points $(1, 0)$, $(0, 2)$ and $(-1, 0)$. Join these points to make a triangle and label the triangle T. On your graph plot the image of triangle T under each of the following translations:

$\begin{pmatrix} 5 \\ 0 \end{pmatrix}$ and label the image A.        $\begin{pmatrix} 1 \\ -5 \end{pmatrix}$ and label the image B.

$\begin{pmatrix} 4 \\ 4 \end{pmatrix}$ and label the image C.        $\begin{pmatrix} -5 \\ 3 \end{pmatrix}$ and label the image D.

$\begin{pmatrix} 0 \\ -6 \end{pmatrix}$ and label the image E.        $\begin{pmatrix} -4 \\ -2 \end{pmatrix}$ and label the image F.

**2** This diagram shows eight separate translations of the shaded triangle. Write down the column vector to describe each translation.

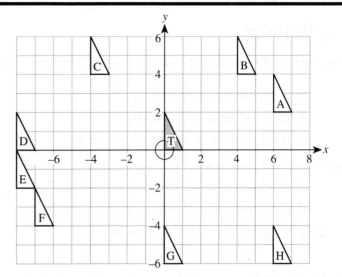

**3** Study the figure below.

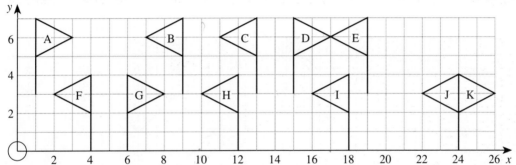

The table gives details of twelve reflections. Using the figure, copy and complete this table.

|   | Object | Reflection in line | Image |
|---|--------|--------------------|-------|
| **a** | A | x = 5 | B |
| **b** | F | x = 5 |  |
| **c** | G |  | F |
| **d** | A | x = 7 |  |
| **e** | D |  | B |
| **f** |  | x = 9 | H |
| **g** | K |  | J |
| **h** |  | x = 12 | G |
| **i** |  | x = 18 |  |
| **j** |  | x = 10 | A |
| **k** | J |  | G |
| **l** |  | x = 17 |  |

What would be the co-ordinates of the image of flag C under a reflection in the line
**a** x = 101  **b** x = a?

**4** Draw $x$ and $y$ axes from 5 to $-5$. Plot the points $(0, 5)$, $(4, 4)$, $(0, 0)$ and join them to form a triangle. Label this triangle A.

**a** Reflect triangle A in: (i) $x = 0$ and label the image B   (ii) $y = x$ and label the image C.

**b** Reflect triangle C in $x = 0$ and label the image D.

**c** Triangle D can be mapped onto triangle B by a reflection in a certain line. Draw this line on your graph. Write down the equation of this line.

**5** The diagram shows a flag in nine different positions. Each flag can be rotated onto one or more of the other flags. For example, flag A can be rotated onto flag F through $90°$ clockwise about $(-1, 0)$.

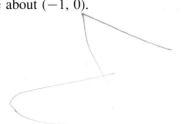

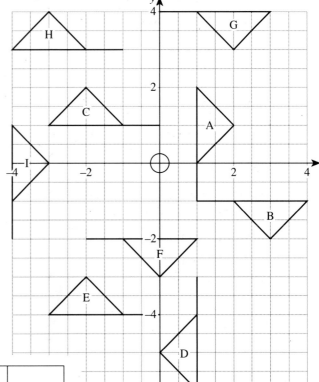

The table below shows details of thirteen rotations. Copy this table and complete it by using the diagram.

| Object | Rotation | | Image |
| | centre | angle | |
| --- | --- | --- | --- |
| B | $(0, -2)$ | $90°$ clockwise | |
| A | $(1, -2)$ | $180°$ | |
| D | | | B |
| G | $(1, -1)$ | $90°$ anticlockwise | |
| F | | | I |
| I | $(-3, -3)$ | | |
| | $(0, 2\frac{1}{2})$ | | G |
| D | $(-1, -4)$ | | |
| | $(3, 1)$ | | D |
| | $(-3, 0)$ | $90°$ anticlockwise | |
| | $(-1\frac{1}{2}, -2\frac{1}{2})$ | | D |
| | $(-\frac{1}{2}, 3\frac{1}{2})$ | | |
| C | | $90°$ anticlockwise | |

**6** Draw $x$ and $y$ axes from 4 to $-4$. Draw the lines $y = x$ and $y = -x$ and plot the point A (3, 2). Rotate A about (0, 0) through
**a** 90° clockwise.
**b** 90° anticlockwise.
**c** 180°.
Write down the co-ordinates of the image in each case. Use your answers to work out the co-ordinates of the image of (16, 61) rotated through the same angles.

For Questions 7 and 8, draw $x$ and $y$ axes from 5 to $-5$, using the same scale for both axes.

**7** **a** Plot the points (4, 2), (4, 5) and (2, 5), and join them to form triangle T.
A denotes a reflection in $x = 1$.
B denotes a rotation of $+90°$ about centre (5, 0).
C denotes a rotation of $-90°$ about centre (0, $-1$).
**b** A(T) $\rightarrow$ P. Draw and label triangle P.
**c** B(T) $\rightarrow$ Q. Draw and label triangle Q.
**d** C(Q) $\rightarrow$ R. Draw and label triangle R.
**e** Describe fully the single transformation that maps triangle R onto triangle T.

**8** **a** Plot the points (5, 1), (5, 2) and (2, 1), and join them to form triangle T.
A denotes a reflection in $y = -1$.
B denotes a translation along $\begin{pmatrix} -2 \\ 2 \end{pmatrix}$.
C denotes a reflection in $x = 1$.
**b** A(T) $\rightarrow$ R. Draw and label triangle R.
**c** B(T) $\rightarrow$ U. Draw and label triangle U.
**d** C(R) $\rightarrow$ S. Draw and label triangle S.
**e** Describe fully the single transformation that maps triangle S onto triangle U.

# 11.2 Enlargements

When an object is enlarged, its size is altered but its shape remains unchanged.

> *NOTE*
>
> To apply an enlargement, we must be given:
> - The centre of enlargement.
> - The scale factor of enlargement.

(An enlargement can also mean a **reduction** in size, in which case the scale factor is less than 1.)

## Activity 45

1 The diagram shows triangle XYZ transformed onto triangle X'Y'Z' by an enlargement from centre C.

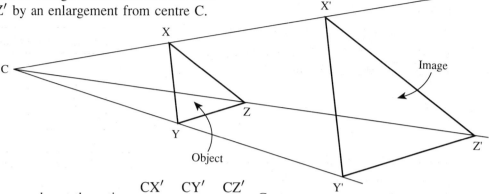

**a** By measuring, work out the ratios: $\dfrac{CX'}{CX}$, $\dfrac{CY'}{CY}$, $\dfrac{CZ'}{CZ}$. Comment.

**b** What factor increases the length of each of the sides of the triangle XYZ? Your answer is called the 'scale factor of enlargement'.

**c** **Investigate** the relative area of each triangle.

2 This diagram shows triangle PQR transformed onto triangle P'Q'R' by an 'enlargement' from centre O.

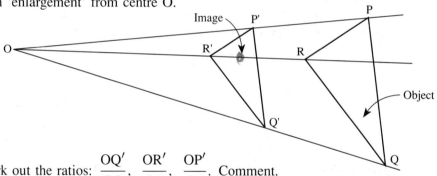

**a** By measuring, work out the ratios: $\dfrac{OQ'}{OQ}$, $\dfrac{OR'}{OR}$, $\dfrac{OP'}{OP}$. Comment.

**b** What factor reduces the length of each of the sides of the triangle PQR? Your answer is called the 'scale factor of enlargement'.

**c** **Investigate** the relative area of each triangle.

> **NOTE**
>
> When applying an enlargement:
> - If necessary, plot the given shape and the centre of enlargement.
> - Draw straight lines from the centre through each vertex.
> - Plot the image.
>   (Object distance from centre of enlargement × Scale factor =
>     Image distance from centre of enlargement)

## Exercise 65

For each of Questions 1 to 4, draw separate $x$ and $y$ axes from 4 to $-4$, using the same scale on both axes.

**1** Plot the triangle PQR where P $(-1, 1)$, Q $(-\frac{1}{2}, 1)$ and R $(-1, 2)$. Draw the image for each enlargement in the table:

|   | Scale factor | Centre of enlargement |
|---|---|---|
| a | 4 | $(0, 2)$ |
| b | 3 | $(-1\frac{1}{2}, 3)$ |
| c | 5 | $(-1\frac{1}{2}, 1\frac{1}{2})$ |
| d | 2 | $(0, 0)$ |

**2** Plot the triangle LMN where L $(1, 0)$, M $(1, -1)$ and N $(0, -1)$. Draw the image for each enlargement in the table:

|   | Scale factor | Centre of enlargement |
|---|---|---|
| a | $3\frac{1}{2}$ | $(0, 0)$ |
| b | $2\frac{1}{2}$ | $(3, -3)$ |
| c | $1\frac{1}{2}$ | $(4, 2)$ |
| d | $2\frac{1}{2}$ | $(0, -2)$ |

**3** Plot the triangle EFD where E $(0, 0)$, F $(2, 4)$ and D $(2, -2)$. Draw the image for each enlargement in the table:

|   | Scale factor | Centre of enlargement |
|---|---|---|
| a | $\frac{1}{2}$ | $(-1, 1)$ |
| b | $\frac{1}{2}$ | $(-4, 0)$ |
| c | $\frac{3}{4}$ | $(0, 0)$ |
| d | $\frac{1}{4}$ | $(-2, -4)$ |

**4** Plot the triangle RST where R $(2, 0)$, S $(1, 0)$ and T $(0, 2)$. Draw the image for each enlargement in the table:

|   | Scale factor | Centre of enlargement |
|---|---|---|
| a | 2 | $(4, 4)$ |
| b | $\frac{1}{2}$ | $(0, 0)$ |
| c | $\frac{1}{2}$ | $(0, -2)$ |
| d | $1\frac{1}{2}$ | $(-1\frac{1}{2}, 0)$ |

**5** Work out the scale factor of enlargement which transforms:
  **a** A onto B  **b** A onto C  **c** B onto A  **d** C onto A  **e** B onto C  **f** C onto B.

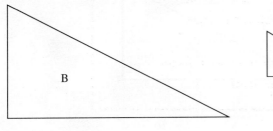

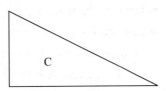

**6** These three photographs of King's College, Cambridge, have been printed from the same negative.

A  B  C

In each photograph, measure the height $h$ from the ground to the highest pinnacle.

**a** For A transformed onto B and for B transformed onto C, work out: (i) the scale factor of enlargement   (ii) the percentage reduction.

**b** If the actual height of the pinnacle is 60 m, work out an estimate of the scale of the photograph labelled A.

**7** The two triangles drawn have the same shape.

**a** Find the scale factor of enlargement which transforms triangle F onto triangle E.

**b** Use your answer to part **a** to work out the length of $x$.

**c** Explain the connection between working with scale factors of enlargements and similar triangles.

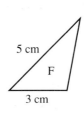
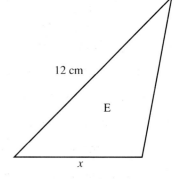

## MASTERMINDER

**8** Find the centre and the scale factor of enlargement which transform triangle P onto triangle Q.

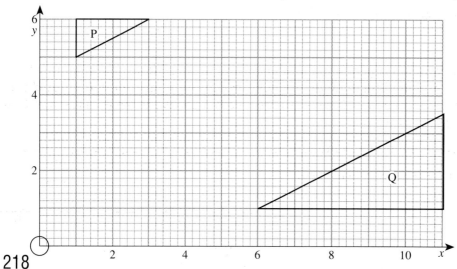

# — 11.3 Loci

The locus of a point is the path which it describes when it moves under given conditions. (Note that the plural of locus is loci.)

## — *Activity 46*

Suppose a number of pupils from the class stand 2 m from a given wall in the classroom. A diagram to show their likely positions is shown below, together with a brief description of their positions. (*Note*: each cross denotes a pupil.)

*Plan (above) view*

Their positions form a straight line which is parallel to the wall and 2 m from it.

A number of pupils from the class should now stand in exactly the positions given in each of the following. Draw separate diagrams for each and give a brief description:

**1**   1 m from the centre of a given desk.

**2**   3 m from a given corner of a room.

**3**   1 m from the given edge of a desk.

**4**   Equidistant from two adjacent corners of a room.

**5**   Equidistant from two opposite corners of a room.

**6**   Equidistant from two adjacent walls of a room.

**7**   Equidistant from two opposite walls of a room.

■ *EXAMPLE 1*

Draw a line and mark on it two points A and B 10 cm apart. Draw the locus of a point which is **a** 4 cm above the line   **b** 5 cm from A. Mark on your diagram two points which are 4 cm above the line and 5 cm from A. Measure the distance between the two points and the distance from B to the point which is the nearer of the two to B.

The diagram should look like this, but drawn to scale:

The two points are 6 cm apart and the point nearer to B is 8 cm from it.

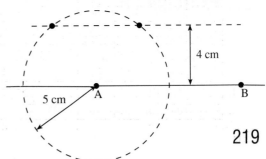

**■ EXAMPLE 2**

Copy the diagram of the letter T to full scale.
Draw the locus of the point which is 1 cm from
the letter.

The locus is :

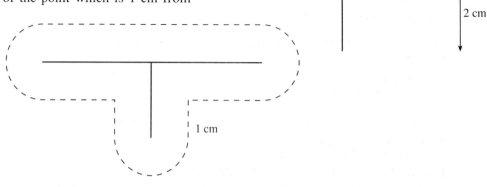

## Constructions with a pair of compasses

● To bisect the angle ABC, use your compasses
as shown.

OB is part of the locus (set of points) which is
equidistant from AB and BC.

● To bisect the line XY, and to construct a right
angle, use your compasses as shown.

PQ is part of the locus (set of points) which is
equidistant from X and Y.

● To draw a line parallel to the given line AB,
use your compasses as shown.

PQ is the locus (set of points) which is, on one
side of AB, equidistant from AB.

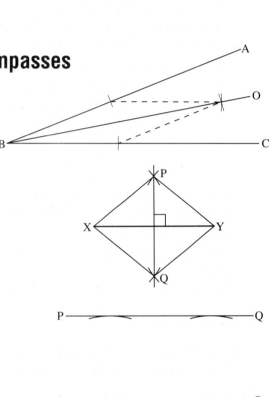

## Exercise 66

Diagrams may be drawn to any suitable scale, if necessary.

1    A line AB is 10 cm long. Draw the locus of the point which is:
    **a** 5 m from A.
    **b** 5 cm from B.
    **c** 5 cm from the midpoint of AB.

2 A line PQ is 12 cm long. Draw the locus of the point which is:
   **a** 6 cm from the midpoint of PQ.
   **b** 6 cm above PQ.
   **c** 6 cm below PQ.

3 A line XY is 16 cm long. Draw the locus of the point which is:
   **a** 4 cm above XY.
   **b** 4 cm below XY.
   **c** 4 cm from the midpoint of XY.

4 Describe as precisely as possible the locus of each of the following:
   **a** A doorknob of an opening door.
   **b** The head of a girl sliding down the bannisters.
   **c** The valve on a bicycle moving in a straight line.
   **d** The centre of the top of an empty icecream cone rolling on a table.

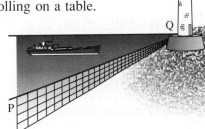

5 PQ is a breakwater, 750 m long, with a lighthouse at Q. By making a suitable scale drawing, find the distance from P of a ship which is 190 m from the breakwater and 280 m from the lighthouse.

6 A ladder is 15 m long and is resting almost vertically against a wall. If the bottom of the ladder is pulled out from the wall, sketch the locus of the middle rung of the ladder.

7 Some treasure is hidden in a field in which there are three trees, an ash (A), a beech (B) and a chestnut (C). BC = 300 m, CA = 210 m and AB = 165 m. If the treasure is at the same distance from the chestnut as from the beech, and 60 m from the ash, make a suitable scale drawing to find out how far the treasure can be from the beech tree.

## MASTERMINDERS

8 Copy the triangle ABC of Question 7, and find by construction the points which are equidistant from A and B and also equidistant from CA and CB. Measure their distances from A.

9 A and B are two points 5 cm apart. Plot the locus of the point P such that AP + PB = 9 cm. (A short piece of string may be useful.)

10 Cut out a triangle from a piece of card. By balancing the card on the edge of a ruler, find the centre of gravity of the triangle. Repeat the experiment and deduce a method to find the centre of gravity by construction.

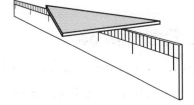

# __ 11.4 Maps and bearings

## __ Bearings

These are measured clockwise from the North.

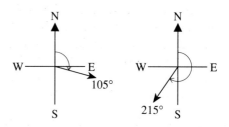

## __ Grid references

Remember to write the Eastings before the Northings.

The shaded grid square in the diagram is denoted by the four-figure grid reference 1030.

The points A, B and C are denoted by the respective six-figure grid references: 115310, 140310, 115320.

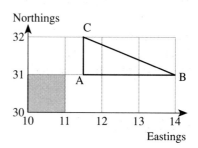

## __ Map scales

The perpendicular distance between two adjacent Eastings (or Northings) is always 1 km.

In the example above the length AB represents a distance of 2.5 km. The shaded area represents 1 km$^2$. The area ABC represents 1.25 km$^2$.

In this section you are expected to find each answer **by drawing and measuring**, unless otherwise asked.

In some questions we use the lines on graph paper to represent the grid lines on a map. This is called a 'map-grid'. For convenience all map-grids will be labelled as shown in Activity 47 (that is, Northings from 20 to 26 and Eastings from 50 to 54).

## Activity 47

1  **a** Copy this map-grid onto a quarter of a
   piece of A4 graph paper, using a scale of
   2 cm between each of the grid lines.
   **b** Show that the scale of your map-grid is
   1 : 50 000.
   **c** On your map-grid draw the line AB
   where A (510250) and B (530210). This
   represents a straight road. From A, Holly
   notes that the bearing of a hill is 100° and
   from B the bearing of the same hill is 005°.
   Find (i) the grid reference of the hill
   (ii) its distance from A and from B
   (iii) the bearing of A from B.

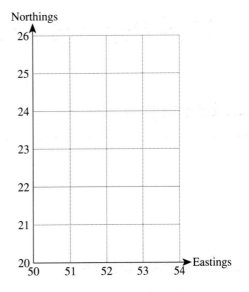

2  **a** Copy the map-grid onto a whole piece of
   A4 graph paper by using a scale of 4 cm
   between each of the grid lines.
   **b** Show that the scale of the new map-grid is
   1 : 25 000.
   **c** Repeat part 1 **c**.
   **d** Comment on the accuracy of your answers
   obtained from both map-grids.

## Exercise 67

Remember that all map-grids are labelled as shown in the previous Activity and that the grid lines
are drawn 2 cm apart for a scale of 1 : 50 000, and 4 cm apart for a scale of 1 : 25 000.

1  From X, the bearing of a hill is 300° and from Y the bearing of the same hill is 210°. If the grid
   references of X and Y are 540210 and 525255 respectively, represent these facts on a map-grid
   using a scale of 1 : 50 000. Use your diagram to find:
   **a** The grid reference of the hill.
   **b** The bearing of Y from X.
   **c** The distance between X and Y.

2  Coastguard station P is at 505260 and coastguard station Q is 5 km due south of P. The coast
   between P and Q is straight. Both stations observe a small boat drifting towards the shore. From
   P the bearing of the boat is 130° and from Q it is 040°. Represent these facts on a map-grid
   using a scale of 1 : 50 000.
   **a** Find the grid reference of the boat.
   **b** Find the shortest distance from the boat to the coast.
   **c** If the boat was drifting at a mean speed of 2 km/h, how long would it take to reach the coast
   by the most direct route?

223

3   Luke runs in a straight line from 520235, at 8 km/h. Where could he be after 15 minutes?

4   A nuclear reactor is to be built inside a large triangular site ABC, whose grid references are 507243, 537253, 517213 respectively. Plot these on a map-grid of scale 1 : 25 000. Join up these points to represent the fencing around the site.
    **a** Find the total length of fencing.
    **b** Find the total area of the site.
    **c** If the reactor is to be placed as far away from all the boundary fences as possible, where should it be built?
    **d** There is a radioactive leak from the reactor. If this affects an area up to 1.5 km from the reactor, shade the area inside the site which is not affected by the radiation.

5   **Investigate** the old naval saying: 'Constant bearing means collision'.

## MASTERMINDER

6   In the sport of Orienteering the object is to visit, in any order and as quickly as possible, a number of check-in points which are marked on a map. As the check-in points are often rather obscure, each competitor has to follow a compass bearing and judge the distance between one check-in and the next.

Imagine you are going to take part in a competition. You are able to run at a mean speed of 12 km/h. You have to start and finish at S (540230) and first go to A (530210) and then to the following in any order:

    B (520220)
    C (510205)
    D (530240)
    E (525235)
    F (505260)
    G (515230)

Assuming that you take a stopwatch with you, make a detailed preparation plan for your race. (No marks will be given unless the shortest route is followed!)

# 11.5 Scale drawing

## Activity 48

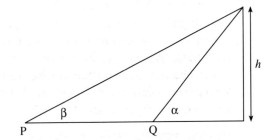

The object of this Activity is to find the height $h$ of a building by measuring the angle of elevation from two places, P and Q, which are a known distance apart.

First make a clinometer (sometimes called an 'inclinometer') as shown below. You will need the following materials:
- A planed piece of wood about 30 cm long which need only be about 2.5 cm by 5 cm.
- A protractor with a 1.6 mm hole drilled in the middle.
- A drawing pin.

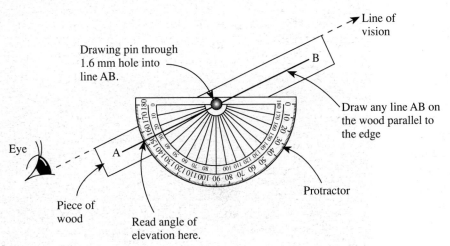

It is very important that the protractor hangs freely so that it comes to rest in the horizontal position.

1   Choose a suitable building and estimate its height.

2   Use your clinometer to measure the angle of elevation from P and from Q. Measure the distance between P and Q.

3   Use your measurements to make a scale drawing and use it to find the height of the building.

4   Use your measurements in the formula shown below, to calculate the height of the building. Use percentages to compare your two answers.

$$\text{Height} = PQ \times \frac{\tan \alpha \times \tan \beta}{\tan \alpha - \tan \beta}$$

5   If your measured angles were only accurate to within $\pm 2°$, find the maximum and minimum possible height of the building to 2 SF.

## —— Exercise 68

1   Each of three fields is in the shape of a quadrilateral ABCD. Their dimensions are shown below. Make scale drawings of each and use them to find the length of the diagonals AC in metres.

| | Actual length in metres | | | | |
|---|---|---|---|---|---|
| | AB | BC | CD | AD | BD |
| a | 95 | 72 | 110 | 90 | 100 |
| b | 38 | 40 | 60 | 39 | 55 |
| c | 22 | 20 | 25 | 15 | 30 |

Explain why the field cannot be drawn unless the length of a diagonal is known.

2   A surveyor has to make a scale drawing of a five-sided plot of land ABCDE. She uses a 'tellurometer' to make accurate measurements from both ends of a base line XY, to each of the five corners.

Her actual measurements are shown below. Use these to make a scale drawing of the plot and hence find the actual length of DC.

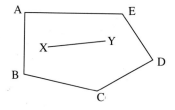

| From | Distance in metres to | | | | |
|---|---|---|---|---|---|
| | A | B | C | D | E |
| X | 39 | 29 | 64 | 126 | 131 |
| Y | 128 | 121 | 90 | 31 | 48 |
| Distance XY = 100 m | | | | | |

3   S is a railway station and T is a tower 25 km due East of S. A straight railway line runs out of S on a bearing of 070°. Make a scale drawing to show the position of the railway line, S and T.
  a X and Y are two points on the railway line each 15 km from T. Mark X and Y on your drawing and hence find the distance XY.
  b A train passes X at 09:07 and Y at 09:32. Find the speed of the train.

MASTERMINDER

**4** A fielder is standing at P, 30 m from a batsman at B. The batsman hits the ball which travels along a line which makes an angle of 20° with BP. Make a scale drawing to show the positions of B and P and the path of the ball.

 **a** The ball travels along the ground at a steady speed of 10 m/s towards a point X on the boundary 50 m from B. At the moment the ball is hit, the fielder starts to run towards X. Find at what speed he must run to field the ball at X.

 **b** If, instead, the fielder had decided to run in a direction perpendicular to BX, would he have been able to field the ball by running at the same speed as before?

# _ 11.6 Drawing three-dimensional figures

To be good at working in three dimensions requires three important skills:

- To be able to sketch a solid effectively.
- To be able to take a solid and imagine how it looks from different angles, such as end elevations, front elevations and plan views.
- To be able to visualize cross-sections of the solid.

Of these, the first two are illustrated by the following diagrams of a house roof.

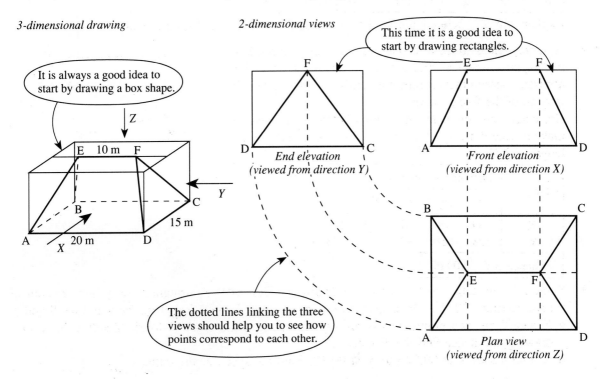

*3-dimensional drawing*

It is always a good idea to start by drawing a box shape.

*2-dimensional views*

This time it is a good idea to start by drawing rectangles.

*End elevation (viewed from direction Y)*

*Front elevation (viewed from direction X)*

*Plan view (viewed from direction Z)*

The dotted lines linking the three views should help you to see how points correspond to each other.

## —— Exercise 69

**1** Copy the three-dimensional diagram ABCDEF which represents a dry ski slope. Make a scale drawing of the two elevations (end elevation from BC) and the plan, if AB = 100 m, AF = 40 m and EF = 20 m.

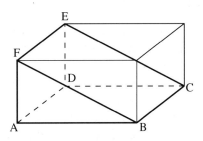

**2** Copy the three-dimensional diagram ABCDEFGH which represents a small lean-to shed.
Make a scale drawing of the two elevations and the plan if AB = 4 m, AE = 2 m, BC = 1.5 m and CG = 3 m.

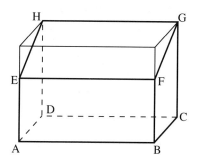

**3** Copy the three-dimensional diagram ABCDEFGHIJ which represents a house with an ordinary pitch roof.
Make a scale drawing of the two elevations and the plan, if AB = 20 m, BC = 6 m, FB = 5 m, and the ridge IJ is 10 m above the ground floor ABCD.

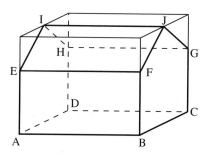

**4** This is the end elevation and plan of a house, with its adjoining garage.
Use these two views to sketch a front elevation and a 'three-dimensional' picture of the property.

End elevation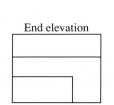

Plan view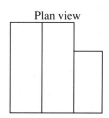

**5** Make a three-dimensional drawing of a pyramid standing on a square base. Draw the two elevations and the plan.

MASTERMINDER

**6** This cuboid represents one of four separate identical blocks of wood. M and N are the midpoints of AD and BC respectively and V is where the diagonals of ABCD intersect.

Each block of wood is made into a different shape. The plan of each shape is shown below. Look carefully at each plan and draw:
- The two elevations.
- The three-dimensional diagram.

Label each vertex carefully.

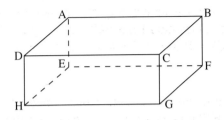

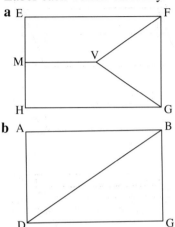

**a**

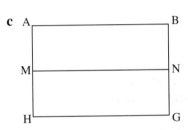

**c**

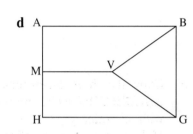

**d**

# 11.7 Networks

Consider a railway network represented like this:

This kind of diagram is called a **route diagram**.

The spots representing the towns are called **nodes**. (There are six nodes in this diagram.)

The routes which form the network by linking nodes are called **arcs**. (There are nine arcs in this diagram.)

The areas separated from each other by the arcs are called **regions**. (This diagram has five regions, A, B, C, D and E – the outside is included.)

The **order** of a node is the number of arcs which meet there. On this network Hereford has order 4 (an **even** node) and Kidderminster has order 3 (an **odd** node).

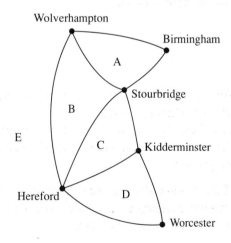

## Exercise 70

For all questions, state the order of the nodes shown and whether they are odd or even nodes.

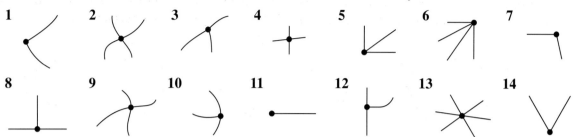

## Traversability

A network is **traversable** if it can be drawn

- without lifting your pencil off the paper, and
- without drawing an arc more than once.

(*Note*: you are allowed to pass through a node more than once.)

### ■ EXAMPLE 1
Is this network traversable?

Drawn in the order ABCADC, this network can be seen to be traversable. (Would it have been traversable if you had started at B?)

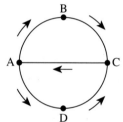

### ■ EXAMPLE 2
Is this network traversable?

With this network, no matter where you choose to start, you will find it to be non-traversable.

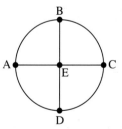

## Activity 49

1   For each of the networks labelled **a** to **h**, find the number of even nodes, the number of odd nodes, and decide whether the network is traversable. Put your answers into a table.

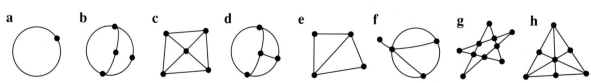

2   Look carefully at the table you made in part 1 to see if you can find a simple rule, concerning the number of odd nodes, for deciding whether or not a network is traversable.

3   Use your 'rule' from part 2 to decide which of the following networks are traversable. For those which you decide are traversable, suggest a suitable starting point and finishing point.

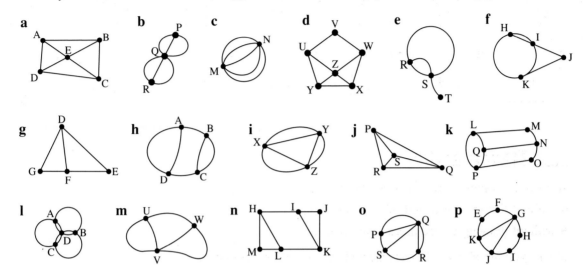

4   a For each of the networks from part 3 find the number of regions $R$, the number of nodes $N$, and the number of arcs $A$. Put your answers into a table.
    b Can you find a formula which connects $R$, $N$ and $A$?

5   Use your formula from part 4 to fill in the gaps for the following networks:

|   | R | N | A |
|---|---|---|---|
| a | 3 | 4 |   |
| b | 5 | 8 |   |
| c |   | 6 | 9 |
| d | 4 | 6 |   |
| e | 6 |   | 8 |
| f |   | 2 | 5 |
| g | 9 |   | 9 |

6   Using the formula from part 4, state whether it is possible to draw the following networks:

|   | R | N | A |
|---|---|---|---|
| a | 4 | 4 | 6 |
| b | 3 | 2 | 4 |
| c | 7 | 5 | 8 |
| d | 6 | 4 | 7 |
| e | 1 | 2 | 1 |

# __ 11.8 LOGO

LOGO is a low level computer language used mainly for drawing. All of the instructions refer to the movement of a 'turtle' (or a pointer).

> *NOTE*
>
> The sign ↵ means that you should press the 'RETURN' **or** the 'ENTER' key.

The following section refers to the use of Logotron and RM Nimbus versions of LOGO. The relatively small differences between these versions are labelled **L** and **RM**.

You need very little knowledge to get going:

**CS** ↵   will obtain a drawing screen.

A good idea with any procedure is to begin with:

| L | RM | *Instructions* |
|---|---|---|
| **ST** ↵ | **CL** ↵ | Clear screen |
| **HOME** ↵ | **CT** ↵ | Centre turtle to face 'due North' |

Simple movement instructions are:

**FD 50** ↵   Move forward 50 units
**RT 45** ↵   Turn right through 45°

(*Note*: the spaces, such as that between the RT and the 45, are as important as the letters; they must be included.)

Try out the following examples on a computer before attempting Exercise 71.

| | L | RM | *Resulting picture* |
|---|---|---|---|
| 1 | **ST** ↵ <br> **HOME** ↵ <br> **FD 50** ↵ <br> **RT 45** ↵ | **CL** ↵ <br> **CT** ↵ <br> **FD 50** ↵ <br> **RT 45** ↵ | |
| 2 | **ST** ↵ <br> **HOME** ↵ <br> **RT 45** ↵ <br> **FD 50** ↵ | **CL** ↵ <br> **CT** ↵ <br> **RT 45** ↵ <br> **FD 50** ↵ | |
| 3 | **ST** ↵ <br> **HOME** ↵ <br> **RT 90** ↵ <br> **FD 50** ↵ <br> **RT 90** ↵ <br> **FD 50** ↵ | **CL** ↵ <br> **CT** ↵ <br> **RT 90** ↵ <br> **FD 50** ↵ <br> **RT 90** ↵ <br> **FD 50** ↵ | |

# ▬ Procedures

The best way to obtain a good basic knowledge of LOGO is to try out a few simple procedures. Sketch the picture you expect **before** running each one.

| L | RM |
|---|---|

**L**

For each procedure type:

      **TO ... ↵**   (A name will be needed here)

[Then type in the procedure you wish to be identified by the above name.] ↵

    **END** ↵

You may now wish to call up your procedure. To do this type the name.

    **... ↵**

The procedure should now be carried out.

### ■ EXAMPLE 1

Suppose we wish to write a procedure to draw a square. Type the following boxed instructions:

```
ST ↵
HOME ↵
TO SQUARE ↵
FD 60 ↵
RT 90 ↵
FD 60 ↵
RT 90 ↵
FD 60 ↵
RT 90 ↵
FD 60 ↵
RT 90 ↵
END ↵
```

To test the procedure, clear the screen using:

```
ST        ↵
HOME ↵
```

Then type:

```
SQUARE ↵
```

A square should now have been drawn.

**RM**

For each procedure type:

      **BUILD '... ↵**  (A name will be needed here)

A new screen will be provided for this procedure to be typed in. Your choice of name will be at the top of the screen, so just press ↵ to complete typing the procedure.

```
...
```

"**ESC**" returns you to the original screen. You may now wish to call up your procedure. To do this type the name.

    **... ↵**

The procedure should now be carried out.

### ■ EXAMPLE 1

Suppose we wish to write a procedure to draw a square. Type the following boxed instructions:

*Main screen*
```
CL ↵
CT ↵
BUILD 'SQUARE ↵
```

*Procedure screen*
```
SQUARE ↵
FD 60 ↵
RT 90 ↵
FD 60 ↵
RT 90 ↵
FD 60 ↵
RT 90 ↵
FD 60 ↵
RT 90 ↵
```

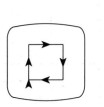

"**ESC**" *to Main screen*
```
SQUARE ↵
```

A square should now have been drawn.

*Note*:

- Most of the following examples feature the REPEAT instruction, which greatly aids the drawing of regular shapes.
- The AND instruction is not really necessary here, but it does help in understanding what is intended.
- The following examples show solely what should appear on the screen. You will still need to define the procedure beforehand, using either:

    **L: TO ... ↵**      **RM: BUILD ... ↵**

Then you will need to call up the procedure afterwards.

Try out the following procedures:

| | L | RM | *Resulting picture* |
|---|---|---|---|
| 1 | **TO TRI ↵**<br>**REPEAT 3 [FD 300 AND**<br>                **RT 120] ↵**<br>**END ↵** | **TRI ↵**<br>**REPEAT 3 [FD 300 AND**<br>                **RT 120] ↵** | 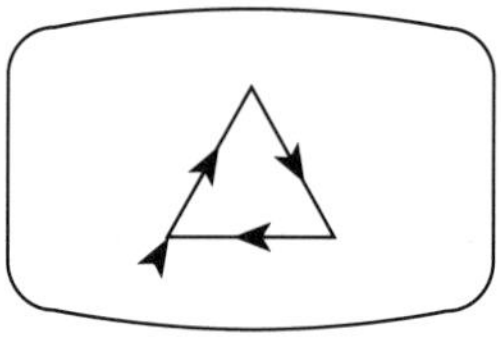 |
| 2 | **TO HEX ↵**<br>**REPEAT 6 [FD 150 AND**<br>                **RT 60] ↵**<br>**END ↵** | **HEX ↵**<br>**REPEAT 6 [FD 150 AND**<br>                **RT 60] ↵** | 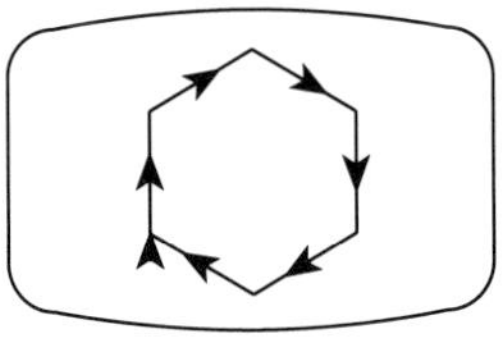 |
| 3 | **TO CIRCLE ↵**<br>**REPEAT 180 [FD 10 AND**<br>                **RT 2] ↵**<br>**END ↵** | **CIRCLE ↵**<br>**REPEAT 180 [FD 10 AND**<br>                **RT 2] ↵** | 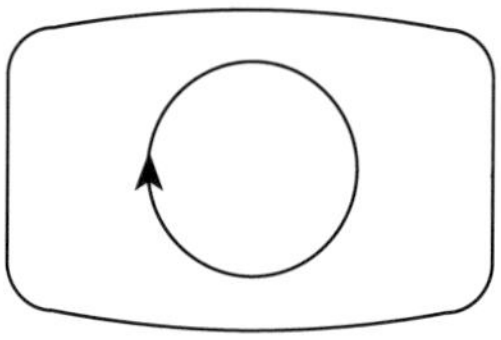 |
| | The next two procedures show how procedures can themselves be part of larger procedures. | | |
| 4 | **TO PATTERN ↵**<br>**REPEAT 4 [TRI AND**<br>                **RT 90] ↵**<br>**END ↵** | **PATTERN ↵**<br>**REPEAT 4 [TRI AND**<br>                **RT 90] ↵** | 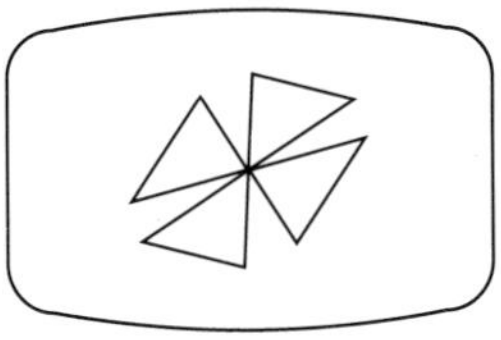 |
| 5 | **TO HEXPATT ↵**<br>**REPEAT 6 [HEX AND**<br>                **LT 60] ↵**<br>**END ↵** | **HEXPATT ↵**<br>**REPEAT 6 [HEX AND**<br>                **LT 60] ↵** | 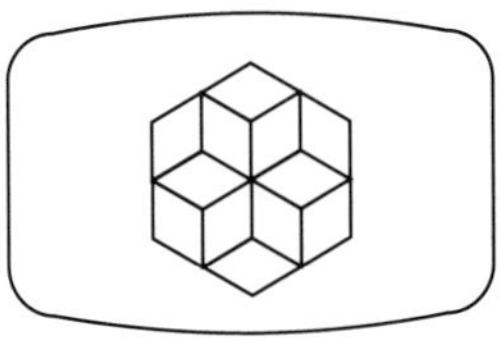 |

# ▬ Exercise 71

For Questions 1 to 6, write and test a LOGO program to:

**1** Draw a square of size 150 units.

**2** Draw a rectangle with sides 150 units and 300 units,

**3** Draw an equilateral triangle of side 200 units.

**4** Draw a parallelogram having sides of 142 units and 156 units which include an angle of 65°.

**5** Draw a regular hexagon of side 135 units.

**6** Draw a regular pentagon of side 140 units.

**7** Copy these shapes by writing LOGO programs:

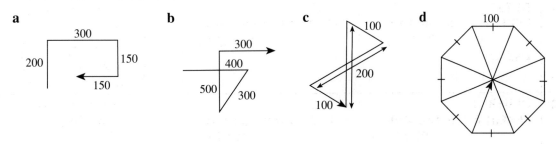

## ▬ Revision Exercise 11

For Questions 1 to 3, draw $x$ and $y$ axes from $-5$ to $+10$, using the same scale for both axes.

**1 a** Plot the points $(1, 2)$, $(1, 4)$ and $(2, 4)$ to form triangle P.

A denotes a translation along $\begin{pmatrix} -5 \\ -4 \end{pmatrix}$.

B denotes a reflection in $y = x$.

C denotes a clockwise rotation of $90°$ about centre $(1, 1)$.

**b** $A(P) \rightarrow Q$.

Draw and label triangle Q.

**c** $B(P) \rightarrow R$.

Draw and label triangle R.

**d** $C(R) \rightarrow S$.

Draw and label triangle S.

**e** Describe fully the single transformation that maps triangle S onto triangle P.

**2** Describe fully the transformations which map:

**a** A onto E    **b** C onto B    **c** D onto C

**d** B onto A    **e** E onto D    **f** B onto D.

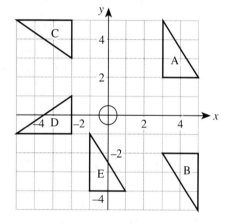

**3** Triangle T has vertices $(2, 1)$, $(4, 1)$, $(4, 2)$.

A is an enlargement, centre $(0, 0)$, scale factor 2.

B is an enlargement, centre $(4, 0)$, scale factor 3.

**a** $A(T) \rightarrow T_1$.

Draw and label triangle $T_1$.

**b** $B(T) \rightarrow T_2$.

Draw and label triangle $T_2$.

**c** To map $T_1$ onto $T_2$ requires an enlargement. Describe this enlargement precisely.

**4** A fierce dog is tethered by a rope 13 m long to a post 5 m from a straight path. If the path is 2 m wide, draw a suitable diagram to illustrate the area of path along which a walker would be in danger.

**5** The diagram shows a school playground and the staff room of the school. (Not drawn to scale.) Each window is 2 m wide and in the middle of each wall. Assume the staff-room walls have negligible thickness.
The teacher on playground duty decides to sit on her swivel chair in the staff room.
**Investigate** where she should place the chair in order to see as much of the playground as possible.

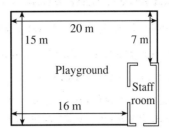

**6** A and B are two artillery guns on either side of a wide river. Each gun has a maximum range of 2 km.
Using a scale of 1 : 50 000, plot the position of A at 510235 and the position of B at 540225.
**Investigate** possible courses for an enemy ship to take when passing the guns.

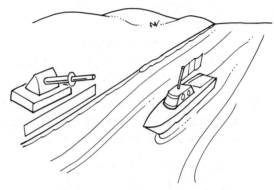

**7** Using a scale of 1 : 50 000, plot the grid references A (515215), B (535245) and C (535205). A party of walkers went from A to B, then on to C and back to A. Their walk took exactly three hours.
**a** What was the total length of their walk?
**b** Work out their mean speed to the nearest km/h.
**c** Estimate the area of land around which they walked.

**8** Find the number of regions $R$, nodes $N$ and arcs $A$ for each network and show that $R+N = A+2$.

**a**    **b**    **c**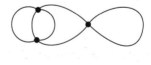

## MASTERMINDERS

**9** Aport and Xport are two towns on a straight stretch of coastline, 20 km apart. The bearing of Xport from Aport is 130°. Ethos is an island 25 km from Aport and on a bearing of 055°. Make a scale drawing to show the positions of the two towns and the island.
**a** A motor boat sets out from Aport at 15:40 and travels to Ethos at 20 km/h. What time will it arrive?
**b** Another boat leaves Xport travelling at 15 km/h, and wishes to arrive at Ethos at the same time as the first boat. When should it leave Xport and on what bearing should it travel?

## Basic Algebra Test 3

**Section A**  (1 mark for each correct answer)

Simplify if possible:

**1** $\frac{2a + 2a}{2a}$

**2** $3x^2 \times x$

**3** $(3y)^2 \times y$

**4** $3y^2 \div 2y$

**5** $\frac{3 + x^2}{x^2}$

**6** $c^2 \div (2c)$

**7** $\frac{1}{r} + \frac{1}{s}$

**8** $1 - \frac{1}{t}$

**9** $\frac{4a^6}{6a^4}$

**10** $\frac{2x}{3} \div \frac{3x}{2}$

**11** $x(2x)^3$

**12** $x^2 - x(x - 1)$

Find the value of each expression when $a = -1$ and $b = -3$:

**13** $-ab^2$

**14** $-(ab)^2$

**15** $(-ab)^2$

**16** $(-a)b^2$

Rearrange to make $x$ the subject:

**17** $m = \frac{x}{y} - b$

**18** $p = q(x - a)$

**19** $a - x = b$

**20** $\frac{a}{x} + 2 = m$

· Factorize completely:

Solve the inequalities:

**21** $x^3 + x^2 - x$

**22** $2x^3y^2 - 4x^2y^3$

**23** $1 - x < \frac{2x}{3}$

**24** $2 - x \geqslant \frac{3x + 1}{4}$

**Section B**  (2 marks for each correct answer)

Simplify:

Rearrange to make $x$ the subject:

**25** $\frac{2}{x + 1} - \frac{3}{x}$

**26** $\frac{a - b}{b - a}$

**27** $ax^2 + b = c$

**28** $\frac{a}{a - x} = c$

Solve for $x$:

**29** $4x^2 - 3 = 6$

**30** $\frac{4x - 13}{3} = -7$

**31** $(x + 2)^2 = 196$

**32** $x^2 - x = 6$

## Puzzlers

**1**  Find the formula relating $m$ matches to $t$ triangles arranged in this way. Use it to find how many triangles would be formed by 1001 matches.

**2**  If $ab = 143$ and $a^2 - b^2 = 48$, find $a^2 + b^2$.

**3**  A pony is tethered to a post at the circumference of a circular field so that it can just reach the centre. What percentage of the field can it graze?

# Coursework: Surveying with a Silva compass

A Silva compass is used to measure a magnetic bearing (that is, the angle between magnetic north and a given direction). When the 'red arrow' is pointed in the given direction and the 'compass housing' is rotated so that the 'black arrow' coincides with the magnetic needle, read off the magnetic bearing. See Figure 1.

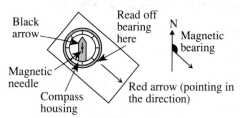

**Figure 1**

1   From a position outside your classroom, use your compass to measure the magnetic bearing of five different objects. Describe, with the aid of a diagram, how you used your compass. Draw a diagram to illustrate your five bearings.

2   From a point P, near to a building XY, measure (i) XP and PY   (ii) the magnetic bearing of X from P and of Y from P. See Figure 2.
    **a** Enter your measurements in a table.
    **b** Make a scale drawing and find the width XY of the building.
    **c** Measure the actual width of the building and calculate the percentage error of your answer in part **b**.

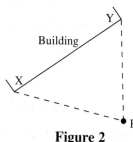

**Figure 2**

3   The aim of this part is to make a scale drawing of a field, represented by ABCD in Figure 3.
    **a** Select a suitable field and place two posts, X and Y, near to the middle and roughly parallel to one side and further apart than half the longest side.
    **b** Copy and complete the table below.

| From | Magnetic bearing of | | | |
|---|---|---|---|---|
|  | A | B | C | D |
| X |  |  |  |  |
| Y |  |  |  |  |
| Actual distance XY   = | | | | |
| Bearing of Y from X   = | | | | |

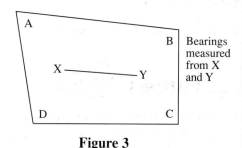

**Figure 3**

    **c** On lined paper, using the lines pointing North/South, make a scale drawing of the field. (Remember to draw XY first and at the correct angle to the lines of your paper.) Find the dimensions of the field.
    **d** Make another scale drawing of the field with the bearings given to you by your teacher. Compare the accuracy of your two drawings.

## EXTENSION

4   By discussing each of the possible errors in your measurements, explain why your scale drawing in part 3 **c** may not be very accurate. Use diagrams to illustrate your answer. (Hint: why do $x$ and $y$ have to be so far apart?)

# Fact Finders: Wimbledon

Every year at Wimbledon, the 'All England Tennis Club' holds the most prestigious and famous tennis tournament in the world. The first championships were held in July 1877. Since then many changes have taken place to accommodate the modern professional game.

The total prize money in 1989 was £3 133 749 rising to £3 874 450 in 1990. Some of the individual prizes for 1990 are listed below with the 1989 prizes in brackets.

| | | | |
|---|---|---|---|
| *Men's Singles:* | Winner | £230 000 | (£190 000) |
| | Runner-up | £115 000 | (£95 000) |
| | 1st round loser | £3450 | (£2550) |
| *Women's Singles:* | Winner | £207 000 | (£171 000) |
| | Runner-up | £103 500 | (£85 500) |
| | 1st round loser | £2675 | (£1975) |
| *Men's Doubles:* | Winners | £94 230 | (£65 870) per pair |
| *Women's Doubles:* | Winners | £81 510 | (£56 970) per pair |

The betting odds for the 1990 championships were:

| | | |
|---|---|---|
| *Men's Singles:* | Boris Becker | 11/8 |
| | Ivan Lendl | 11/8 |
| | Stefan Edberg | 5/1 |
| *Women's Singles:* | Steffi Graf | 4/7 |
| | Monica Seles | 3/1 |
| | Martina Navratilova | 5/1 |

Roscoe Tanner holds the record of 140 mph for the fastest service in the tournament.

The Centre Court is now all-seater with a capacity of 13 110 compared to 14 502 previously. As a result of these changes, the total attendance of the fortnight in 1990 was 30 000 fewer than the 403 706 figure for 1989.

The 1989 men's final was watched by 11.7 million people on BBC 2 whereas the women's final was watched by 9.5 million. The average television audience for each programme during the championships was 3.4 million.

About 650 matches are played on Wimbledon's 18 show courts. Approximately 21 000 balls are used.

Over the fortnight, the crowds consume 23 tonnes of strawberries, 33 000 cups of tea, 75 000 pints of beer and 12 000 bottles of champagne.

240

## — Questions on Wimbledon

1  How many years ago was the first Wimbledon championship?

2  What was the percentage increase in prize money from 1989 to 1990 for:
   **a** The men's singles champion?
   **b** The women's singles champion?
   **c** The men's and women's doubles champions?

3  How much would a male player have received in 1990 if he lost in the first round of the singles but won the men's doubles?

4  How much would a female player have received in 1989 if she was the runner-up in the singles but won the women's doubles?

5  Given that the length of a tennis court is 23.78 m, estimate how long an opponent of Roscoe Tanner would have to react to one of his 'power services' in seconds to 3 SF. (1 mile ≈ 1600 m)

6  What was the percentage decrease in total attendance over the fortnight from 1989 to 1990?

7  Given that the population of the UK in 1989 was about 62 million, estimate the percentage of the UK population that watched the men's singles final that year.

8  How many balls are used on average per match in the championships?

9  In 1990 the costs for food and drink were:

| | |
|---|---|
| Strawberries: | £12 per kg |
| Cup of tea: | £0.50 |
| Pint of beer: | £1.20 |
| Bottle of champagne: | £25 |

What was the mean amount spent on these items by a spectator at the 1990 championships?

10  **Investigate** betting odds and answer the following question:

Michael bets £10 on Stefan Edberg winning the men's singles and £20 on Steffi Graf winning the women's singles title, in 1990. How much did Michael gain or lose overall?

# Multiple Choice Test 1A

**1** How many cm are there in 1 km?

    **a** 100          **b** 1000          **c** 100 000          **d** 1 000 000

**2** The number 5.375 correct to 2 DP is:

    **a** 5.37          **b** 5.4          **c** 5.45          **d** 5.38

**3** The number 437 600 in standard form correct to 3 SF is:

    **a** $4.375 \times 10^5$      **b** $43.8 \times 10^4$      **c** $4.38 \times 10^5$      **d** $4.37 \times 10^5$

**4** The larger angle between North-East and West is:

    **a** 225°          **b** 270°          **c** 315°          **d** 135°

**5** If your final score for this test is 65%, how many questions did you get right?

    **a** 6          **b** 7          **c** 12          **d** 13

**6** The interior angle of a regular ten-sided polygon is:

    **a** 162°          **b** 144°          **c** 126°          **d** 108°

**7** $a^3 \times 3a^2$ simplifies to:

    **a** $9a^5$          **b** $9a^6$          **c** $3a^6$          **d** $3a^5$

**8** If $3a + 4 = 28 + a$, the value of $a$ is:

    **a** 8          **b** 16          **c** 12          **d** 26

**9** If $x = 2$, $y = 3$ and $z = -4$, the value of $\dfrac{xyz}{2(x - z)}$ is:

    **a** 12          **b** $-4$          **c** 2          **d** $-2$

**10** The greatest integer solution to $5x - 3 < x + 9$ is:

    **a** 4          **b** 3          **c** 2          **d** 1

**11** A scalene triangle has angles in the ratio 2 : 3 : 4. The size of the smallest angle is:

    **a** 40°          **b** 20°          **c** 60°          **d** 80°

Questions 12 to 14 refer to the graph below of temperature (°C) against time.

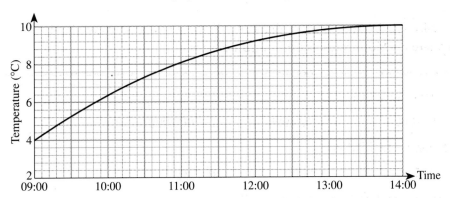

**12** What is the temperature at midday?

   **a** 6.75 °C       **b** 8.2 °C       **c** 9.2 °C       **d** 10 °C

**13** What is the approximate percentage increase in temperature between 10:00 and 14:00?

   **a** 20%       **b** 66%       **c** 67%       **d** 40%

**14** What is the mean temperature increase per hour between 09:30 and 12:00?

   **a** 1.6 °C       **b** 2 °C       **c** 0.5 °C       **d** 0.6 °C

**15** The number 0.003 518 in standard form correct to 3 SF is:

   **a** $3.51 \times 10^{-3}$       **b** $3.52 \times 10^{-3}$       **c** $35.2 \times 10^{-4}$       **d** $3.52 \times 10^{3}$

**16** If $3(r + 2) = 4(r - 1)$, the value of $r$ is:

   **a** 2       **b** 3       **c** $-2$       **d** 10

**17** A shirt is reduced by 15% to a sale price of £14.96. This is a reduction of:

   **a** £2.24       **b** £2.25       **c** £5.28       **d** £2.64

**18** If $10 + \frac{10}{x} = 110$, the value of $x$ is:

   **a** 10       **b** 21       **c** 0.1       **d** 0.01

**19** If $x = 1.2 \times 10^{3}$, $y = 3.5 \times 10^{-2}$ and $z = 4.9 \times 10^{2}$, the value of $\dfrac{2xyz}{(x - z)^{2}}$ in standard form correct to 3 SF is:

   **a** $8.17 \times 10^{-2}$       **b** $8.16 \times 10^{-2}$       **c** $5.80 \times 10$       **d** $4.96 \times 10^{2}$

**20** In which equation is $x$ **not** equal to 8?

   **a** $8x = 64$       **b** $4x - 14 = 18$       **c** $\frac{2x - 1}{3} = 5$       **d** $\frac{128}{x - 4} = 36$

# Multiple Choice Test 1B

**1** How many mm$^3$ are there in 1 cm$^3$?

   **a** 100       **b** 1000       **c** 10 000       **d** 100 000

**2** $y^3 \times y^2$ simplifies to:

   **a** $y^6$       **b** $y^9$       **c** $y$       **d** $y^5$

**3** The larger angle between the hands of a clock at 18:05 is nearest to:

   **a** 210°       **b** 200°       **c** 180°       **d** 170°

**4** Part of a car journey is shown here.

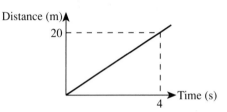

   The car's speed is:

   **a** 10 m/s       **b** 40 m/s       **c** 80 m/s       **d** 5 m/s

**5** 15 000 × 6000 in standard form is:

   **a** $9.0 \times 10^7$       **b** $90 \times 10^6$       **c** $9.0 \times 10^5$       **d** $0.9 \times 10^6$

**6** The angle sum of a nine-sided polygon is:

   **a** 1260°       **b** 450°       **c** 2520°       **d** 1620°

**7** A train journey is shown here.

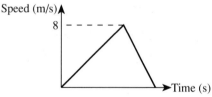

   If the train has travelled 1200 m, the time of the journey is:

   **a** 5 minutes       **b** $2\frac{1}{2}$ minutes       **c** 10 minutes       **d** 15 minutes

**8** The value, to 3 SF, of $(1.03)^5$ is:

   **a** 1.01       **b** 5.15       **c** 1.16       **d** 1.15

**9** If $2 = \frac{3}{x} - 4$, $x$ is:

   **a** 2       **b** $\frac{1}{2}$       **c** 6       **d** $-1\frac{1}{2}$

**10** The smallest possible solution of $\frac{x}{3} - 1 \geqslant 2$ is:

   **a** 9       **b** 3       **c** 7       **d** 1

**11** A rectangular field is $(2x + 1)$ m long and $x$ m wide. If the perimeter is 14 m, the area is:
    **a** $5\,\text{m}^2$      **b** $10\,\text{m}^2$      **c** $14\,\text{m}^2$      **d** $15\,\text{m}^2$

**12** The population $P$ of an insect colony at time $t$ is shown here.

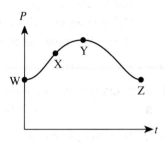

    The population of the insect colony increases most rapidly at:
    **a** W      **b** X      **c** Y      **d** Z

**13** A computer decreases in value by 55%. If it is now valued at £157.50, its value before the decrease was:
    **a** £350      **b** £1575      **c** £3500      **d** £286

**14** In the diagram, O is the centre of the circle.

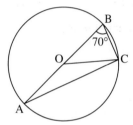

    Angle OAC is:
    **a** $18°$      **b** $20°$      **c** $22°$      **d** $40°$

**15** The internal angle of a regular octagon is:
    **a** $135°$      **b** $140°$      **c** $120°$      **d** $158°$

**16** A red blood cell is $7 \times 10^{-6}$ m in diameter. Approximately how many could be placed in a straight line across a human hair of diameter 0.06 mm?
    **a** 9      **b** 90      **c** 900      **d** 9000

**17** In this triangle, the gradient of AB is:
    **a** $\frac{12}{13}$      **b** $\frac{5}{12}$      **c** $\frac{5}{13}$      **d** $\frac{12}{5}$

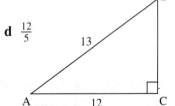

**18** A 295 g can of soup costs 35p. The price per gram is approximately:
    **a** 8p      **b** 0.1p      **c** 0.8p      **d** 12p

**19** The time for a speed-boat to travel 8 miles at 40 mph is:
    **a** 5 minutes      **b** 12 minutes      **c** 20 minutes      **d** 24 minutes

**20** The solution to the simultaneous equations, $y = 7 - 2x$, $y = 2x + 1$, is:
    **a** $(3, -2)$      **b** $(2, 3)$      **c** $(1.5, 4)$      **d** $(4, 1.5)$

# Multiple Choice Test 2A

**1** If £1 can be exchanged for Fr 10.8, how many pounds can be exchanged for Fr 594?

    **a** 55         **b** 550         **c** 5.5         **d** 108

**2** In snail racing, the equivalent of the 'four minute mile' is 24 inches in 3 minutes. What is this speed equal to in mm per second to the nearest whole number? ( 1 inch $\approx$ 25 mm)

    **a** 4         **b** 3         **c** 10         **d** 200

**3** In this triangle, the length of side $x$ is:

    **a** 4.33 cm         **b** 8.66 cm         **c** 2.5 cm         **d** 7.5 cm

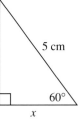

**4** In this triangle, the angle $\theta$ is approximately:

    **a** 67.4°         **b** 22.6°         **c** 42.7°         **d** 47.3°

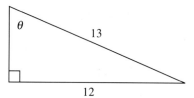

**5** If $2(x - 1) + 1 = 3(2x - 1)$, the value of $x$ is:

    **a** 1         **b** 0.25         **c** 2         **d** 0.5

**6** If $3^x = 750$, the best approximate value of $x$ is:

    **a** 10         **b** 6         **c** 5         **d** 4

**7** Which values of $y$ satisfy the inequality $4y - 3 < 5$?

    **a** $y < \frac{1}{2}$     **b** $y > \frac{1}{2}$     **c** $y < 2$     **d** $y > 2$

**8** The radius of a wheel of circumference 4 m is approximately:

    **a** 64 cm         **b** 127 cm         **c** 63 cm         **d** 113 cm

**9** The diameter of a circle of area 100 cm$^2$ is approximately:

    **a** 32 cm         **b** 16 cm         **c** 5 cm         **d** 11 cm

**10** The volume of a cylinder of diameter 8 cm and height 2 m is:

    **a** $3200\pi$ cm$^3$     **b** $12\,800\pi$ cm$^3$     **c** $1600\pi$ cm$^3$     **d** $51\,200\pi$ cm$^3$

**11** In this triangle, the length of side $x$ is:

   **a** 4 cm       **b** 5 cm       **c** 6 cm       **d** 8 cm

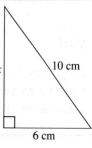

**12** What is the value of $s$ if $v^2 = u^2 + 2as$, given that $v = 10$, $u = 4$, and $a = 6$?

   **a** 19       **b** 7       **c** 28       **d** 6

**13** If $a + \frac{2b}{c} = d$ is rearranged to make $b$ the subject, $b$ is equal to:

   **a** $\frac{1}{2}(dc - a)$       **b** $\frac{1}{2}(dc + ac)$       **c** $\frac{1}{2}(dc - ac)$       **d** $2(dc - ac)$

**14** If AB is the diameter of the circle, angle $\theta$ is:

   **a** 90°       **b** 70°       **c** 110°       **d** 35°

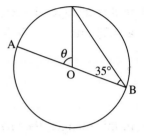

**15** Which of the following statements is/are true?

   I     $\sin 30° = 0.5$

   II    $\sin 45° = \cos 45°$

   III  $\tan 45° > \cos 60°$

   **a** I only       **b** I and II only       **c** All three       **d** None

**16** A car travels 180 miles using 4.5 gallons of petrol. How far will it travel on 3.5 gallons?

   **a** 80 miles       **b** 100 miles       **c** 120 miles       **d** 140 miles

**17** The bearing of X from Y is 150°. The bearing of Y from X is:

   **a** 060°       **b** 300°       **c** 210°       **d** 330°

**18** A 10 cm square is inscribed inside a circle. The area of the circle in $cm^2$ is:

   **a** $50\pi$       **b** $100\pi$       **c** $25\pi$       **d** $150\pi$

**19** If £1 is represented by 1 second, approximately how long will £1 billion be represented by? (1 billion = $10^9$)

   **a** 1 day       **b** 12 days       **c** 32 years       **d** 317 years

**20** A train travels at 100 km/h. If the diameter of its wheels is 1 m, what is the approximate number of revolutions made in 1 minute?

   **a** 531       **b** 265       **c** 1061       **d** 3600

# Multiple Choice Test 2B

**NOTE**

For Chapters 5 to 7.
Calculators are allowed. Do **not** write on this page. Show all your working clearly.
Write down the **letter** which represents the correct answer.

**1**   On a map of scale 1 : 50 000, a 15 km road would be of length:

    **a** 3 cm          **b** 30 cm          **c** 300 cm          **d** 3000 cm

**2**   A right-angled triangle has sides in the ratio 3 : 4 : 5. The sine of the smallest angle is:

    **a** 0.8          **b** 1.25          **c** 0.75          **d** 0.6

**3**   If $4 = 2(x - 1)$, $x$ is:

    **a** 1          **b** 2          **c** 3          **d** 9

**4**   £1 can be exchanged for Ptas 225. How many pounds could be exchanged for Ptas 2700?

    **a** £120          **b** £22.50          **c** £12          **d** £1.20

**5**   In Figure 1, the cosine of 45° is:

    **a** $\frac{1}{2}$          **b** 1          **c** $\frac{1}{\sqrt{2}}$          **d** $\sqrt{2}$

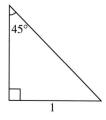

**Figure 1**

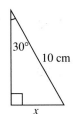

**Figure 2**

**6**   In Figure 2, the length of $x$ is:

    **a** 9 cm          **b** 7 cm          **c** 6 cm          **d** 5 cm

**7**   If $cx - b = d$, $x$ is:

    **a** $c(d + b)$          **b** $(d - b) \div c$          **c** $\frac{b + d}{c}$          **d** $(d - b)c$

**8**   The area of an equilateral triangle of side 5 cm is approximately:

    **a** 10 cm$^2$          **b** 11 cm$^2$          **c** 12 cm$^2$          **d** 13 cm$^2$

**9**   The Channel Tunnel can be built in 4 years by 25 000 men. How long would it take 20 000 men to build?

    **a** 6 years          **b** 3 years          **c** 5 years          **d** 4 years

**10** The distance between points (1, 2) and (4, 6) is:

    **a** 3 units      **b** 4 units      **c** 5 units      **d** 6 units

**11** The circumference of a circle is $10\pi$ metres. The radius is:

    **a** 500 cm      **b** 50 cm      **c** 100 cm      **d** 1000 cm

**12** A rectangle has sides 10 m and 20 m. The angle between the diagonal and the shorter side is approximately:

    **a** 63°      **b** 65°      **c** 67°      **d** 69°

**13** The circumference of a circle is $20\pi$ metres. The area in m$^2$ is:

    **a** $400\pi$      **b** $200\pi$      **c** $100\pi$      **d** $40\pi$

**14** A square of side length 10 cm has a circle inscribed inside to touch each of the four sides. The area outside the circle but inside the square is approximately:

    **a** 21 cm$^2$      **b** 25 cm$^2$      **c** 50 cm$^2$      **d** 22 cm$^2$

**15** The volume in m$^3$ of a cylinder with a diameter 2 m and height 3 m is:

    **a** $3\pi$      **b** $12\pi$      **c** $36\pi$      **d** $18\pi$

**16** An athlete runs on average 10 km a day. In a week he runs approximately:

    **a** 16 miles      **b** 44 miles      **c** 60 miles      **d** 1000 miles

**17** $x = 2$, $y = 3$, $z = -4$. The value of $(zy)^2 \div x$ is:

    **a** $-18$      **b** $-72$      **c** 6      **d** 72

**18** In this diagram, the largest angle is:

    **a** 60°      **b** 80°      **c** 100°      **d** 90°

**19** The curved surface area of a cylinder radius 4 cm and height 10 cm is:

    **a** $80\pi$ cm$^2$      **b** $40\pi$ cm$^2$      **c** $250\pi$ cm$^2$      **d** $160\pi$ cm$^2$

**20** The angle of depression from the top of an 80 m high lighthouse to a ship 100 m away is approximately:

    **a** 51°      **b** 39°      **c** 30°      **d** 72°

# Multiple Choice Test 3A

> **NOTE**
>
> For Chapters 8 to 11.
> Calculators are allowed. Do **not** write on this page. Show all your working clearly.
> Write down the **letter** which represents the correct answer.

**1** The only possible equation for this graph is:

   **a** $y = 2x - 1$    **b** $y = 3x + 1$    **c** $y = 2x$    **d** $y = x^2$

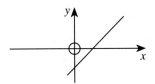

**2** If $w = \dfrac{x + y}{z}$, what is the maximum value of $w$, given that $x = 2.5 \pm 0.1$, $y = 1.3 \pm 0.1$ and $z = 0.6 \pm 0.1$?

   **a** 7.6        **b** 5.7        **c** 8        **d** 7.2

**3** The multiplying factor to decrease a number by 12% is:

   **a** 1.12        **b** 0.88        **c** 0.12        **d** 1.88

**4** The VAT on a £250 violin at $17\frac{1}{2}\%$ is:

   **a** £42.50        **b** £37.50        **c** £293.75        **d** £43.75

**5** What is the interest earned on $500 saved for two years at 10% per annum, assuming all interest is kept in the account?

   **a** $105        **b** $100        **c** $605        **d** $150

**6** The cash price of a tape-recorder is £160. Sophie pays an initial deposit of 10% of the cash price followed by 12 equal monthly payments of £15.
The amount of interest she pays over the year is:

   **a** £30        **b** £36        **c** £20        **d** £5

**7** The following temperatures were read on consecutive days; $3\,°C$, $4\,°C$, $-2\,°C$, $-3\,°C$, $0\,°C$, $2\,°C$, $3\,°C$. The mean temperature over this period was:

   **a** $0\,°C$        **b** $1\,°C$        **c** $2\,°C$        **d** $1.5\,°C$

**8** The probability of snow in Manchester on a particular day is 0.05. The probability that it does **not** snow in Manchester on this day is:

   **a** 0.05        **b** 1.05        **c** $\frac{1}{0.05}$        **d** 0.95

**9** A letter is randomly selected from the sentence, 'A thing of beauty is a joy for ever'. The probability that it is an 'e' is:

   **a** $\frac{1}{9}$        **b** $\frac{2}{27}$        **c** $\frac{3}{26}$        **d** $\frac{3}{28}$

**10** If the point (3, 5) is reflected in the $x$ axis, its image is at:

   **a** $(-3, 5)$        **b** $(-3, -5)$        **c** $(3, -5)$        **d** $(5, 3)$

**11** If the point (3, 5) is translated along vector $\begin{pmatrix} -3 \\ -5 \end{pmatrix}$, its image is at:

   **a** $(-3, -5)$      **b** $(0, 0)$      **c** $(6, 10)$      **d** $(-6, -10)$

**12** On a map the distance 24 km is represented by a 6 cm line. The scale of this map is:

   **a** $1 : 4000$      **b** $1 : 40\,000$      **c** $1 : 400\,000$      **d** $1 : 4\,000\,000$

**13** The probability of throwing two prime numbers on two consecutive throws of a fair six-sided die is:

   **a** $\frac{1}{6}$      **b** $\frac{1}{4}$      **c** $\frac{4}{9}$      **d** $\frac{2}{3}$

**14** The number of magazines sold by a shop on a Monday is shown below:

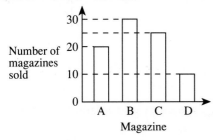

What proportion of all the magazines sold are of type C?

   **a** $\frac{5}{17}$      **b** $\frac{5}{13}$      **c** $\frac{5}{16}$      **d** $\frac{6}{17}$

**15** In Question 14, the cost of each magazine A, B, C and D is £1.25, £0.50, £1.50 and £2.00 respectively. The total value of all the magazines sold that Monday was:

   **a** £102.50      **b** £97.50      **c** £105      **d** £110

**16** If a card is randomly selected from an ordinary pack of playing cards, the probability that it is a King or a Queen is:

   **a** $\frac{1}{13}$      **b** $\frac{1}{169}$      **c** $\frac{4}{27}$      **d** $\frac{2}{13}$

**17** Three people toss a coin. If the first two outcomes were tails the probability that the third person will throw a head is:

   **a** $\frac{1}{2}$      **b** $\frac{1}{8}$      **c** $\frac{1}{4}$      **d** $\frac{1}{3}$

**18** If the point (1, 4) is reflected in the line $y = x$ and then reflected in the $y$ axis, its image is at:

   **a** $(4, 1)$      **b** $(4, -1)$      **c** $(-4, 1)$      **d** $(-4, -1)$

**19** For the following network, $R + N + A$ is:

   **a** 12      **b** 13      **c** 14      **d** 15

**20** A sales assistant in a bakery is paid £3 per hour normal time and £4.50 per hour overtime. He usually works a 30 hour week. If he works a 40 hour week, his total wage for that week is:

   **a** £180      **b** £135      **c** £120      **d** £165

# Multiple Choice Test 3B

**NOTE**

For Chapters 8 to 11.
Calculators are allowed. Do **not** write on this page. Show all your working clearly.
Write down the **letter** which represents the correct answer.

**1** The line $y = 3x + 1$ cuts the $y$ axis at:

   **a** $(0, -1)$       **b** $(0, 3)$       **c** $(0, 1)$       **d** $(3, 0)$

**2** Fred earns a basic rate of £3.50 per hour and £6.00 per hour overtime. His total wage for 36 hours at basic rate and 4 hours overtime is:

   **a** £140       **b** £150       **c** £240       **d** £506

**3** Ten boys have a mean age of 15.5 years. If one is 11 years old, the mean age of the others is:

   **a** 15 years       **b** 16 years       **c** 17 years       **d** 18 years

**4** The bearing of a church, at grid reference 540210, from a school at grid reference 510180 is:

   **a** 045°       **b** 225°       **c** 030°       **d** 060°

**5** The gradient of the line $2x + 3y = 4$ is:

   **a** 2       **b** $-2$       **c** $-\frac{3}{2}$       **d** $-\frac{2}{3}$

**6** A lazy girl taking this test decides to guess all the answers. Her approximate score is likely to be:

   **a** 6       **b** 7       **c** 8       **d** 5

**7** A point moves such that its distance from a fixed point is always the same. The shape described by the point is a:

   **a** Square       **b** Circle       **c** Triangle       **d** Rhombus

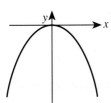

    **Figure 1**                 **Figure 2**

**8** In Figure 1, the equation of the graph is:

   **a** $y = -x^2$       **b** $y = x^2$       **c** $y = \frac{1}{x}$       **d** $y = -\frac{1}{x}$

**9** In Figure 2, the equation of the graph is:

   **a** $y = -\frac{2}{x}$       **b** $y = \frac{1}{x}$       **c** $y = -x^2$       **d** $y = 2x^2$

**10** The probability of throwing a six and a one with two dice is:

    **a** $\frac{1}{18}$          **b** $\frac{1}{36}$          **c** $\frac{1}{6}$          **d** $\frac{7}{36}$

**11** If $a = 2.5 \pm 0.1$, $b = 1.3. \pm 0.1$ and $c = 1.1 \pm 0.1$, the minimum value of $(a + b) \div c$ is:

    **a** 3          **b** 3.6          **c** 4          **d** 3.8

**12** To increase a number by 5%, the number is multiplied by:

    **a** 1.5          **b** 0.05          **c** 1.05          **d** 1.005

**13** A railway tunnel has a constant cross-sectional area of $800\,\text{m}^2$ and is 0.2 km long. Its volume is:

    **a** $16\,000\ \text{m}^3$      **b** $1600\ \text{m}^3$      **c** $160\,000\ \text{m}^3$      **d** $1\,600\,000\ \text{m}^3$

**14** To decrease a number by 15%, the number is multiplied by:

    **a** 0.15          **b** 0.015          **c** 0.085          **d** 0.85

**15** The length of diagonal PQ in the unit cube below is:

    **a** $\sqrt{3}$ units      **b** $\sqrt{2}$ units      **c** $\frac{2}{3}$ units      **d** 2 units

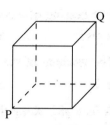

**16** The probability that it rains on any day is 0.2. The probability that it does not rain on Monday is:

    **a** 0.2          **b** 0.8          **c** 0.5          **d** 0.04

**17** The graph of $x + 2y = 3$ cuts the $x$ axis at:

    **a** $(3, 0)$      **b** $(0, 3)$      **c** $(1\frac{1}{2}, 0)$      **d** $(-3, 0)$

**18** The median of 2, 6, 33, 21, 9, 6, 7, 12 is:

    **a** 12          **b** 6          **c** 8          **d** 27

**19** A man's Tax Allowance is £5015 and he pays tax at the rate of 25p in the pound. If his salary is £17 015, his monthly tax bill is:

    **a** £750.00      **b** £667.92      **c** £354.48      **d** £250.00

**20** A £500 television is bought by Hire Purchase over one year at an interest rate of 12% per annum on the cash price. After paying a 10% deposit, each monthly payment is:

    **a** £45.67      **b** £42.00      **c** £42.50      **d** £46.17